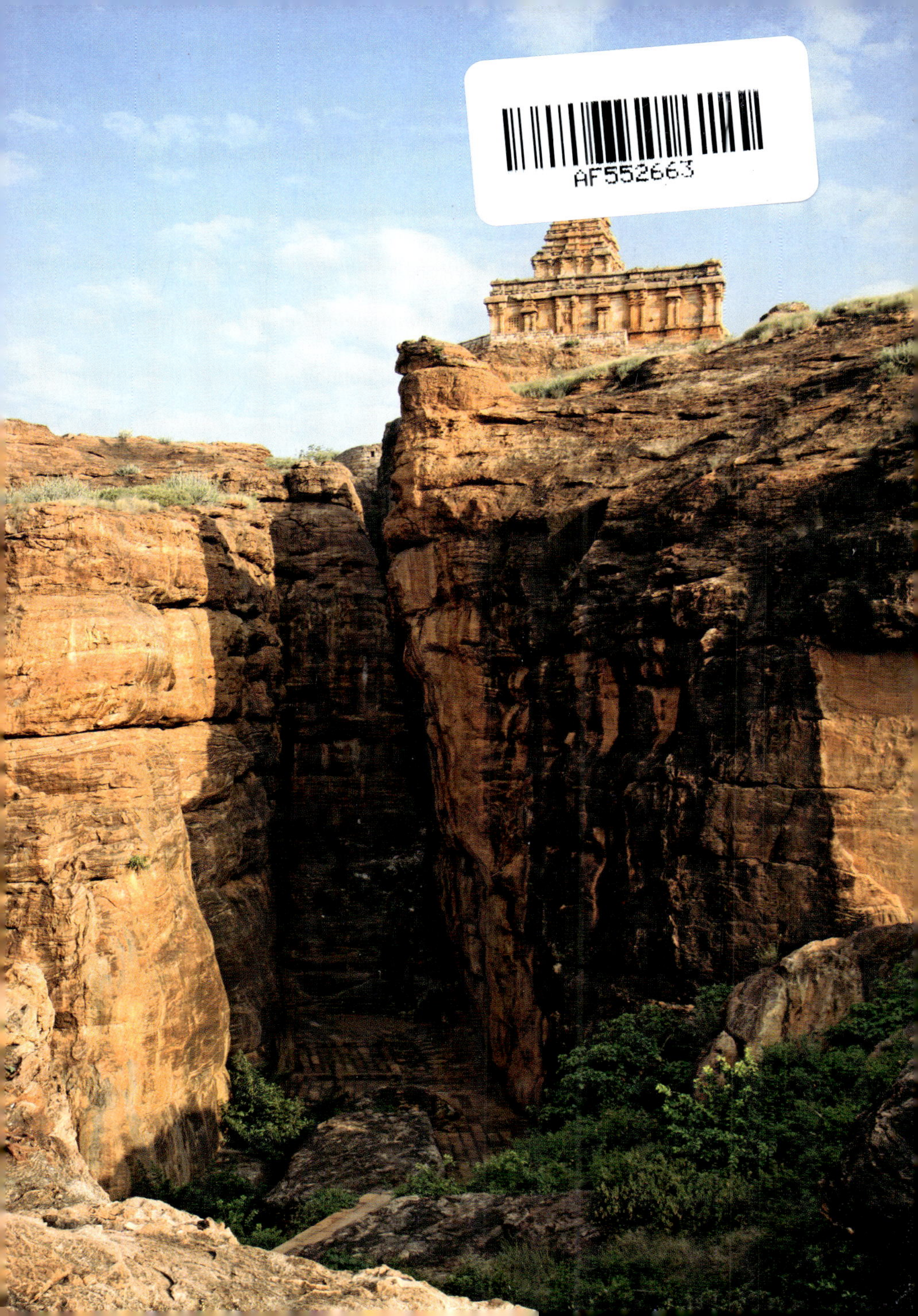

Previous page: Upper Shivalaya at the summit of the North Fort, Badami
Opposite: Tower of the Galaganatha temple, Pattadakal
Following pages: Amorous couple beneath tree; column bracket from Cave 3, Badami; ceiling panel from Cave 2, Badami

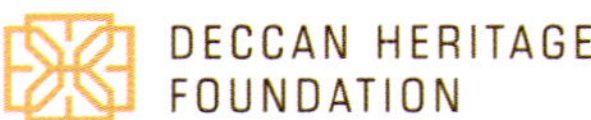

Striving to promote and implement the preservation and conservation of the historic monuments and cultural heritage of the Deccan within a holistic environment and social context

Deccan Heritage Foundation Ltd.
Suite 1, 3rd Floor
11-12 St. James's Square
London
SW1Y 4LB

Deccan Heritage Foundation India
Ground Floor, 27 Castle Chambers,
Castle Street, Ashok Nagar, Bengaluru - 560025.
Email id: admin@deccan-heritage-foundation.org
Website: www.deccan-heritage-foundation.org

The Deccan Heritage Foundation would like to acknowledge the generous support of John and Fausta Eskenazi, who have made this publication possible

ISBN 978-81-8495-600-9
First Jaico Impression 2014
Fifth Jaico Impression 2025

Processing
Commercial Art Engravers Pvt Ltd

Printing
JAK Printers Pvt Ltd

Published by
JAICO PUBLISHING HOUSE
A-2, Jash Chambers, 7-A Sir Phirozshah Mehta Road,
Fort, Mumbai 400 001
jaicopub@jaicobooks.com
www.jaicobooks.com

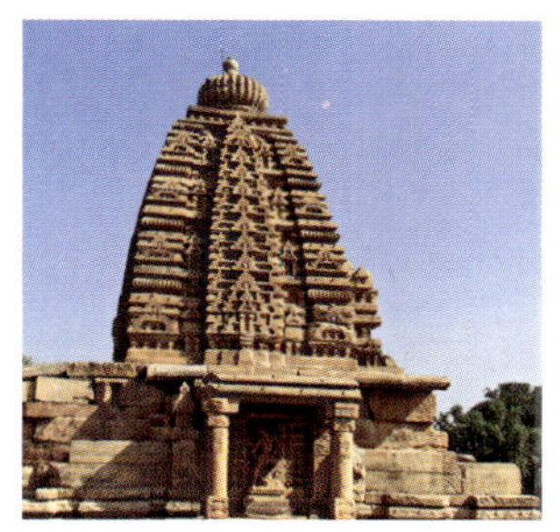

Badami, Aihole, Pattadakal

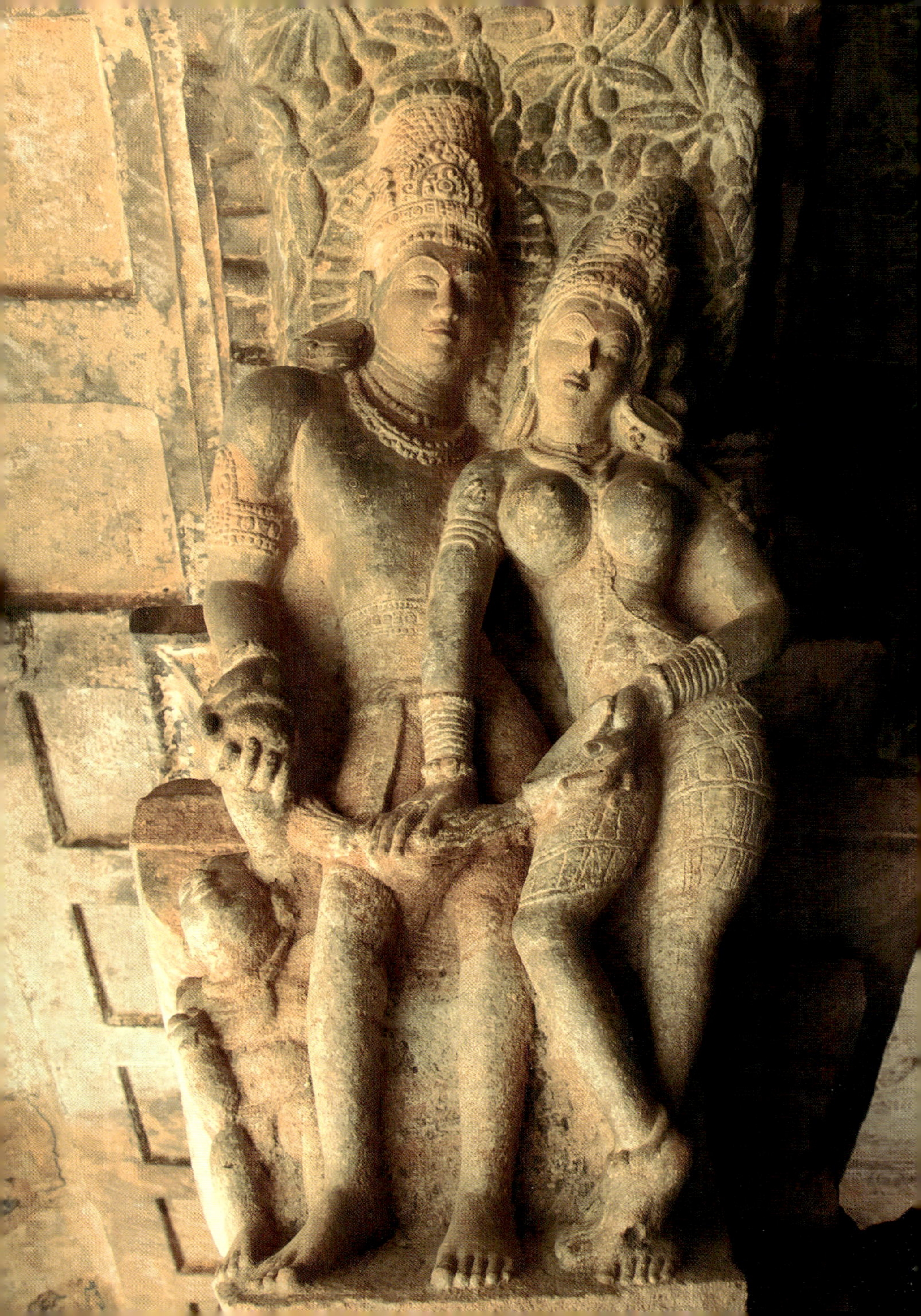

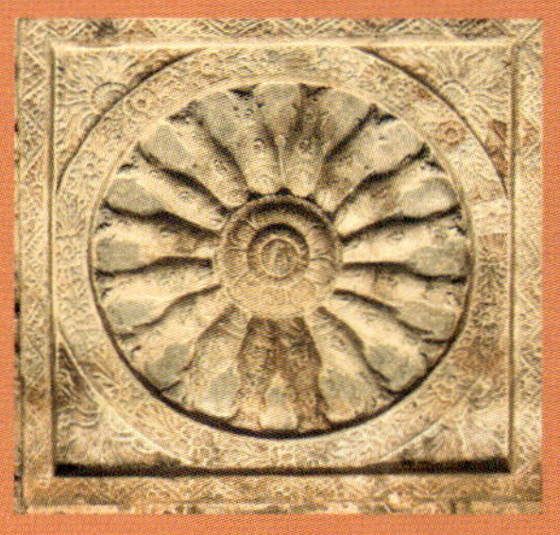

BADAMI, AIHOLE, PATTADAKAL

George Michell

PHOTOGRAPHY Surendra Kumar

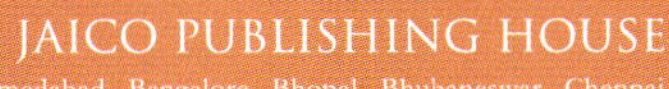
JAICO PUBLISHING HOUSE

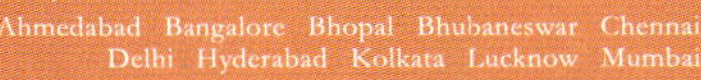
Ahmedabad Bangalore Bhopal Bhubaneswar Chennai
Delhi Hyderabad Kolkata Lucknow Mumbai

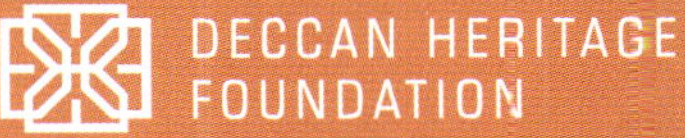

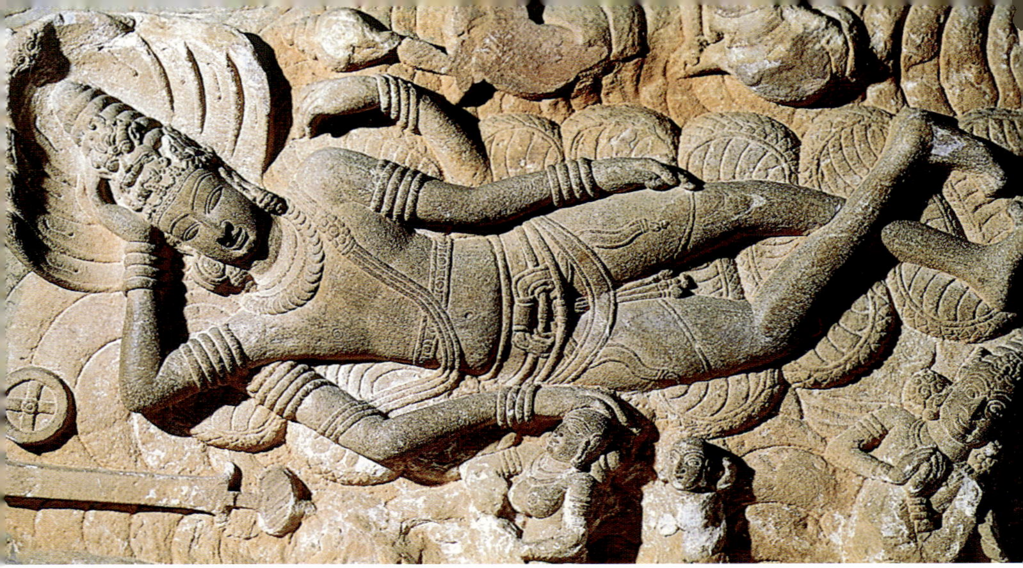

Contents

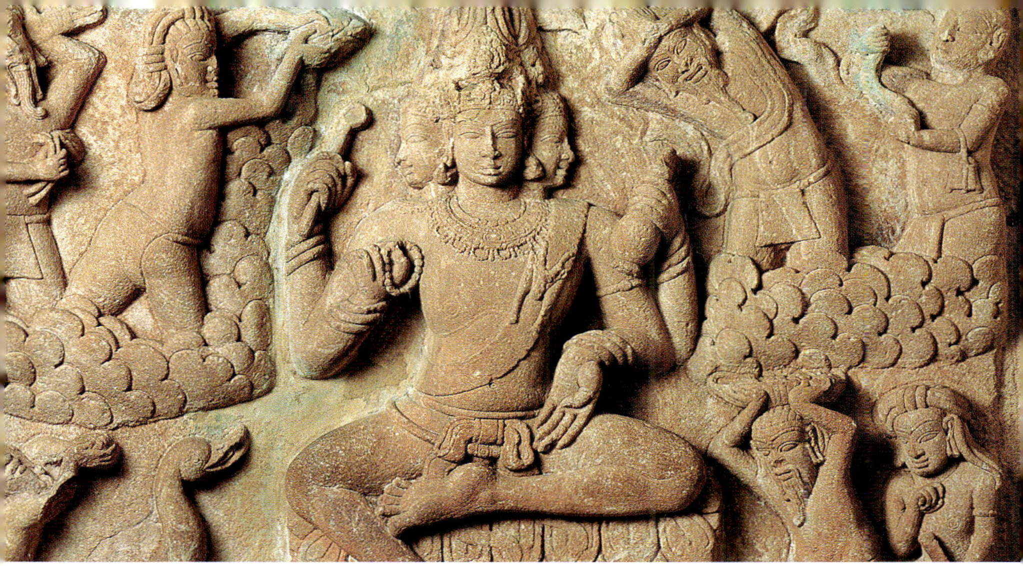

Sleeping Vishnu and seated Brahma - two ceiling panels from the Hucchappayyagudi Aihole, now in the Chhatrapati Shivaji Maharaj Vastu Sangrahalaya, Mumbai

Aihole

Pattadakal

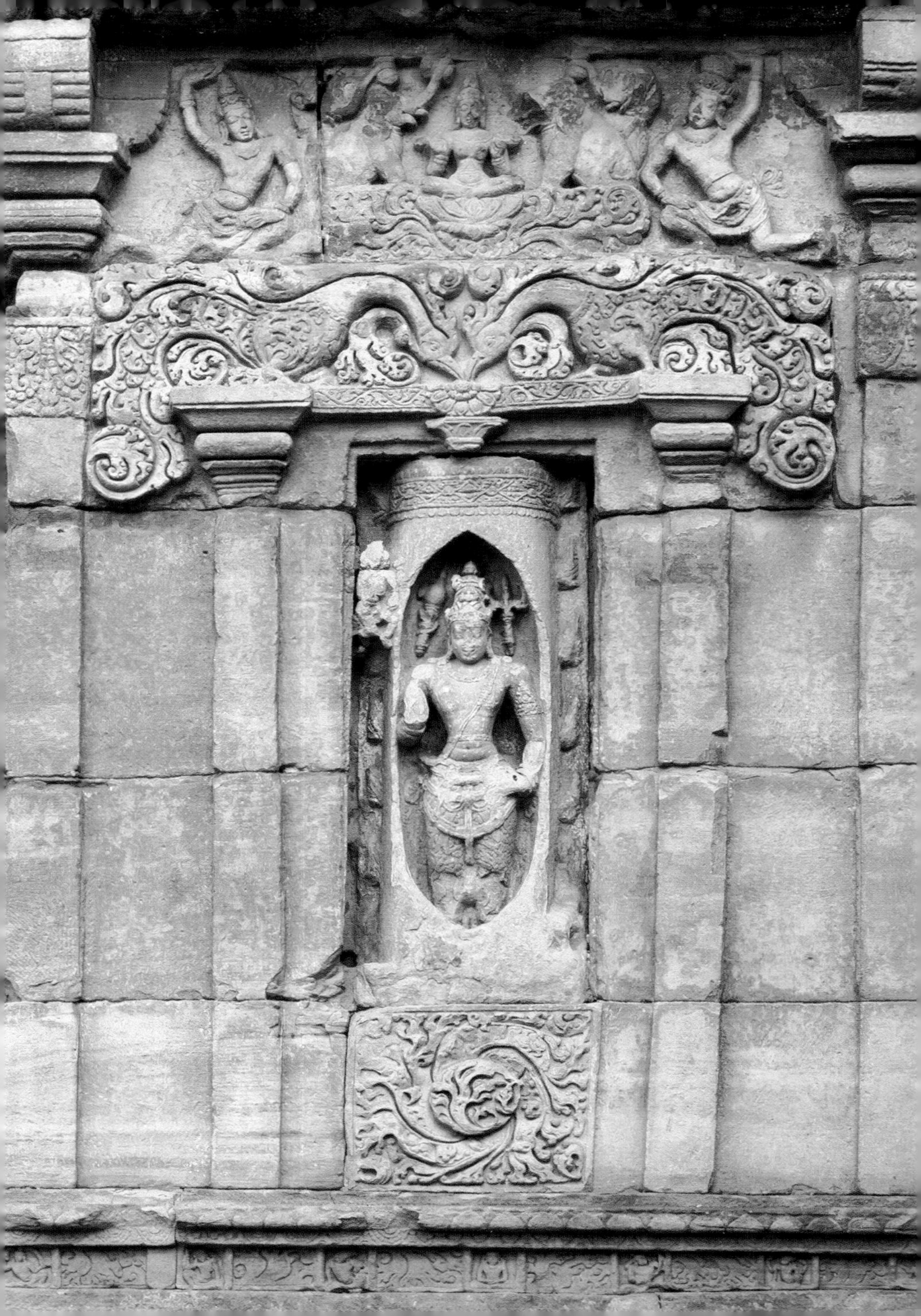

PREFACE

Badami, Aihole and Pattadakal are renowned for their magnificent temples, particularly those associated with the Early Chalukya rulers in the 6th-8th centuries CE. Unsurpassed for their remarkably complete condition, varied architectural styles, and wealth of sculptures, these temples are to be counted among the earliest, most artistically beautiful religious monuments of the Deccan. The temples are excavated into red sandstone cliffs and also built out of sandstone blocks, thereby bridging the transition from rock-cut to constructed techniques. They are located in and around the towns of Badami and Aihole and the village of Pattadakal, on or near the Malprabha river in present-day Bagalkot District of northern Karnataka. Visitors are encouraged to spend at least three days in the area so as to explore the various sites and monuments described here. The spectacular rocky setting offers numerous scenic walks leading to out-of-the-way spots with delightful natural springs and unique prehistoric remains.

The author's acquaintance with the Badami temples dates from his first trip to India in 1965–6, when still an architecture student in Melbourne. In his further studies at the School of Oriental and African Studies, University of London, he selected Badami's structural buildings as the subject for a PhD thesis, spending two seasons in the area in the early 1970s preparing measured architectural drawings. It is therefore with considerable pleasure that the author returns here to introduce these temples to the general traveler and lover of Indian art. Expanding on the original dissertation, this volume covers both the rock-cut and structural monuments of the Early Chalukyas, as well as the temples of later rulers in the Badami area. Nor is the coverage limited to architecture, since the magnificent sculpted panels and carved ornamentation with which the buildings are adorned are also noticed here.

George Michell

Opposite: Shiva appearing out of the *linga*; wall panel from the Virupaksha temple, Pattadakal

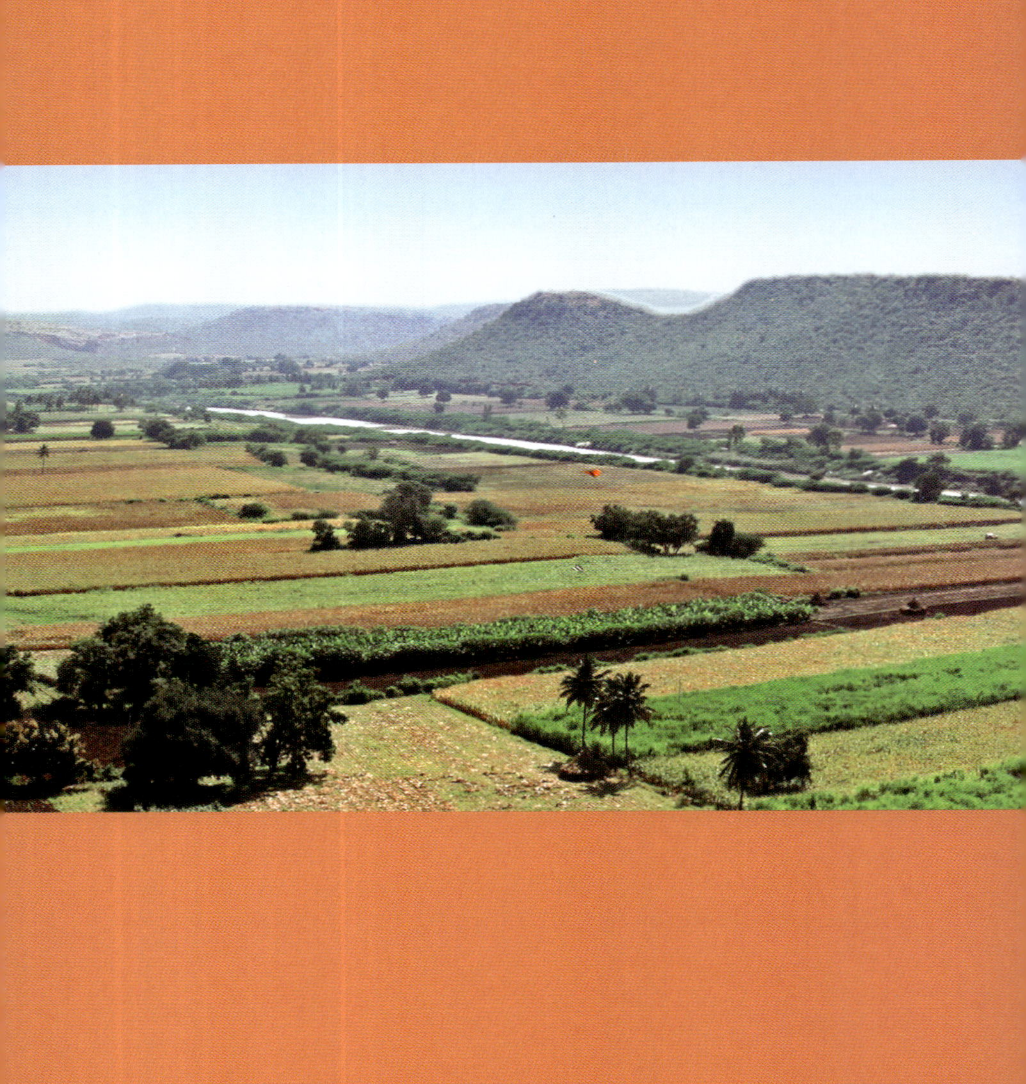

INTRODUCTION

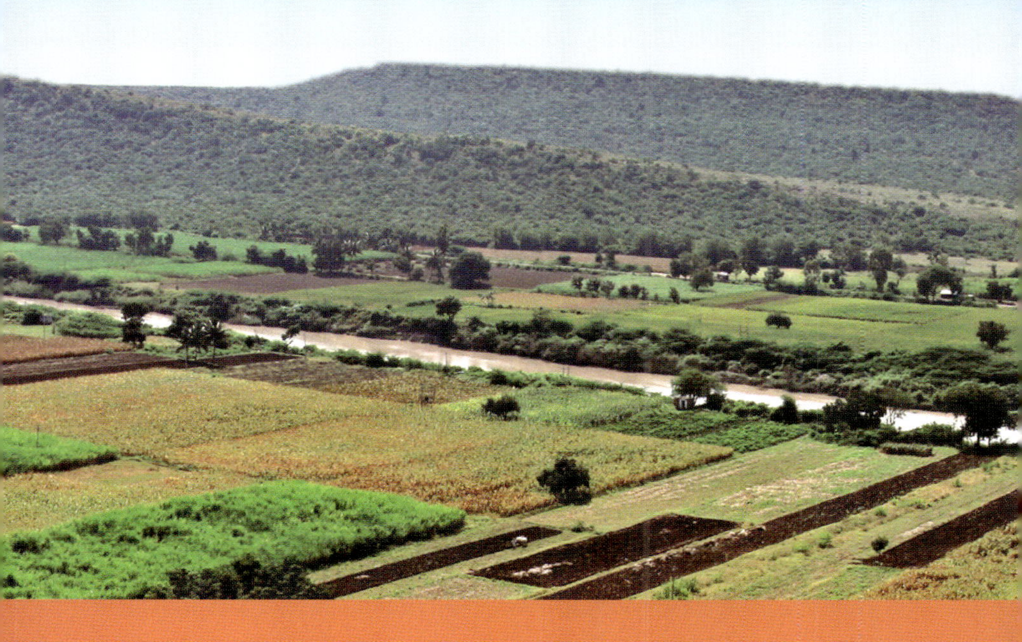

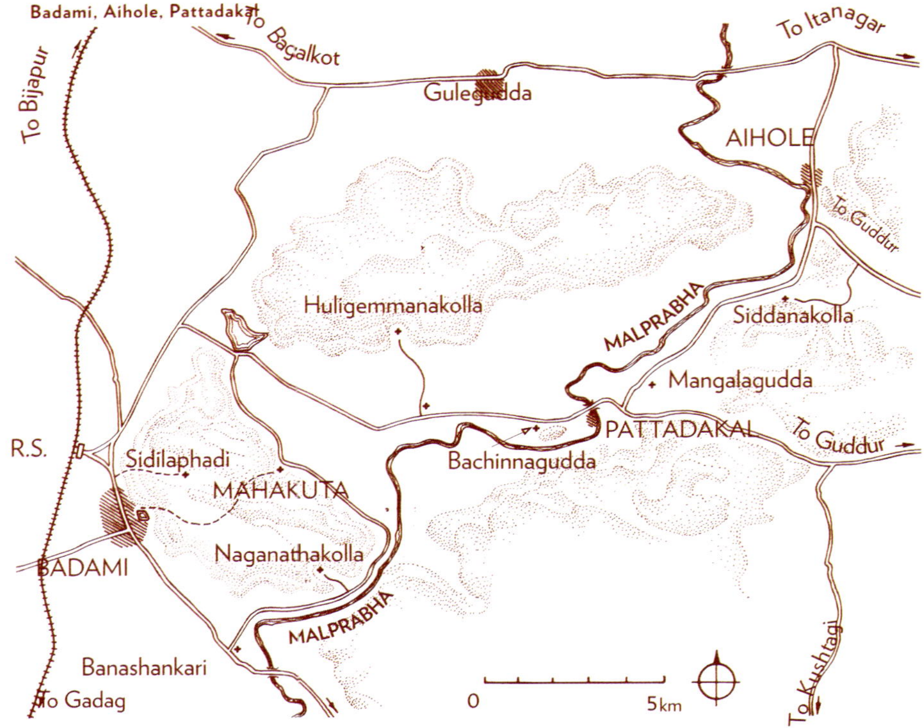

THE MALPRABHA VALLEY

The realm of the Early Chalukyas in Karnataka is mainly confined to a valley, some 25 kilometres long, through which the Malprabha river flows in a north-easterly direction. Little more than 8 kilometres wide at its broadest point, the valley is fringed with sandstone bluffs, some with dramatic cliffs and spectacular ravines. This secluded zone is today richly irrigated, and must once have been densely populated, since it served as the core of a kingdom that in its day extended across most of the Deccan. In addition to its plentiful supply of water, the Malprabha valley also benefits from natural protection since it is hemmed in by rugged cliffs. The strategic value of this setting was well appreciated by the Early Chalukyas, as well as their successors, some of whom erected defensive fort walls, bastions and watchtowers on the edges of the rocky outcrops. Wars and invasions are long past and the Malprabha valley is a now peaceful, rural area that derives much charm from its comparatively isolated situation.

Preceding pages: Panoramic view of the Malprabha valley

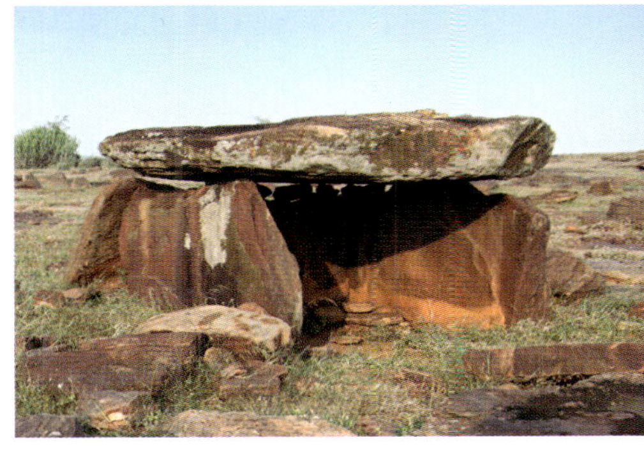

Dolmen on Meguti hill, Aihole

With its natural advantages of river and surrounded cliffs, it is hardly surprising that the Malprabha valley should have been the setting for human habitation from earliest times. This is borne out by the number of **Prehistoric Remains** that have been discovered here. These take the form of lithic burials known as dolmens, as well as representations of animals, birds and even human figures painted or pecked onto the surfaces of natural rock-shelters. The chronology of these burials, paintings and pictographs spans the Palaeolithic, Microlithic and Megalithic periods, extending back to the 2nd and 1st millennia BCE.

Another advantageous feature of the Malprabha valley are the **Water Sources** trapped just beneath the level top of the surrounding hills. These result in a number of waterfalls and natural springs that feed rocky cisterns and man-made tanks known as *kollas*. Such well-watered locales never run dry even in the hottest months, and for this reason many have become tirthas, or holy pools, sacred to particular Hindu cults. Among these are Mahakuta, reached by road or a footpath from Badami, Siddanakolla on the outskirts of Aihole, and Huligemmanakolla near to the road leading to Pattadakal. In contrast, Badami, the former capital of the Early Chalukyas and still the largest town in

Spring at Siddanakolla

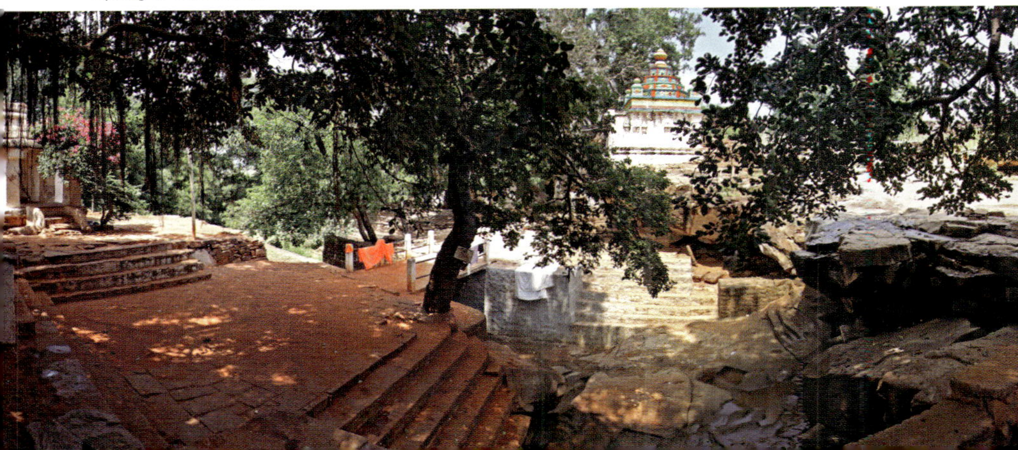

the region, is situated at one end of an artificial tank with strikingly green waters trapped by a stone-faced *bund*. This dam-wall bridges a gap of about 300 metres between two ends of a natural horseshoe of sandstone cliffs located at the south-western end of the Malprabha valley. The pilgrimage shrine at Banashankari, a short distance from Badami, faces towards an immense, rain-fed tank.

And then of course there is the **Malprabha River** itself. Towards the middle of the valley the river takes a sharp turn so as to run northwards (in the direction of the Himalaya range, in local imagination). This auspicious point served as an ideal setting for a group of Early Chalukya temples that now enjoys international renown, having been inscribed in 1987 on UNESCO's prestigious World Heritage List. As for Aihole, the second largest town in the area, this is located just a short distance from the right bank of the Malprabha, where the cliffs almost converge at the north-eastern end of the valley.

THE EARLY CHALUKYAS AND THEIR SUCCESSORS

Before the advent of the Early Chalukyas in the middle of the 6th century CE the Malprabha valley region came under the sway of the Satavahanas and Kadambas. However, virtually nothing can now be seen of these earlier occupants. Recent excavations beneath the hill of Bachinnagudda near Pattadakal revealed brick structures and coins datable to the 3rd–4th centuries but these traces have now been covered up. Nothing has yet been discovered of the Kadamabas who were present here in the 5th–6th centuries. In contrast, there is an abundance of historical information available about the **Early Chalukyas**. Thanks to the many inscriptions engraved on temple walls and columns in the Badami area, as well as on copper-plates discovered at various sites throughout Karnataka and Andhra Pradesh. Both Sanskrit and Kannada languages are used in these records, but the script is mostly Southern Indian and the dates are invariably in the Shaka era (Shaka year 1 = 78 CE). It is perhaps worth noting that the Badami kings are usually designated as the Early Chalukyas in order to distinguish them from a dynasty established at Kalyana in the extreme north of Karnataka near the border with Maharashtra during the 11th and 12th centuries, generally known as the Later

Varaha with sun and moon; regal emblem of the Early Chalukyas: column detail from the Ladkhan temple, Aihole

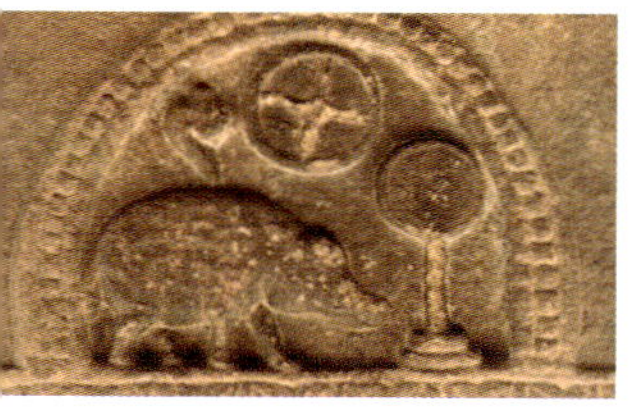

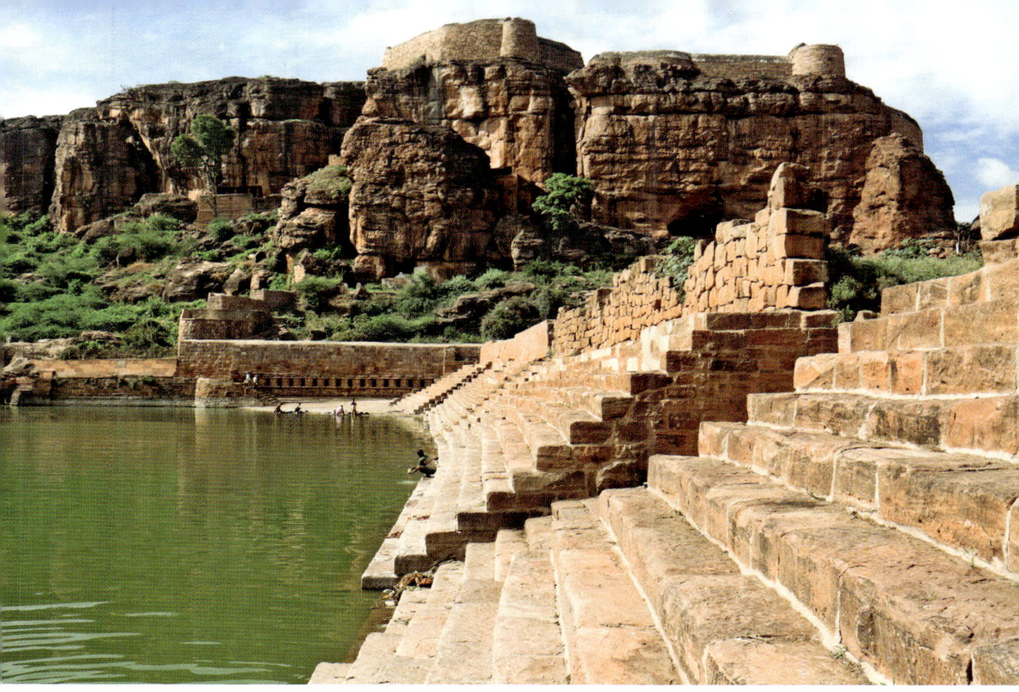

Steps leading down to the tank at Badami; founded by Pulakeshin I, with the South Fort in the distance

Chalukyas. In spite of this correspondence of names, the two royal families do not seem to have been directly related in any way.

Pulakeshin I (r. 544–67) is generally regarded as the founder of the Early Chalukya line. An inscription record of this king engraved on a boulder in Badami records the fortification of the hill above "Vatapi" in 544. Pulakeshin's choice of this location for his capital was no doubt dictated by strategic considerations since Badami is protected on three sides by rugged sandstone cliffs. The regal emblem adopted by Pulakeshin I and his immediate successors, as revealed on their coins and dynastic seals, was Varaha, the boar incarnation of Vishnu. However, the kings of this line were never adherents of a single Hindu cult and the gods Vishnu, Shiva and Surya all received veneration. Buddhism and Jainism also flourished at various times under Early Chalukya patronage.

On the death of Pulakeshin I, his son **Kirttivarman I** (r. 567–98) ascended the throne. This king embarked upon a policy of expanding Early Chalukya power throughout peninsular India. Among the architectural projects associated with his reign are the rock-cut temples in the cliffs above Badami, one of which was completed in 578 by his younger brother **Mangalesha**. Succeeding as regent when Kirttivarman I's eldest son, the future Pulakeshin II, was still a minor, Mangalesha (r. 598–610) subdued the

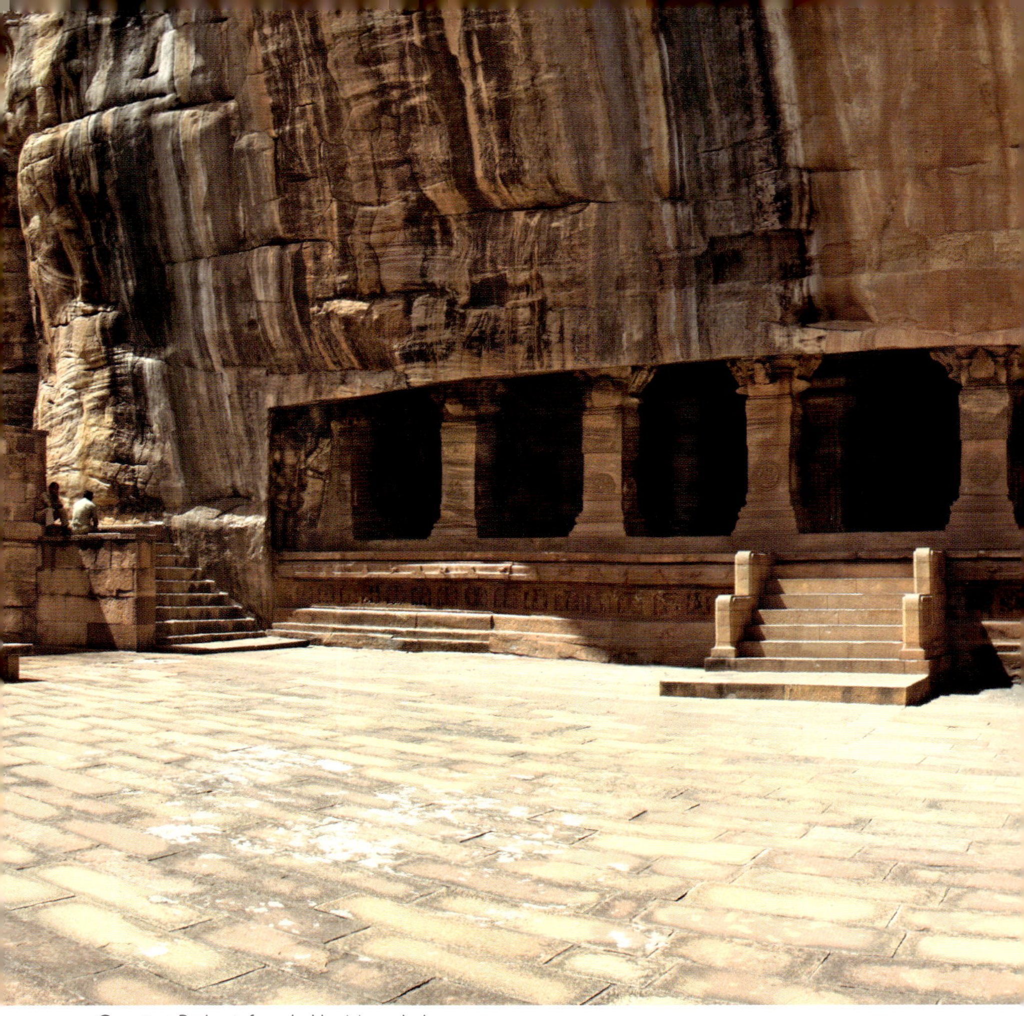

Cave 3 at Badami, founded by Mangalesha

Kalachuri rulers of Maharashtra, thereby extending the Early Chalukya realm to the north. In 602 Mangalesha set up a pillar at Mahakuta to commemorate his mastery over his neighbours. But Mangalesha was eventually challenged and killed by **Pulakeshin II** (r. 610–42), who emerged as one of the great Early Chalukya kings. This figure augmented the reputation of the Early Chalukya kingdom by sending an ambassador bearing gifts to the Sasanian court of Khusrau II in Iran in 626, and in about 633 successfully repelling the advances into the Deccan of Harshavardhana of Kanauj, the most powerful ruler of Northern India at the time. Pulakeshin then turned his attention to the recalcitrant chiefs of Andhra Pradesh, whom he subdued, thereby

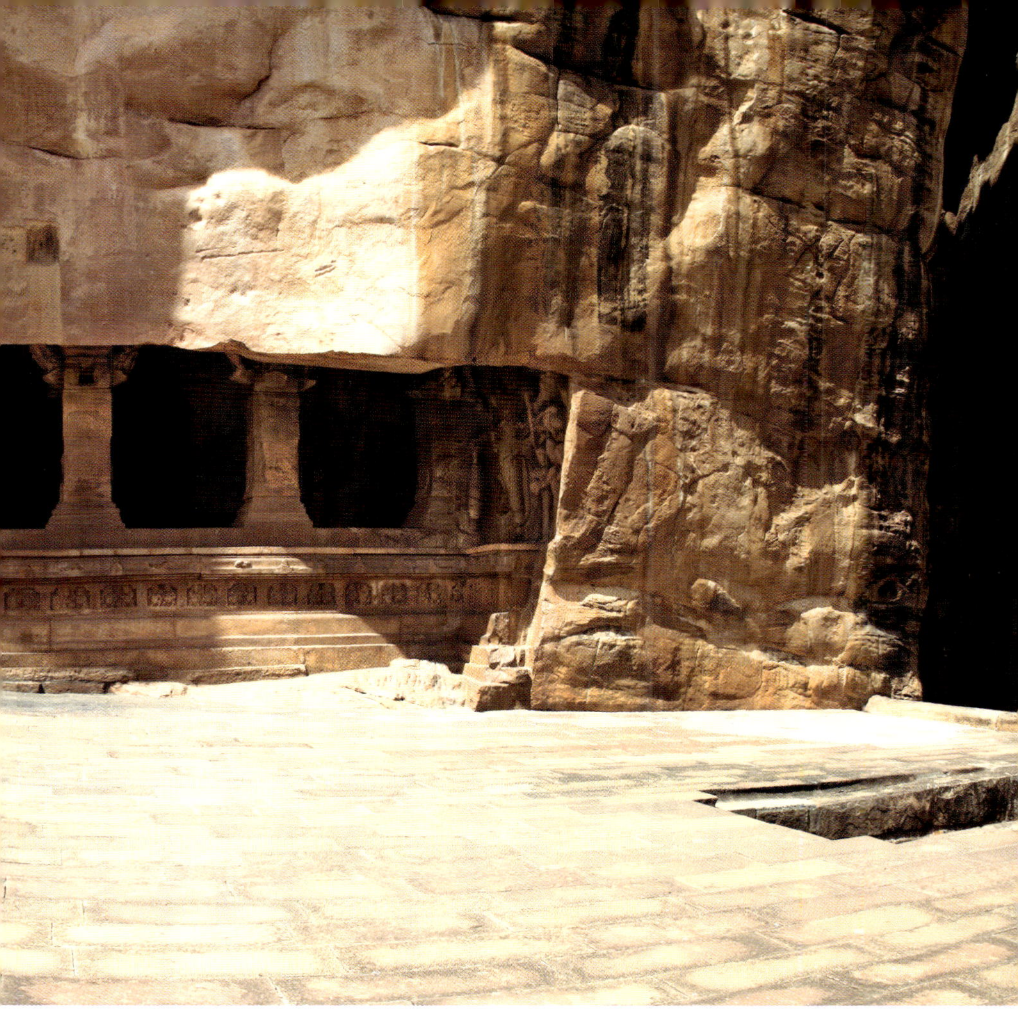

laying the foundation for an eastern branch of the Early Chalukya family. The Tamil territory of the Pallavas to the south of Badami was the next zone to attract Pulakeshin II's attention. After an attempt to besiege Kanchipuram, the Pallavas retaliated. In about 642, the Pallava king Narasimhavarman I invaded the Early Chalukya domains, killing Pulakeshin II and occupying Badami. for more than a decade. Confirmation of the Pallava presence in Badami is provided by an inscription on a boulder near to the Archaeological Museum beside to the north of the tank.

The Pallavas remained in control of Badami for almost 15 years, and it was only under Vikramaditya I (r. 655–81) that the invaders were finally expelled.

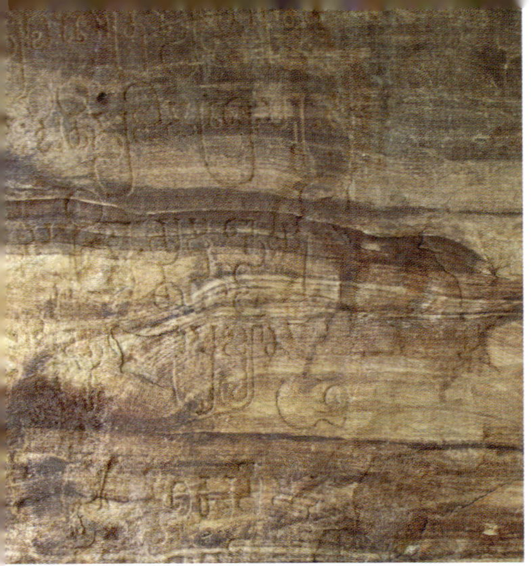

Inscription of Narasimhavarman I on a boulder at Badami recording the Pallava invasion

After repressing disloyal feudatories within his domain, Vikramaditya I undertook various campaigns against the Pallavas between 670 and 675. Most of Vikramaditya I's inscriptions are found in the Andhra country, suggesting that the Early Chalukyas were based in this part of the Deccan during and immediately after the years of the Pallava occupation. Unlike his predecessors, the next ruler Vinayaditya (r. 681–96) presided over an affluent and peaceful realm. The reign of his son and successor **Vijayaditya** (r. 696–734) was the longest of any Early Chalukya ruler, as well as one of the most prosperous of the whole period. Like his father, Vijayaditya associated his son, the future Vikramaditya II, with him in the rule of the kingdom. In 732 Vikramaditya returned from a warring mission against Kanchipuram, having inscribed the name of his father on the Kailasanatha temple there. Vijayaditya is the first known Early Chalukya king to erect a religious monument at Pattadakal. This was dedicated to Shiva under the name Vijayeshvara, in homage to the king himself.

The military campaigns of **Vikramaditya II** (r. 734–45) are described in the inscription on a pillar set up in 755 by his son Kirttivarman II at Pattadakal. In about 745 two sister-queens of Vikramaditya II celebrated a victory of their husband over the Pallavas by erecting a pair of matching temples at Pattadakal. Building activity at this site continued under **Kirttivarman II** (r. 745–57), but during his reign the Early Chalukya kingdom was threatened by the Rashtrakutas of Maharashtra. An inscription of 753 by Dantidurga, who successfully expanded Rashtrakuta sovereignty throughout much of the Deccan, speaks of the destruction of Badami as an accomplished fact. Kirttivarman II seems to have been active for some years after the Rashtrakuta invasion, for in 757 he issued an edict

Pillar inscription at Pattadakal, giving details of the conquests of the father and grandfather of Kirttivarman II

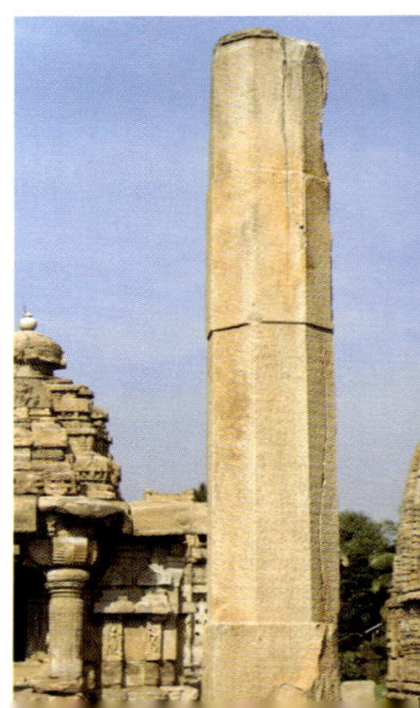

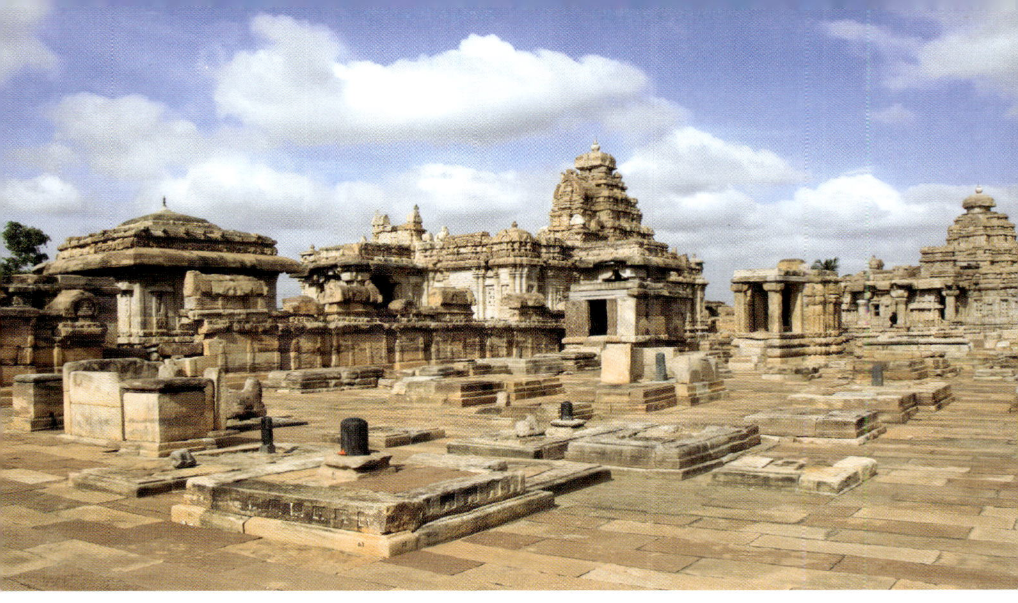

Virupaksha and Mallikarjuna temples, Pattadakal, built by two sister queens of Vikramaditya II

from his 'victorious camp' on the Bhima river. After this nothing more is heard of this last royal figure of the Early Chalukya line.

The emergence of the **Rashtrakutas** signals a new era in the history of Badami, which from this time onwards lost its status as a capital, the centre of power in the Deccan having shifted northwards to Maharashtra. Even so, the few modestly scaled temples erected in Aihole and Pattadakal during the late 8th and early 9th centuries suggest that the Malprabha region retained something of its former importance. The same seems to be true under the **Late Chalukyas**, judging from the abundance of constructional activity during the 11th and 12th centuries in both Badami and Aihole. The temples erected here during this period testify to the presence of a substantial population that enjoyed considerable wealth and influence.

At the very end of the 13th century the Malprabha region, together with much of the Deccan, was ravaged by the conquering armies of the Delhi sultans. After the invaders were driven out, Badami became part of the territory fought over by the Bahmani sultans and the **Vijayanagara Emperors**, the latter established at their great capital on the Tungabhadra river, approximately 125 kilometres south-east of Badami. Two inscriptions in Badami recording additions to the fort walls of the fort on the north side of the town date from 1339 and 1543, during the reigns of the first and last Vijayanagara emperors. respectively. After the catastrophic defeat of the Vijayanagara army in January 1565, at a site on the Krishna river less than 50 kilometres from Aihole, the Malprabha region was absorbed into the kingdom of the **Adil Shahi Sultans** of Bijapur. Evidence of their rule over this zone is provided by a splendid domed tomb in Badami erected by one of their local governors in the early 17th century.

From the Adil Shahis, Badami passed into the hands of the Mughals, who in 1686 took possession of Bijapur and its kingdom. By the middle of the 18th century the Mughal presence in the Deccan had waned and the Malprabha region was contested by the Nizams of Hyderabad and the Peshwas, or Prime Ministers, of the Marathas of Pune in Maharashtra. In 1778 Badami was taken by Haidar Ali, usurper of the Mysore kingdom to the south, but eight years later the town surrendered to the allied forces of the Nizams and the Peshwas after a bitter siege lasting four weeks. At the beginning of the 19th century Badami was the residence of Madhavraj Rastia, an estate-holder under the Peshwas, who shamelessly exploited the local population. Maratha control of Badami was brought to an end in 1818 when General Thomas Munro attacked the town and took it after a considerable effort. Thereafter the Malprabha region was absorbed into the British Dominions of the Bijapur District of the Bombay Presidency. This last phase of Badami's history was briefly interrupted in 1840 when a blind brahmin named Narasimha Dattatreya, accompanied by a fierce band of Arab mercenaries, entered Badami, taking possession of the town and its treasury, and proclaiming himself king. However, within less than one week a modest British force restored the peace by dislodging Narasimha and imprisoning his followers.

MULTIPLE TEMPLE STYLES

Temple architecture in Badami, Aihole and Pattadakal is characterized by a remarkable variety of styles and constructional techniques. This concentration of multiple idioms within the confines of limited zone such as the Malprabha region is to be found nowhere else in India. The location of the Early Chalukya kingdom in the heart of the Deccan helps explain how the Early Chalukya sites came to be a unique meeting place for the distinctive Dravida and Nagara temple building traditions of Southern and Northern India respectively. Not only are these discrete styles represented in temples built side by side, as in Aihole and at Pattadakal, attributes of both these styles even came to incorporated within individual monuments, resulting in a uniquely hybrid idiom. The Malprabha region also witnessed the evolution of a number local temple idioms, here characterized as the Karnataka style and Malprabha tradition.

As already noticed, the Early Chalukya monuments bridge the transition from rock-cut excavation to free-standing construction, beginning with the **Cave-Temples** in Badami and Aihole in the second half of the 6th century. The four examples in Badami are both Shaiva (Cave 1) and Vaishnava (Caves 2 and 3), as well as Jain (Cave 4), in dedication. The cave-temples employ monolithic columns with fluted shafts and cushion-like capitals, with large-scale sculptural compositions occupying the wall spaces in between. These features betray a dependence on earlier Buddhist and Shaiva rock-cut sanctuaries in Maharashtra, as at Ajanta and Elephanta. The layouts of the Badami cave-temples, however, are somewhat different, since they each consist of an outer colonnaded verandah leading to an inner *mandapa*, or columned hall. These sometimes assume impressive dimensions, as in Cave 3, the largest of the Badami rock-cut monuments, and the only one to be provided with an actual date. Small, cell-like sanctuaries are excavated into the rear walls of the *mandapas*. The Hindu and Jain cave-temples in Aihole, the former known as Ravanaphadi, present a different scheme, with triple-bayed openings on three sides of square interior halls. These openings lead to small sanctuaries on axis with the entrances, with chambers opening off to the side embellished with sculptural compositions. Though many of the columnar elements and carved themes of rock-cut monument survive in later structural temples, the layouts just described are not repeated.

The first structural temples date back to the reign of Pulakeshin II in the first decades of the 7th century, after which almost all religious monuments in

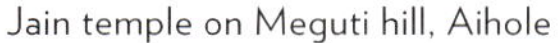

Jain temple on Meguti hill, Aihole

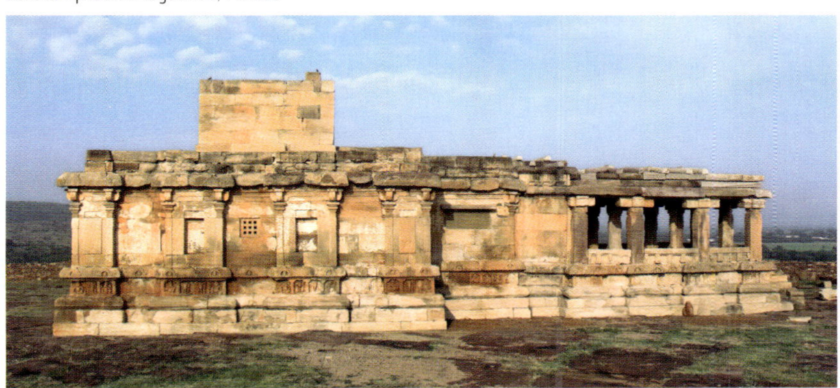

the area were assembled out of dry stone masonry rather than being excavated into cliffs. Significantly, these temples are all built in the **Dravida Style**. Since no earlier Dravida styled monuments are known at other sites in Southern India, it is tempting to propose that this idiom is an Early Chalukya invention, even though eventually it came to be dispersed throughout Karnataka, Andhra Pradesh and Tamil Nadu, evolving over more than 1,000 years. In the Badami region the Dravida style lasted for the whole of the Early Chalukya period, lasting into the Rashtrakuta and Late Chalukya eras.

The earliest example of the Dravida style is the Jain temple on the flat-topped summit of Meguti hill in Aihole, dated 634. Though now only incompletely preserved, the outer walls of the passageway that surrounds the sanctuary on four sides presents the essential attributes of the Dravida manner, being divided vertically into basement mouldings, walls with alternating

Interior of the Ravanaphadi, Aihole

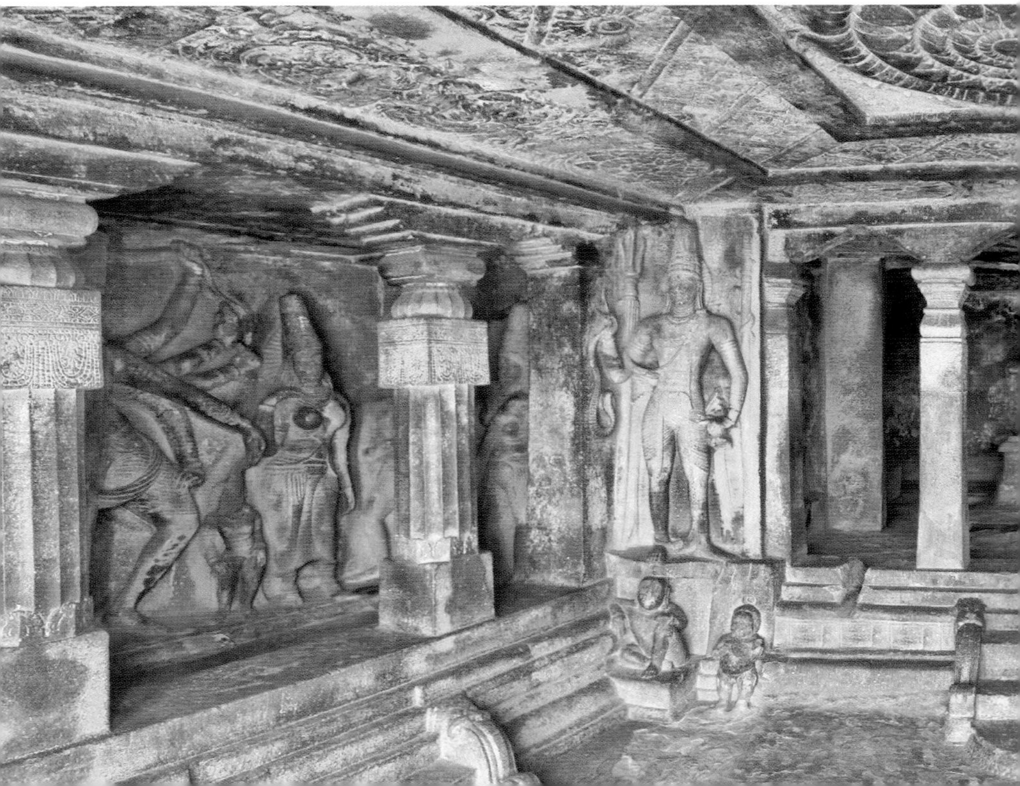

projections and recesses defined by shallow pilasters, and capping *kapota*, or eave, with a parapet now mostly lost. No doubt the sanctuary was once surmounted by a tower that repeated many of the elements of the walls below. (The rooftop chamber seen today is a later replacement.) The sanctuary is approached through an open *mandapa*, with balcony seating between the peripheral columns.

For the next stage in the evolution of the Dravida idiom it is necessary to turn to Badami monuments. The Upper Shivalaya, though now ruined, consists of a rectangle of walls containing a sanctuary surrounded by a passageway on three sides, preceded by a triple-aisled *mandapa*. The outer walls are divided vertically in the manner already described, while the parapet incorporates rudimentary model roof forms, such as barrel-vaulted *shalas* and square-domed *kutas*. Similar components are employed in the tower over the sanctuary,

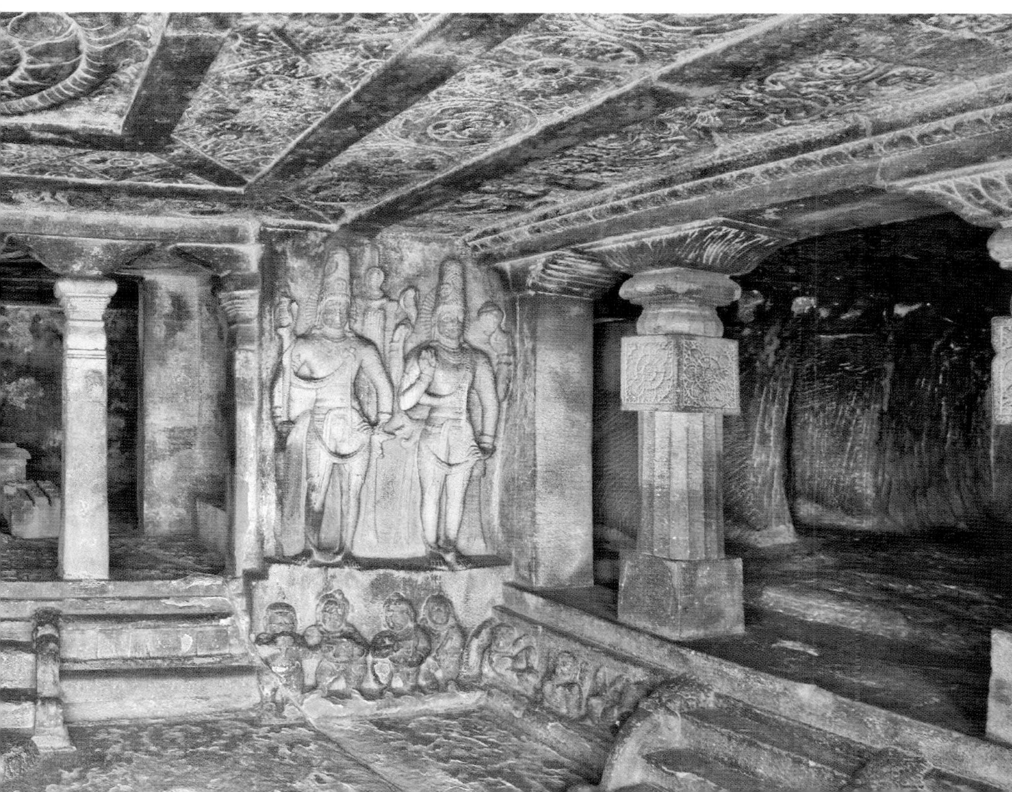

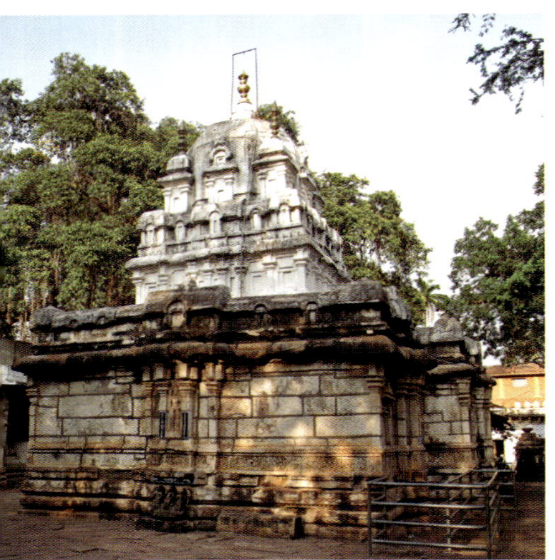

Mahakuteshvara temple, Mahakuta

which is crowned by an enlarged *kuta*-roof with *kudus*, or horseshoe-shaped, false windows, on each face. The more evolved, better preserved Mallegitti Shivalaya temple in Badami gives the best possible idea of the mature early stage of the Dravida manner. This is laid out in a simple sequence of sanctuary, without passageway, triple-aisled *mandapa*, and single-bayed entrance porch. The outer walls are divided vertically in typical fashion into three zones, with fully articulated *shala* and *kuta* parapet elements. Perforated windows set into the side walls of the *mandapa* are flanked by secondary, shorter wall pilasters carrying aquatic monsters with flowing tails known as *makaras*. The whole composition is crowned with a single-storeyed tower topped with an octagon-to-domed roof framed by a quartet of corner model pavilions, each with its own individual *kuta*-roof.

The next phase in the development of the Dravida style coincides with the restoration of Chalukya power in the Malprabha region in the second half of the 7th century. The Mahakuteshvara temple and matching Mallikarjuna temple, both at Mahakuta, each consist of a sanctuary surrounded by a passageway on three sides, opening into a spacious, triple-aisled *mandapa* approached through an entrance porch, with a small Nandi pavilion standing freely in front. The outer walls of both temples are raised high on a series of basement mouldings embellished with narrative friezes. Perforated stone windows are headed by pediments employing both Dravida and Nagara elements, confirming that the Nagara style was already familiar to temple architects by this time (see below). Double sets of pilasters frame major sculpted icons on the wall projections, while prominent *shalas* and *kutas* mark the parapet. Like the earlier Malegitti Shivalaya, the towers at Mahakuta are topped by octagon-to-dome roofs.

The Dravida mode under the Early Chaluykas attains a climax in the early 8th century, as is obvious from the monuments at Pattadakal, beginning with the Sangameshvara temple, left unfinished at the death of Vijayaditya in 734,

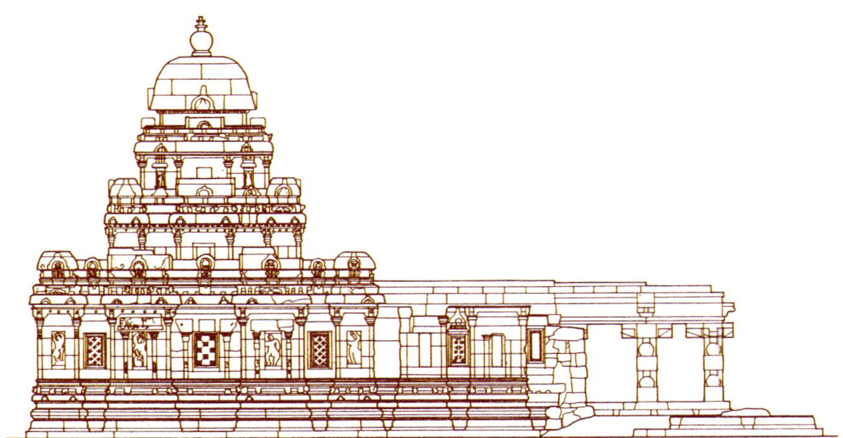

Sangameshvara temple, Pattadakal

and continuing with the Virupaksha and Mallikarjuna temples, under construction from about 745 onwards during Vikramaditya II's reign. Here can be seen the transformation of the Dravida temple into a formally planned complex, with the principal shrine set in a walled compound lined with subshrines, aligned with a free-standing Nandi pavilion and entrance gate. This architectural scheme owes much to Pallava influence from Tamil Nadu, in particular from the early 8th-century Kailasanatha temple at Kanchipuram, a monument visited by Vikramaditya II. The elevations of the three Pattadakal temples just mentioned present a considerable advance on earlier practice. Their outer walls employ multiple projections framed by single, then double, and finally triple, sets of pilasters, with perforated stone windows in the intervening recesses. The *mandapa* walls are interrupted on three sides by projecting porches with balcony seating sheltered by deep curving eaves. Lines of prominent *shalas* and *kutas* constitute the parapets that rise above. The towers over the sanctuaries employ two or three diminishing square storeys, complete with their own pilastered walls and parapets, capped with *kutas* or hemispherical roofs. Frontal projections on the towers are conceived as enlarged *gavakshas*, or horseshoe-shaped arches, which are a borrowing from contemporary Nagara architecture. The *mandapa* interiors are expanded into five aisles defined by rows of columns in both directions. Many of these features are also to be found in the Papanatha temple at Pattadakal,

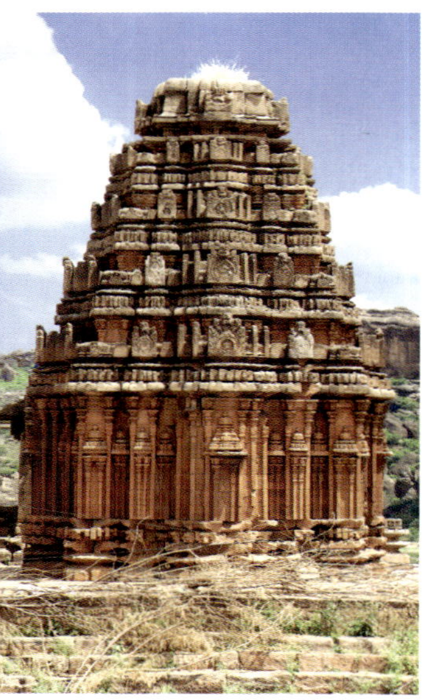
Yellamma temple, Badami

the only Early Chalukya monument at this site with a pair of interconnecting *mandapas*. Dating from the very end of the Early Chalukya era, the Papanatha presents a unique blend of disparate elements: niches headed with Nagara *gavaksha* pediments; parapet with Dravida styled *shalas* and *kutas*; and modest Nagara type tower with *gavaksha* frontal projection.

After these grandly conceived, elaborately finished Dravida monuments it is something of an anticlimax to consider the later history of this idiom under the Rashtrakutas in the later 8th and 9th centuries, and then under Late Chalukyas in the 11th and 12th centuries. While the Dravida temples assigned to these later periods to some extent imitate their predecessors, they present an overall simplification of design and hardening of detail. This is well seen in the Jain temple at Pattadakal, with its closely paired, slender pilasters, and sharply modelled capitals and brackets. The porch here has columns with squat circular shafts and similarly shaped capitals. The same features are seen in the two Rashtrakuta shrines of the Kunti group in Aihole.

Among the many Dravida monuments from the Late Chalukya era in the Malprabha region is the Yellamma temple overlooking the tank in Badami. Erected in 1139, its exterior is enhanced by narrow projections defined by slender pilasters; secondary pairs of pilasters carry pediments with *kutas* as well as Nagara styled *shikharas*. These elements are repeated in the four-storeyed tower that rises above. An idea of the monumental possibilities of the Late Chalukya idiom may be had from the Gauri temple in Aihole. This 12th-century monument has a spacious *mandapa* with porch projections on three sides. Four columns in the middle have ornate, 16-sided shafts topped by double capitals. Wall niches are headed by Nagara styled *shikhara*-towers in shallow relief. A feature to be found in a number of other Late Chaluyka temples in Aihole is the free-standing portal, with a pair of columns carrying a decorated lintel. Such portals generally serve as entrances to stepped tanks.

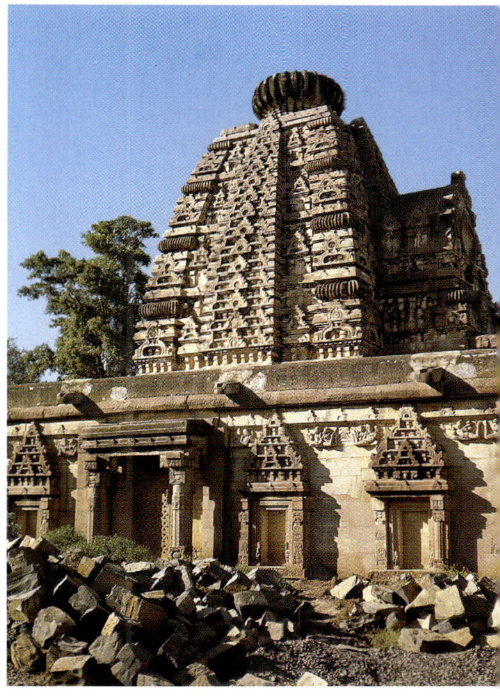

Svarga Brahma temple, Alampur, Andhra Pradesh

Compared with the long career of the Dravida mode in the religious architecture in the Malprabha region, the **Nagara Style** is relatively short-lived, being restricted to the late 7th and first half of the 8th centuries, after which it altogether disappears from the Malprabha region. An import from Northern India, the Nagara style was most likely adopted by the Early Chalukyas when based in the Andhra country during the Pallava occupation of Badami. Evidence for this is provided by the temples at Alampur, near the confluence of the Tungabhadra and Krishna rivers, some 250 kilometres east of Badami. The temples here are topped by curved, *shikhara*-type towers covered with meshes of *gavaksha* motifs, and crowned with prominent ribbed *amalaka* finials. That the Alampur monuments belong to the late 7th century is confirmed by the Svarga Brahma temple there. Like its neighbours, it consists of a *linga* sanctuary surrounded by a passageway and preceded by a triple-aisled *mandapa*, contained within a rectangle of walls, with projecting porches on three sides. Exactly this scheme is found in the dilapidated Galaganatha temple at Pattadakal, which may be regarded as an imitation Alampur monument dating from the same time. A more evolved version of the Nagara idiom is seen in the early 8th-century Kashivishvanatha temple, also at Pattadakal. Here, a complex mesh of *gavaksha* motifs completely covers the curving facets of the *shikhara* spire. The sanctuary walls beneath have shallow projections (without pilasters), headed by pediments composed of interlocking full and split-*gavaksha* motifs.

The Kashivishvanatha contrasts with a number of more rudimentary, but probably contemporary Nagara styled temples, such as those found at Pattadakal and Mahakuta. These each consist of a small sanctuary with a

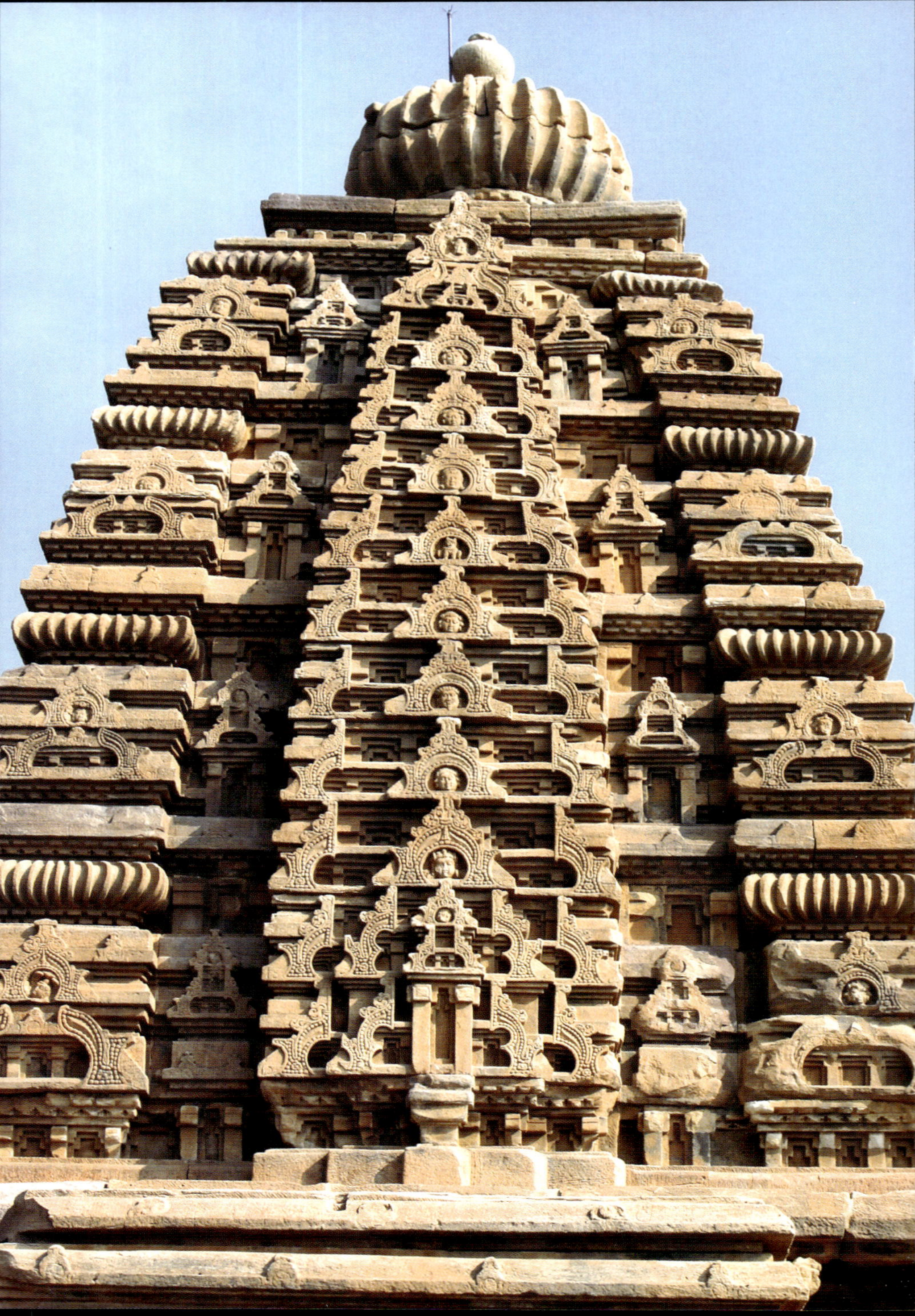

Opposite: Tower of the Galaganatha temple, Pattadakal

curved *shikhara*-tower fronted by an enlarged *gavaksha* framing an icon of Shiva, approached through a walled vestibule or open porch. Nagara styled towers of the same type also surmount the Papanatha temple at Pattadakal, already referred to, as well as a number of monuments in Aihole, such as the Chakragudi, Hucchimalligudi and Durga temple. The last of these is laid out on a unique, apsidal-ended plan topped by an incomplete Nagara styled tower. Wall niches in its outer colonnaded verandah are headed by elaborate pediments employing both Dravida and Nagara components.

In contrast with the Dravida and Nagara styles, which were widely dispersed throughout Southern and Northern India respectively, the Malprabha region also witnessed the development of an architectural mode, here termed the **Karnataka Style.** Temples of this type are recognized by their pyramidal square towers with superimposed eave-like tiers. The principal shrines in the Mallikarjuna and Galaganatha complexes in Aihole, as well as several small examples at Mahakuta, demonstrate that this mode was current in the Malprabha valley during Early Chalukya times. In the temples of the Rashtrakutas, these eave-like tiers are reduced to multiple, sharply-cut mouldings separated by deep recesses, as in the Badigargudi in Aihole. This Karnataka style continued to evolve under the Late Chalukyas, as is evident from the small temples around the tank in Badami, and the many examples which dot the streets of Aihole.

To this array of architectural idioms may be added another, which may be regarded as an expression of a local **Malprabha Tradition.** Temples of this type employ sloping stone roofs, with the joints covered with log-like stone strips, in obvious imitation of thatch and wooden construction.

Ladhkan temple, Aihole

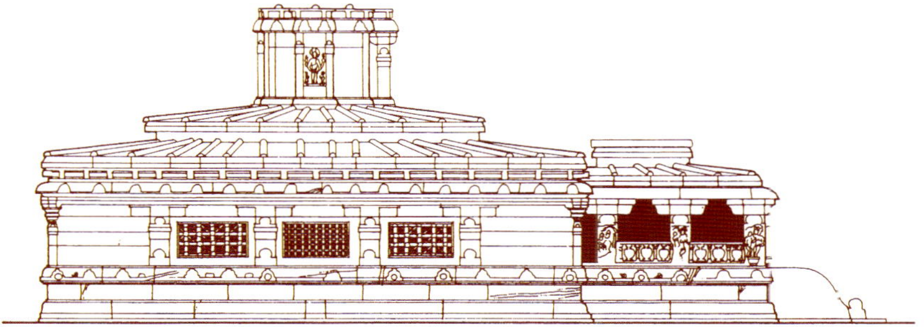

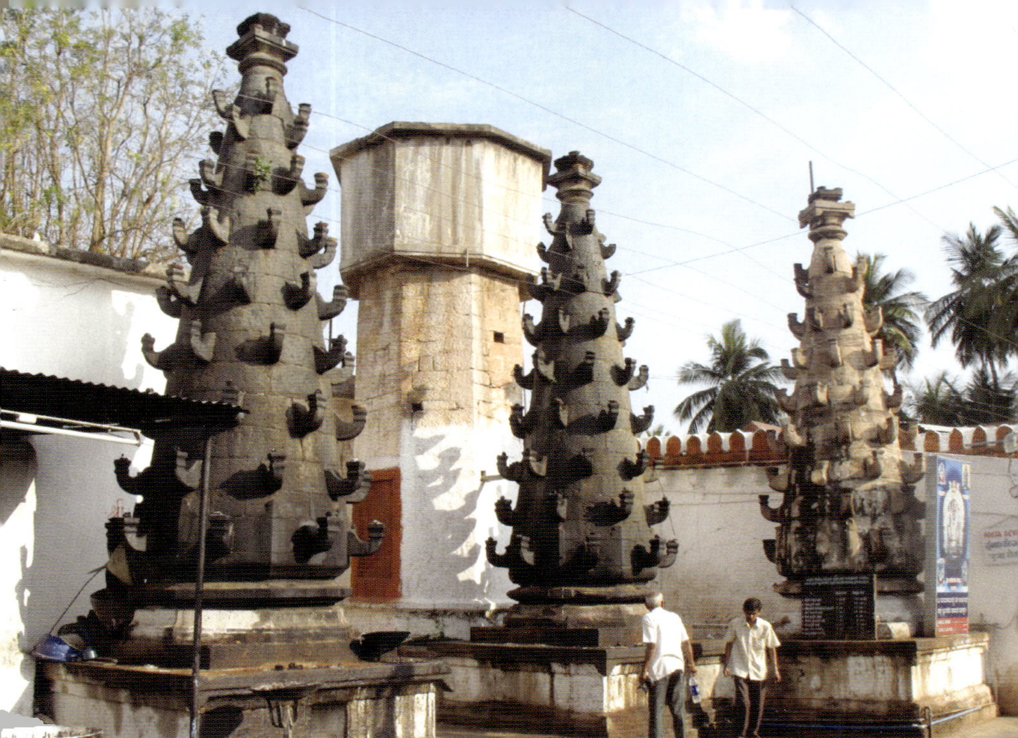

Dipa-stambhas at Banashankari

The outstanding example of this tradition is the early 8th-century Ladkhan temple in Aihole. This unique building has a central bay with a raised roof supporting a small shrine, surrounded on four sides by double tiers of sloping roofs with protective strips. The adjacent, slightly earlier Gaudargudi has a sanctuary approached through a single-bayed *mandapa* surrounded on four sides by an open colonnade, also roofed with sloping slabs. The four temples of the Kunti Group in Aihole repeat this scheme, though each building here is only partly open. The same roofing pattern is even repeated in the Durga temple, in spite of its apsidal-ended plan. The great Dravida style monuments at Pattadakal, which have already been noticed, also employ double tiers of sloping roof slabs with protective strips, though these are mostly concealed behind the parapets. This emphasis on sloping roofs becomes a prominent feature of later architecture, as in the Late Chalukya period porch addition to the Bhutanatha temple overlooking the end of Badami's tank.

No account of temple architecture in the Malprabha region would be complete without mentioning the **Maratha Style** that was introduced during the course of the 18th century. While the chief example of this mode, the goddess sanctuary at Banashankari, is in itself of little architectural interest, the temple has within its walled compound an imposing trio of *dipa-stambhas*, or lamp-columns. These distinctive Maratha features consist of octagonal tapering columns with projecting curved brackets for oil lamps. Similar brackets embellish the lamp-column that protrudes from the roof of the triple-stage arcaded tower that overlooks the vast tank in front of the temple.

A PROFUSION OF SCULPTURAL THEMES

Nowhere else in India during the 6th, 7th and first half of the 8th centuries is there such as concentration of high quality, well preserved stone art as that found on the Early Chalukya monuments. These masterly sculptures illustrate a full spectrum of Hindu icons, as well as a rich narrative tradition that draws on the *Ramayana* and the *Mahabharata*, and also the Krishna legend. To this must be added the imagery associated with Buddhism and Jainism, even if the former was suppressed at some stage in the Early Chalukya era. This predominantly Hindu iconography coexists with an abundance of accessory motifs that fulfill a magical protective purpose within temples, and which draw on what might be described as a substratum of pan-Indian folk beliefs. Almost all these themes disappear in the later monuments of the region, the exception being the standing and seated Tirthankara icons that were installed in the Jain monuments founded during the Late Chalukya era.

Early Chalukya Art is characterized by figures with robustly modelled torsos and limbs. The impression of solidity is to some extent alleviated by the delicately worked costumes, jewellery and headdresses, the swaying postures of lithe maidens and goddesses, and the dynamic postures of gods, such as Shiva dancing or spearing the demon Andhaka. Animals, too, form part of this art, as can be seen in the friezes of lions and elephants, and the extended lion and *yali* brackets that carry roof beams. The deep carving of these figures and animals contrasts with the shallow decorative reliefs that adorn the shafts of *mandapa* columns and sides of beams and ceilings.

Wall Panels at the ends of the outer verandahs of the Badami cave-temples are conceived as majestic, grandly-scaled compositions. Those of Cave 3 illustrate Vishnu as Vaikuntha, seated on the coils of Shesha, as well as Varaha, Narasimha and Trivikrama. In contrast, those of Cave 1, which is dedicated to Shiva, depict this god dancing, Shiva with Nandi, and syncretistic images of Harihara and Ardhanarishvara, the last two at either end of the verandah. Further Shaiva themes are seen in the Ravanaphadi in Aihole, where an expanded

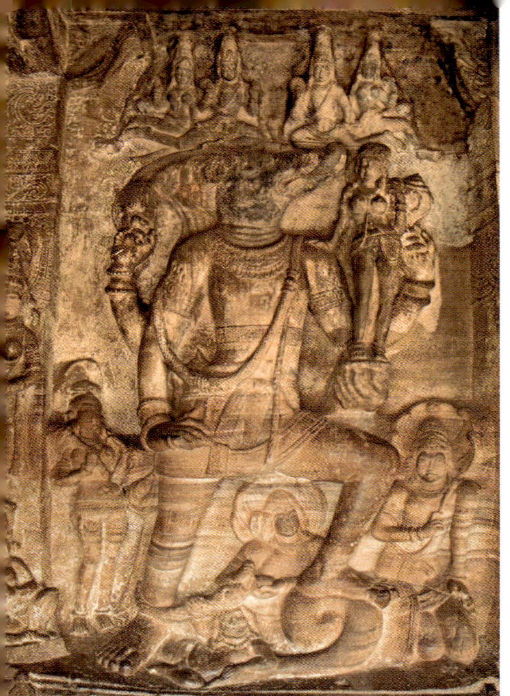
Varaha; wall panel from Cave 3, Badami

Opposite: Vaikuntha; wall panel from Cave 3, Badami

tableau portrays Shiva dancing in the company of Parvati, Ganesha and the Saptamatrikas. The antechamber to the *linga* sanctuary in the Aihole cave is flanked by panels depicting Varaha, and Durga slaying Mahisha. This juxtaposition of Vaishnava and Shaiva icons within the same monument is also found in the wall panels of structural monuments. The Malegitti Shivalaya in Badami, for instance, is enhanced by a pair of matching icons of Vishnu and Shiva.

However, the cult dedications of the different sacred monuments are more often expressed through a restricted range of subjects.Thus the nearby Upper Shivalaya betrays its Vaishnava affiliation from the panels showing Krishna holding up Mount Govardhana, and the same god subduing the serpent demon Kaliya. In contrast, the Shaiva dedication of the twin Mahakuteshvara and Mallikarjuna temples at Mahakuta is apparent from the multiple icons of Shiva that occupy the wall panels. The same is true of the smaller, Sangameshvara temple at the same site, which has representations of Lakulisha, Ardhanarishvara and Harihara on its outer walls. This same trio of images is found on the small Kadasiddheshvara temple at Pattadakal. The horrific, skeletal figures of Kala and Kali guarding the outer gate to the Mahakuta complex are, however, unique; most likely they postdate the Early Chalukya era.

Wall panels on the major temples at Pattadakal encompass a full range of Shaiva themes, though occasional Vaishnava figures are also incorporated. The Sangameshvara, for instance, depicts Shiva in various aspects, including the god spearing Andhaka, dancing in the skin of the elephant demon, and standing together with Bhringi. The Virupaksha temple is unsurpassed for the number and variety of icons on its outer walls, but here there is a mingling of Shaiva and Vaishnava themes, best seen on the frontal (east) facade, where matching panels portray Shiva appearing out of the *linga*, as well as Vishnu as Trivikrama. Among the multiple appearances of

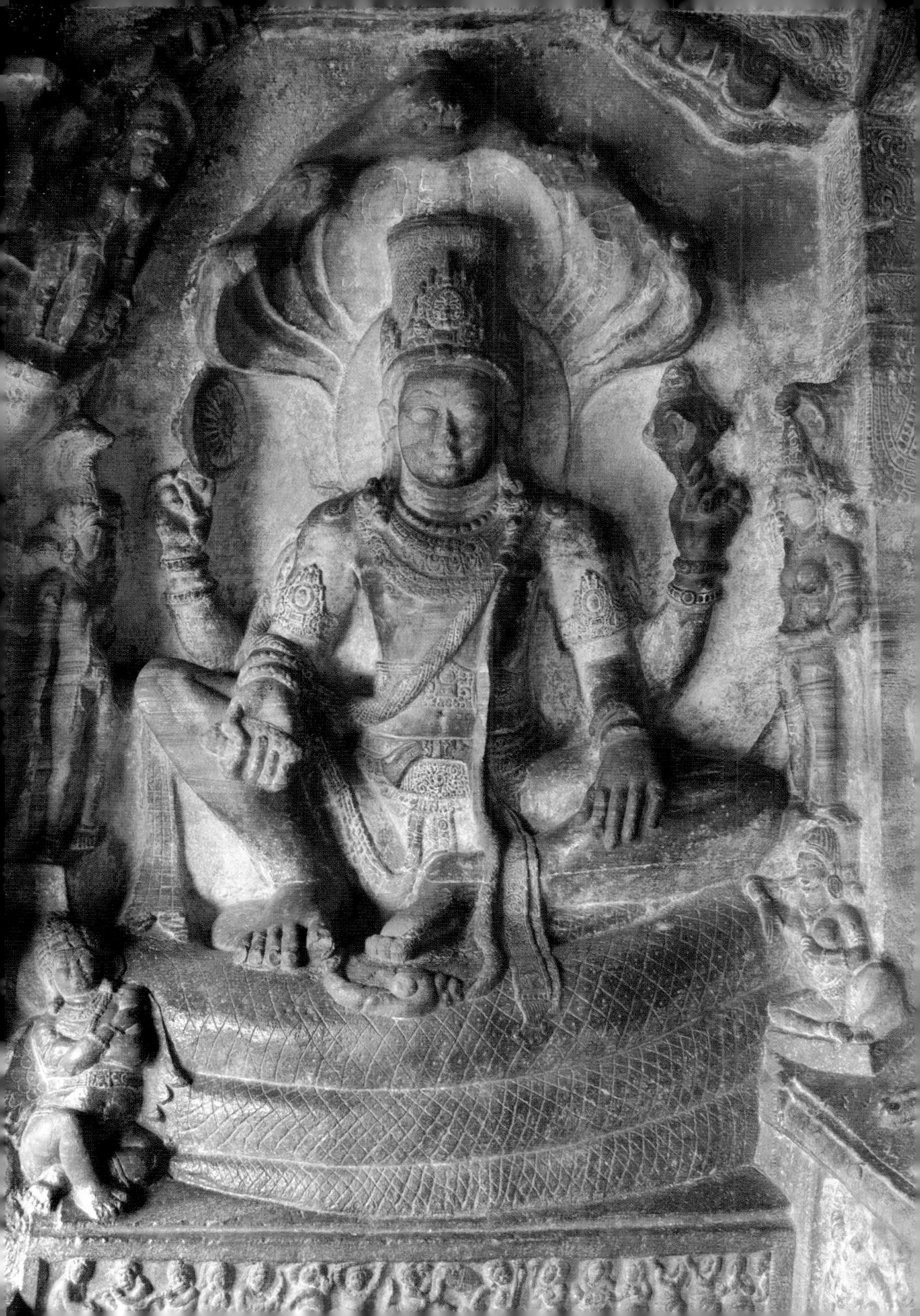

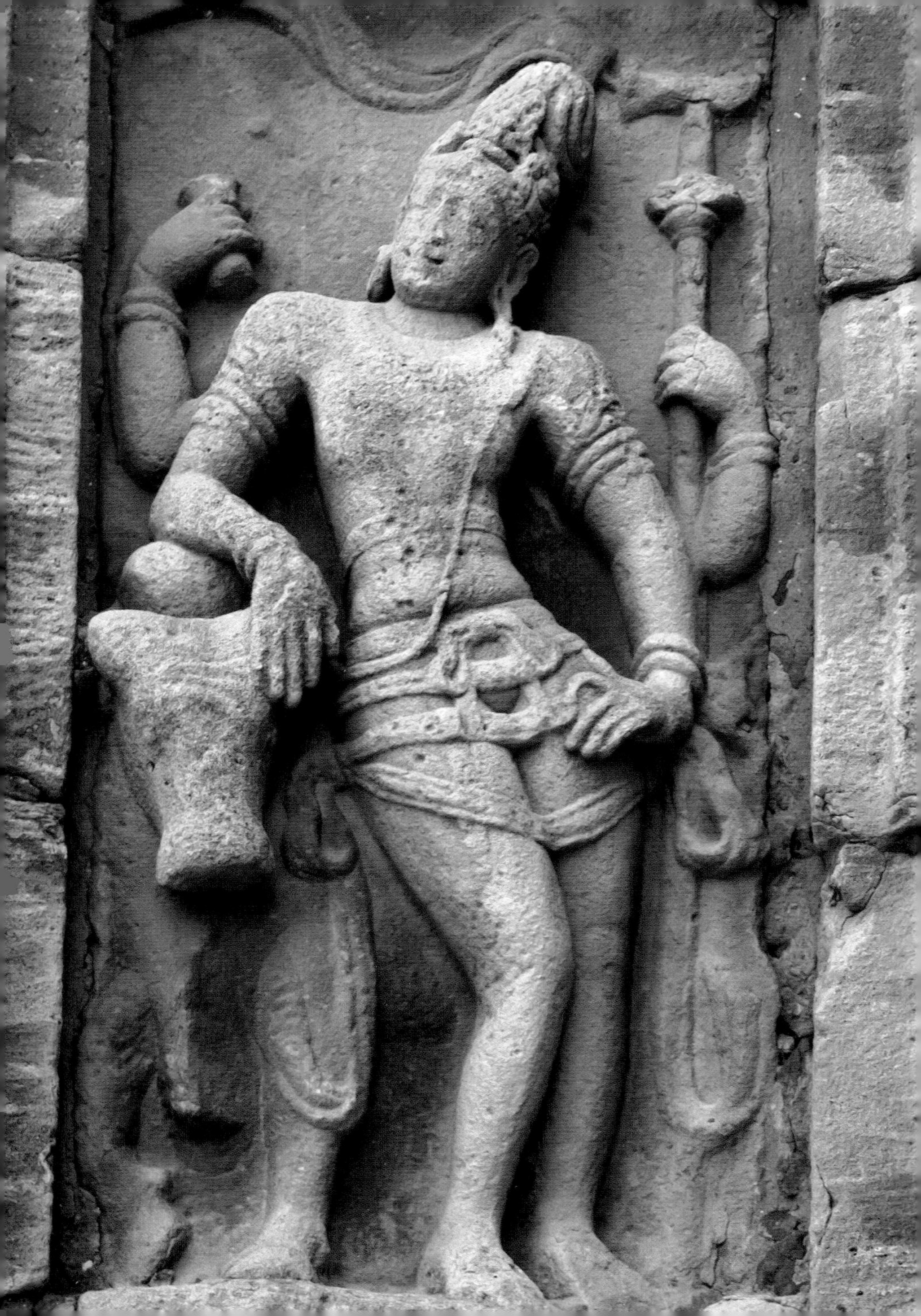

Opposite: Shiva with Nandi; wall panel from the Virupaksha temple, Pattadakal
Below: Ramayana wall panels from the Papanatha temple, Pattadakal

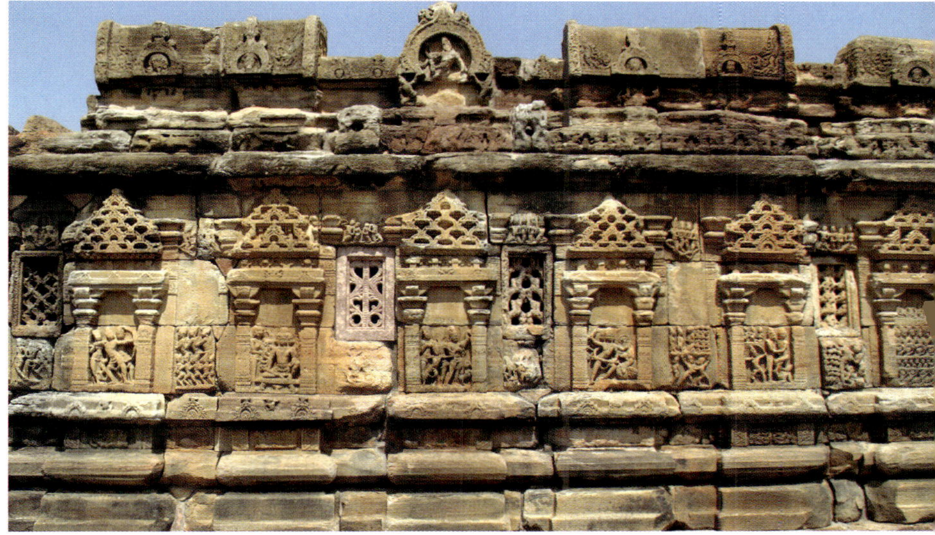

Shiva on this monument is an eight-armed version of the god, Nataraja, and Shiva with Parvati while leaning on Nandi, as well as Bhikshatana, Bhairava and Harihara. Among the Vaishnava icons is a striking, eight-armed image holding various weapons. This sequence is interrupted by three *Ramayana* panels at the south-west corner of the *mandapa* wall. To this repertory must be added the panels on the side walls of the porches, showing Ardhanarishvara, Shiva and Parvati on Kailasa, and Shiva with sages. Here, too, should be mentioned a remarkable panel depicting Durga killing Mahisha installed in a minor shrine within the temple *mandapa* One of the greatest masterpieces of Early Chalukya art, this cut-out, almost three-dimensional composition, shows both goddess and demon with dramatically twisted torsos. A similar range of imagery is found on the wall panels of the twin Mallikarjuna temple, though many of these are unfinished.

The wall panels on the Papanatha temple at Pattadakal are of particular interest for their narrative scenes. Many on the south side illustrate *Ramayana* episodes, beginning with the fire sacrifice conducted by Dasharatha, and ending with climactic battle between Rama and Ravana. Though a lesser number of panels on the north side are dedicated to the Kiratarjuniya story, these too present energetic compositions, with Arjuna and Shiva fighting.

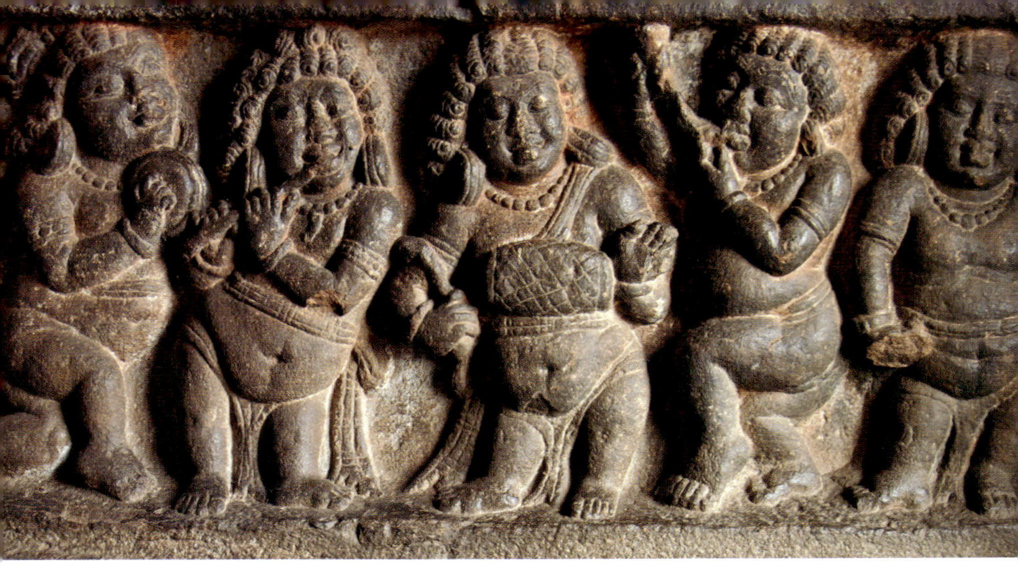

Gana musicians; basement panel from Cave 2, Badami

The only monument in Aihole supplied with a similar range of imagery is the Durga temple. The panels set into the niches of its outer colonnaded verandah illustrate a broad range of Shaiva and Vaishnava themes that gives no hint of the original dedication of the monument to the god Surya.

Basements in Early Chalukya temples are sometimes also the vehicles for elaborate sculptural compositions. Lines of impish *ganas* in playful and occasional obscene poses enliven the outer facades of the Badami cave-temples. Narrative friezes relating the Krishna legend are found on the basement of the Upper Shivalaya in Badami, while crowded courtly scenes and battle episodes, many of them unidentified, adorn the basements of the Mahakuteshvara and Mallikarjuna temples at Mahakuta. Among the similar friezes on the Durga temple (as seen within the colonnaded verandah) is a composition showing a ship with a curved prow carrying travelers, most likely Arabian-sea merchants. Porches of the larger Pattadakal temples are embellished with lions and elephants. Carved with a striking naturalism, the animals are often shown in violent combat, especially those on the entrance porch of the Papanatha temple.

Another important aspect of Early Chalukya temple art is that displayed on **Columns, Brackets and Doorways**. Columns in the Badami cave-temples have their shafts covered with a seemingly inexhaustible repertory of decorative motifs. They include looped and jewelled garlands hanging from monster masks, and roundels filled with animal, bird and human torsos in fanciful foliate surrounds. Brackets angling outwards from the columns of Cave 3 are fashioned as human couples in naturalistic, affectionate poses

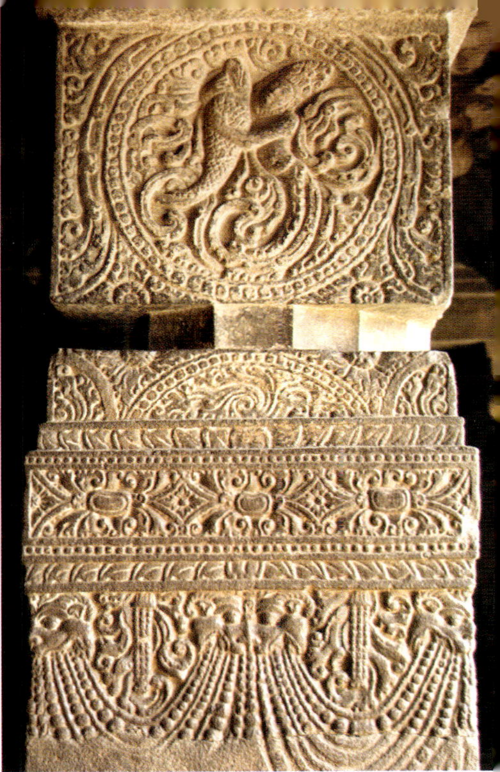

Column decoration; Cave 1, Badami

beneath flowering trees. The charm of these composition is irresistible. Similar amorous figures are seen on the outer columns of many of the Aihole temples. The repeated instances of a horse-headed woman embracing a male companion possibly refer to a local legend, now forgotten. Ganga on the *makara*, and Yamuna on the tortoise, also make an appearance, as on the columns beside the entrance to the Ladkhan temple. The river goddesses that flank the doorway to the Rashtrakuta period Aralibasappa temple in Aihole testify to the survival of this theme into late times. Columns in the Pattadakal temple are also carved with couples in elaborate courtly dress, often in affectionate embrace. More unusual topics, such as Vishnu riding on Garuda, and Ravana shaking Mount Kailasa, grace the columns of the Virupaksa temple porches.

Columns either side of doorways are usually supplied with guardian figures, sometimes sculpted in almost three dimensions, as in the larger of the Pattadakal temples. Sumptuously dressed and crowned, and leaning on heavy clubs, these protectors are often shown with fierce expressions as if to frighten off unwanted visitors.

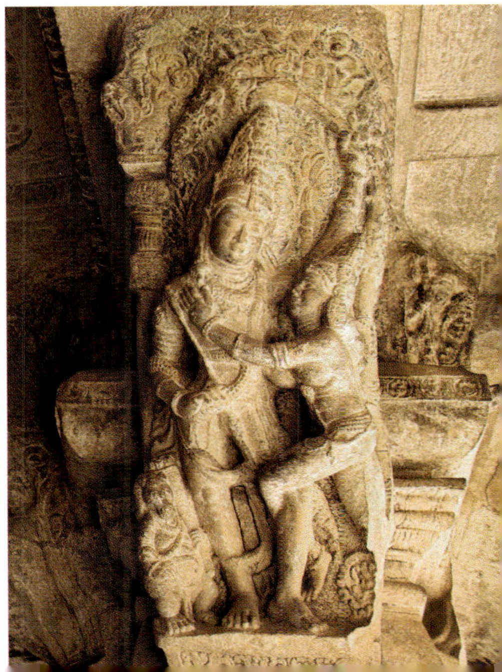

Embracing couple beneath tree; bracket from Cave 3, Badami

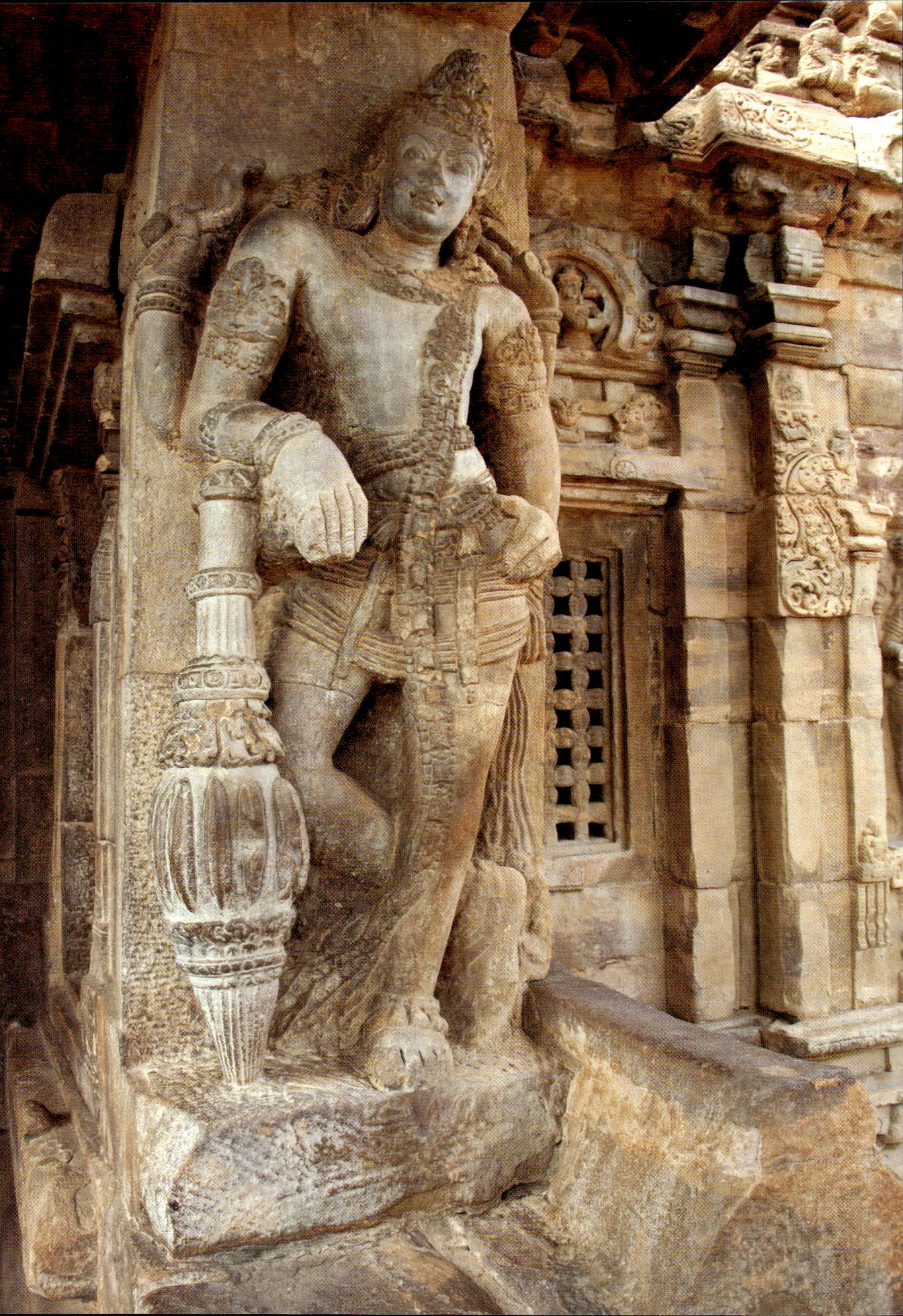

Opposite: Guardian figure in the south porch of the Virupaksha temple, Pattadakal

In the doorway of the Durga temple in Aihole these guardians appear together with river goddesses and female attendants. Flying Garuda, depicted head-on and clutching a pair of long cobra-bodies, is a common theme, even in Shaiva monuments. Pilasters at either side of doorways sometimes support pairs of *makaras* with luxuriant foliated tails, as can be seen within the entrance porch of the Papanatha temple at Pattadakal. Paired *makaras* with hanging tails are among the few Early Chalukya motifs that persist into later times, as in the sanctuary doorway of the Rashtrakuta period Jain temple at Pattadakal.

A wealth of ornamental and narrative reliefs adorns the columns shafts of the Virupaksha and Mallikarjuna *mandapa* interiors. In addition to a profusion of jewelled and foliate motifs derived from those already noticed in regard to the Badami cave-temples, there are scenes illustrating *Ramayana*, *Mahabharata* and Krishna stories, as well as *Panchatantra* compositions. Episodes from these and other legends extend across several faces of a column, and sometimes even continue onto an adjacent column. Courtly tales of the era, not all of which can now be understood, also find visual expression here. Beams, too, are the vehicles for ornamental carving, nowhere better seen than in the foliate patterns and undulating stalks with lotus blossoms within various temples in Aihole.

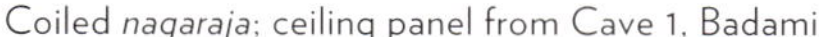

Coiled *nagaraja*; ceiling panel from Cave 1, Badami

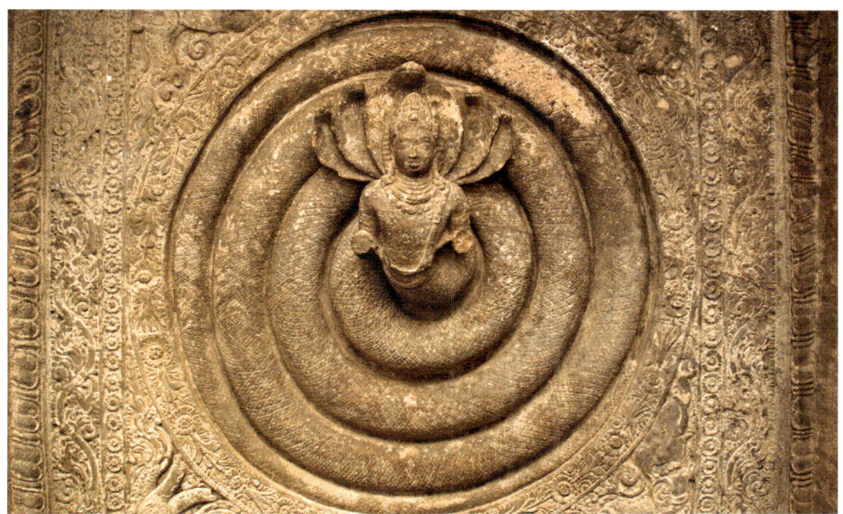

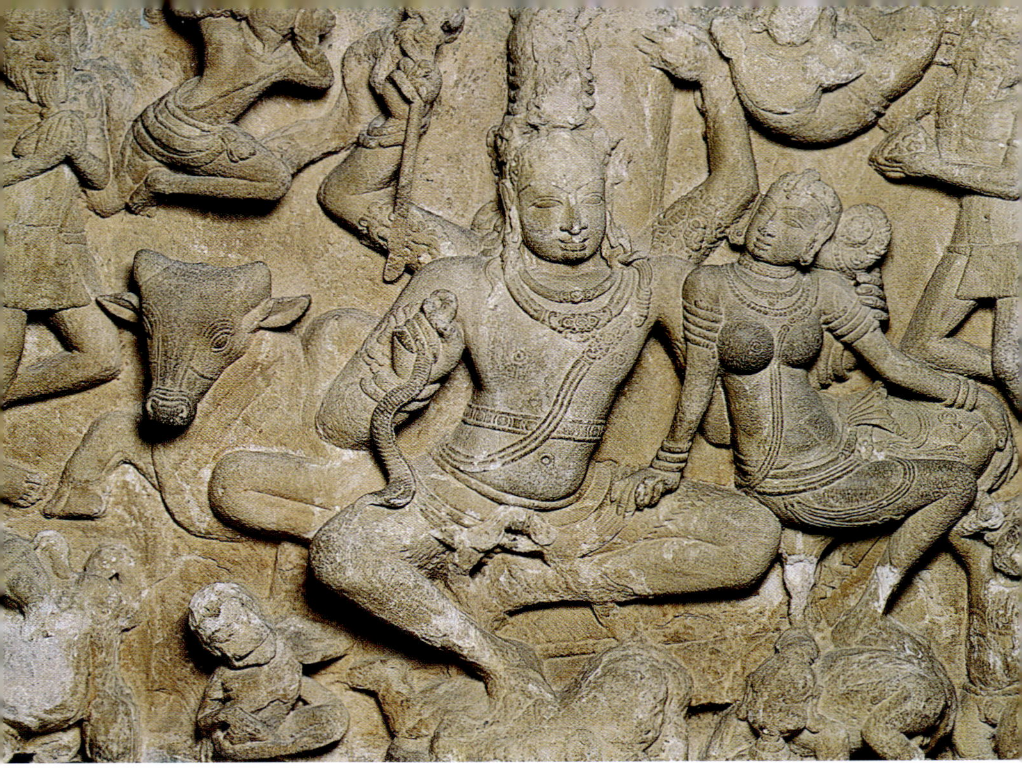

Shiva on Nandi; ceiling panel from the Hucchappayyagudi; Aihole, now in the Chhatrapati Shivaji Maharaj Vastu Sangrahalaya, Mumbai

Nowhere is the glory of Early Chalukya sculptural art better displayed than in the splendid **Ceilings** of temple interiors, both rock-cut and structural. The series begins with those in the Badami cave-temples embellished with coiled *nagaraja* (Cave 1), wheel with fish-spokes (Cave 2), and Shiva and Parvati riding on Nandi, and Brahma surrounded by the Dikpalas (Cave 3). These topics are repeated in the great temples at Pattadakal, together with dancing Shiva, as well as a sole instance of Surya riding in the chariot (east porch of Virupaksha temple). The habit of representing Shiva, Vishnu and Brahma in a trio of matching ceiling panels is already present in the Jambulinga temple in Badami, to be repeated on several occasions in Aihole, most notably in the Hucchapayyagudi (panels now in the Chhatrapati Shivaji Maharaj Vastu Sangrahalaya, Mumbai). Couples, their legs kicked backwards in the act of flying through the clouds, are another popular ceiling theme, the finest examples being those from the Durga temple (now in the National Museum, New Delhi). Icons of dancing Shiva fill the horseshoe-shaped arched projections on the frontal faces of many temple towers, as at Pattadakal.

To this wide-ranging repertory of sculptural themes must be added the Seated Nandis placed inside *mandapas* (Ladkhan temple in Aihole and Papanatha temple at Pattadakal), or in purpose built, free-standing pavilions (Mahakuteshvara and Mallikarujna temples at Mahakuta, and Virupaksha temple at Pattadakal). These naturalistic sculptures perfectly capture the bulk and pose of actual bulls. No less sophisticated are the striking images of Lajja Gauri, which portray a squatting lotus-headed goddess displaying her sex. Whether fully carved, as in the example now in the Archaeological Museum, Badami, or cut in relief, as at Siddanakolla, these extraordinary icons are best understood as manifestations of an ancient fertility cult that survived into Early Chalukya times.

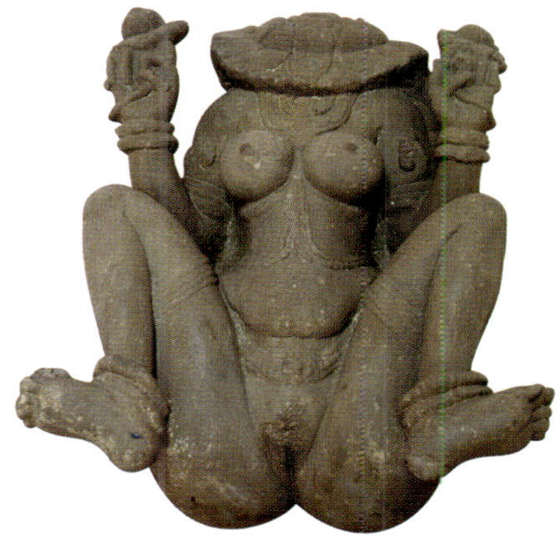

Lajja Gauri from Naganathakolla; now in the Archaeological Museum, Badami

Nandi in the Mallikarjuna temple; Mahakuta

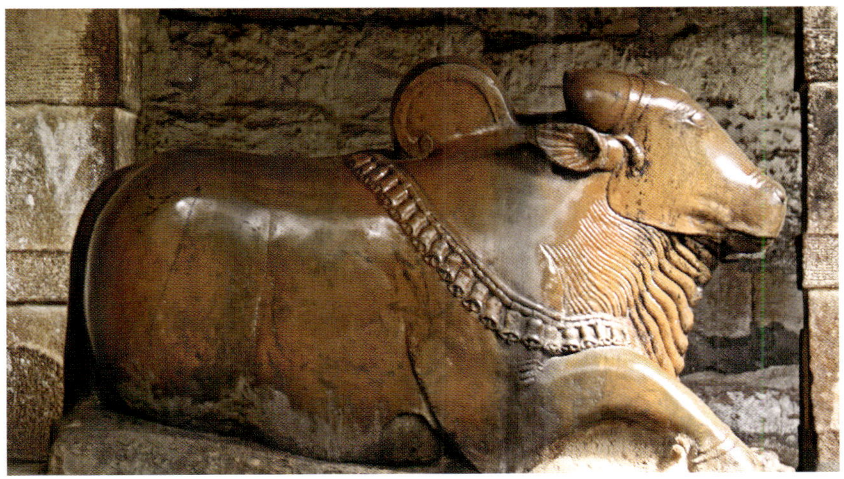

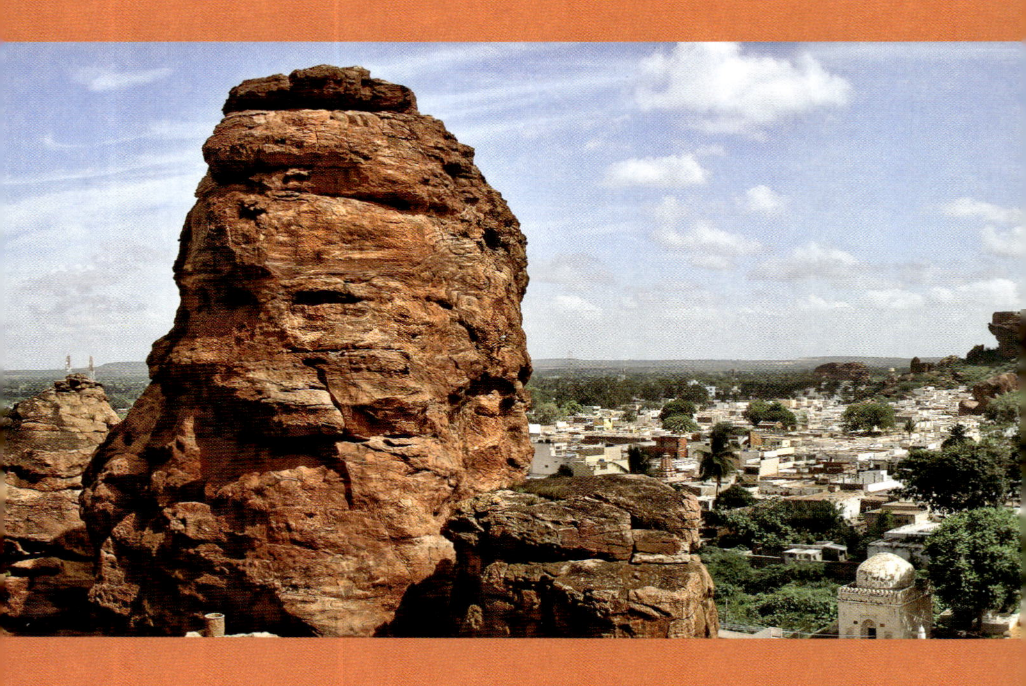

BADAMI

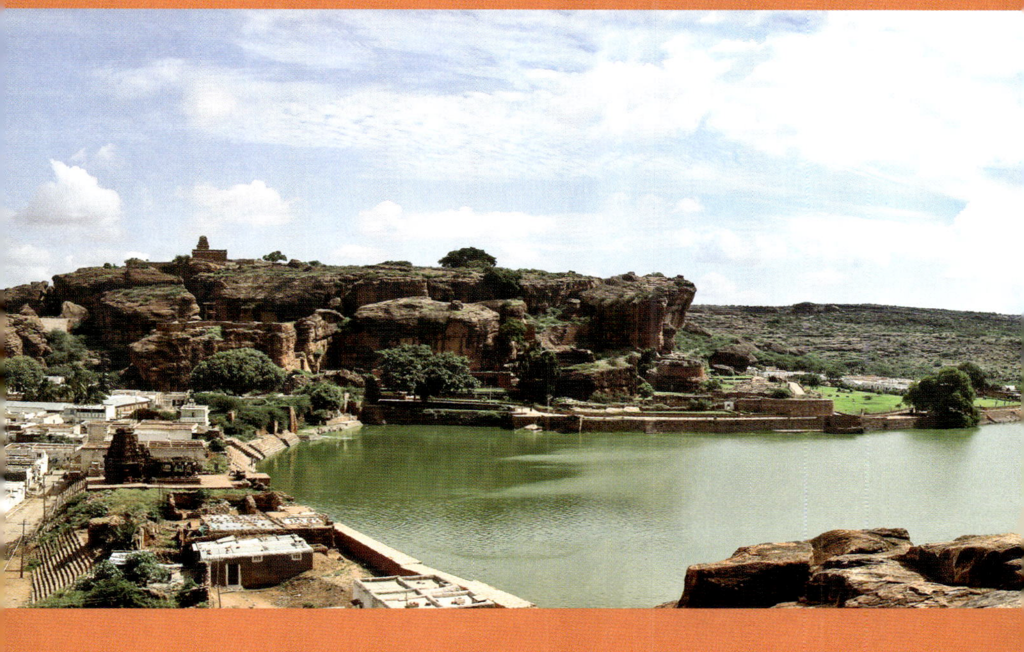

Preceding Pages: View of Badami from the South Fort
Opposite: Steps leading to the cave-temples in the South Fort, Badami

As Vatapi, capital of the Early Chalukyas, the town of Badami is of interest for its ancient historical associations, as well as for its surviving religious monuments, both rock-cut and structural, dating from the 6th-8th centuries. Shrines, tombs, fortifications, gateways and granaries belonging to later times confirm the sustained importance of Badami under the governors of the Later Chalukya, Vijayanagara, Adil Shahi and Maratha rulers. These vestiges are cut into the cliff faces and perched on the summits of the rugged rocky bluffs that frame the town and its tank in a majestic horseshoe of deep red sandstone. They are also found tucked away in the streets of town and upon the dam wall of the rain-fed tank, known in ancient texts as Agastyatirtha, which demarcates the eastern limit of the habitations. The southern and northern extremities of the rocky bluffs, soaring high above the flat-roofed houses, are known respectively as the South and North Forts, from the citadels dating from later times with which they are crowned.

Further sites of archaeological and historical interest are discovered in the hills on the outskirts of Badami. They include rock-shelters with prehistoric paintings at Sidilaphadi and Ranganathagudda, as well as rock carvings beside a tiny natural pool at Aralitirtha. The sacred spring at Mahakuta, on the other flank of the rocky outcrop beyond the tank, serves as the focus for a complex of Early Chalukya shrines that is still in worship. A short distance from Badami is Banashankari, the most popular pilgrimage destination in the region, and the locus of a great annual fair held in January.

SOUTH FORT

The tour described here begins at the foot of the South Fort (car park, ticket office and entrance gate). From here a stepped path ascends to a sequence of four rock-cut monuments, generally referred to simply as 'caves', numbered 1 to 4. Cut directly into the sheer cliff of the South Fort, these monuments are to be counted among the first great achievements of the Early Chalukya architects and sculptors. In addition to its artistic significance, Cave 3 is the only one to be provided with an inscription, making it the earliest dated Hindu cave-temple in the Deccan. The four cave-temples are disposed along the stepped path (patrolled by aggressive monkeys!), with Cave 1 at the bottom and Cave 4 at the top. In spite of this numbering, it is not known precisely in what chronological order the cave-temples were cut into the cliff. Though the columns, beams and brackets in the four caves resemble constructed architecture, these features are monolithic throughout.

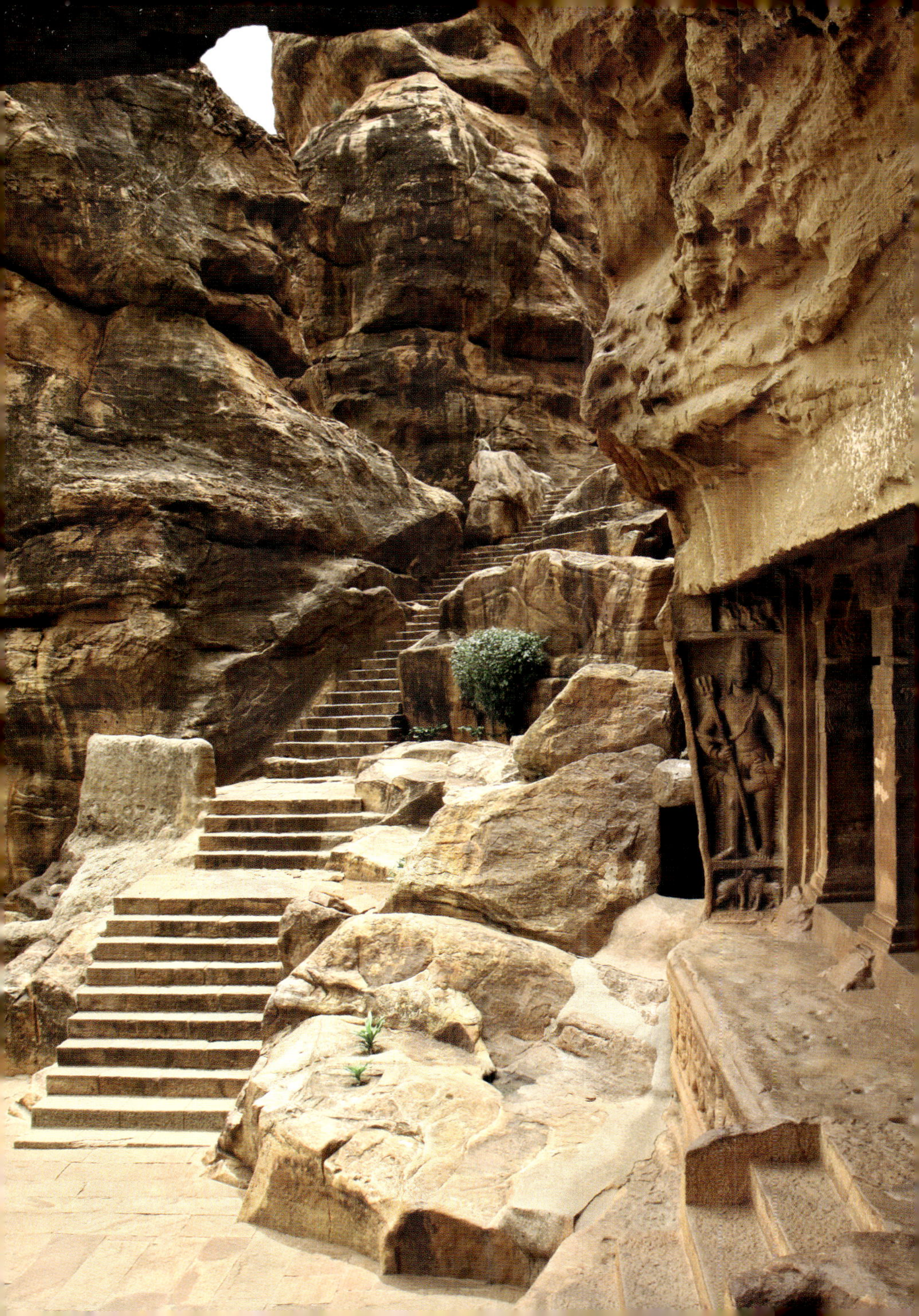

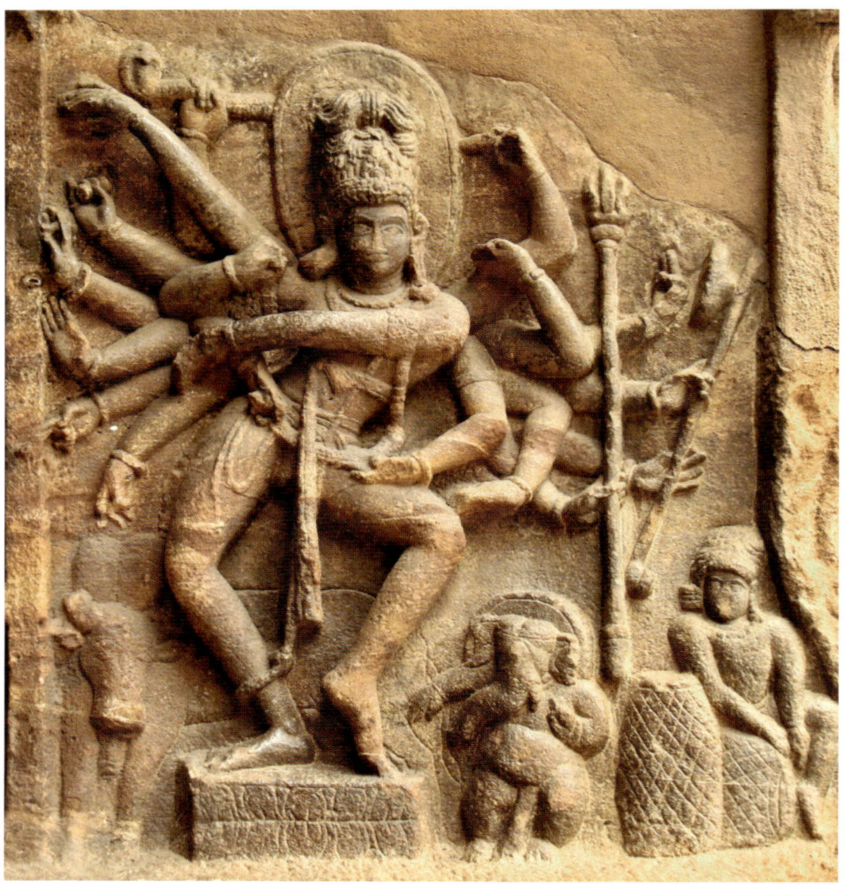

Dancing Shiva beside Cave 1

Cave 1 is the only rock-cut sanctuary in Badami to be dedicated to Shiva. This is immediately apparent from the imposing 18-armed dancing god sculpted onto the rock face directly to the right of the cave-temple's entrance. Portrayed with elaborate matted hair, and with one arm thrust vigorously across the chest, the image expresses the dynamic posture of the god's cosmic dance. To one side is a small chamber, within which is an icon of Durga savagely spearing Mahisha. On the corresponding left-hand side of the entrance is a two-armed guardian figure, holding a trident, with a bull-elephant visual pun beneath.

The five columns that give access to the front verandah of Cave 1 are adorned with delicately carved jewelled garlands and roundels filled with fanciful foliate designs. Sculpted panels at the ends of the verandah illustrate two syncretistic icons of the Shaiva canon: on the left, Harihara in the company of Parvati and Lakshmi; and on the right, Ardhanarishvara accompanied by skeletal Bhringi and Nandi on the male side, and a female attendant carrying a jewel casket on the female side. The second row of columns in Cave 1 are characterised by part-fluted shafts and cushion-like capitals. Transverse beams are carried on brackets fashioned as open-mouthed *makaras* disgorging human figures and *yalis*. Carved onto the ceiling over the central bay is a magnificent *nagaraja*, with a coiled serpent body surrounding a human torso; flying couples are seen at either side. Two additional rows of columns beyond the verandah, also with exquisite ornament, lead to a *mandapa* with a small *linga* sanctuary cut into the rear wall. A small Nandi is placed in front.

Consecrated to Vishnu, **Cave 2** is somewhat smaller and less refined than its predecessor; furthermore, it gives the impression of being a later and smaller copy of Cave 3 (described below). The outer columns of Cave 2

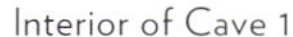

Interior of Cave 1

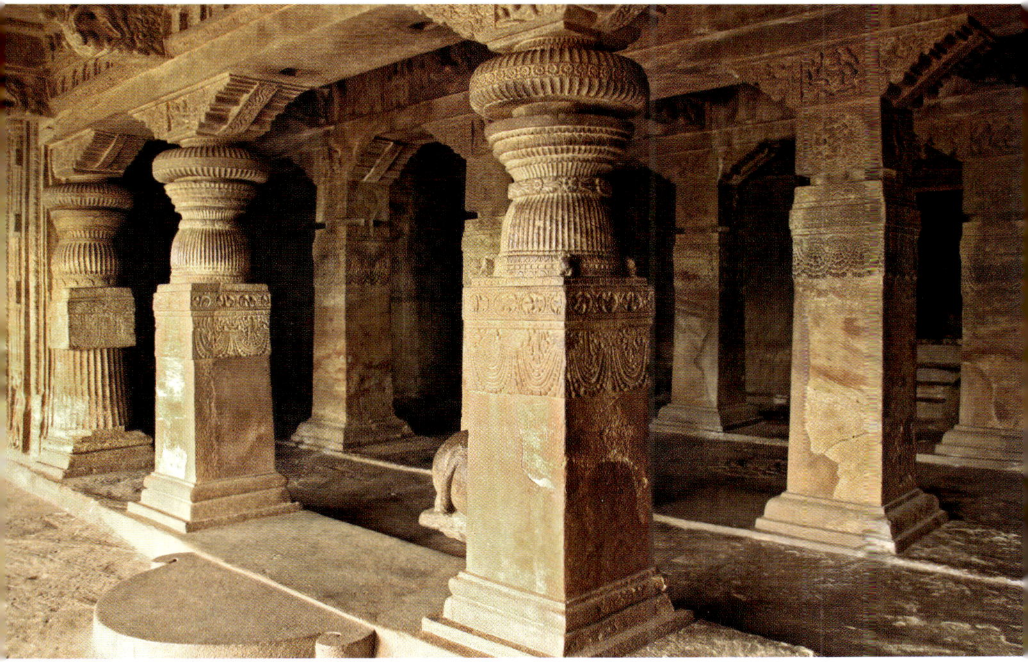

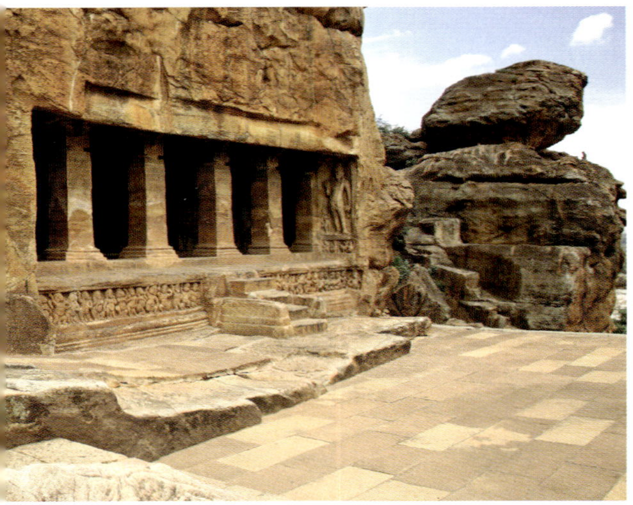
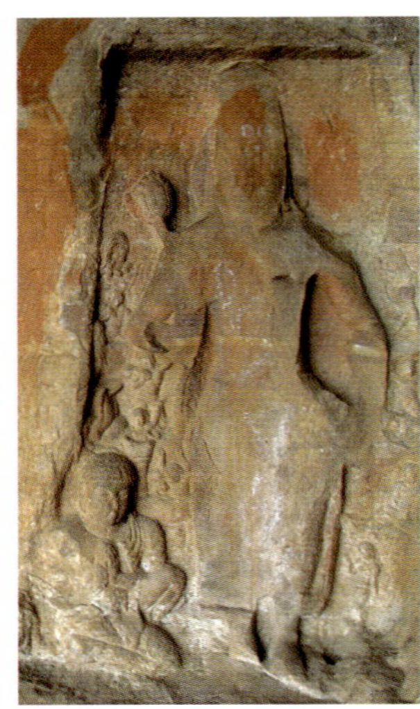
Left: Exterior of Cave 2 *Right:* Mutilated figure of Padmapani in a natural cavern between Caves 2 and 3

are elevated on a plinth enlivened with a frieze of *ganas*. At either end of the facade are two-armed guardian figures holding small flowers. End panels within the verandah depict Vishnu as Varaha (left), and Trivikrama with diminutive Vamana (right). Friezes at the tops of the walls illustrate Vaishnava narratives, such as the churning of the ocean, the birth of Krishna, Krishna as a cow-herd surrounded by animals, and Vishnu asleep on Shesha. Ceiling panels in the verandah show a fish-spoked wheel over the central bay; at either side are swastika compositions, with one showing flying couples. The interior *mandapa* of the cave-temple has rows of columns leading to a sanctuary cut into the rear wall, but there is no image to be seen. A full lotus flower, possibly for offerings, is cut into the rocky floor in front.

Steps ascend to a terrace with a splendid view across the town and the tank towards the North Fort. To the rear is a **Natural Cavern**, within which a mutilated carved figure of Padmapani holding a lotus can be made out. A seated devotee to one side of the Bodhisattva is better preserved. A few metres from the cavern is a narrow gap in the rock face, closed by a doorway (permanently locked). Steep steps from here ascend to the ramparts and circular bastions that constitute the **Citadel** at the summit of the North Fort, attributed to Tipu Sultan's brief occupation of Badami.

Passing through a gateway in a transverse wall, the steps lead to a broad paved terrace (modern) in front of **Cave 3**, the largest and most elaborate Early Chalukya rock-cut monument. This presents an extended colonnaded facade cut dramatically into the cliff face, with no transition between man-made work

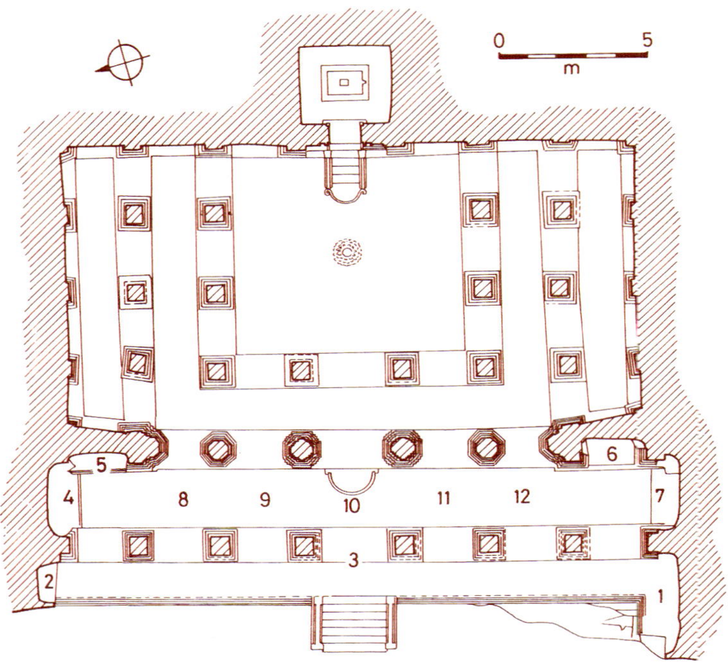

Wall Panels

1. Trivikrama
2. Vishnu
3. Garuda (underside of eave)
4. Vishnu on Shesha
5. Varaha
6. Harihara
7. Narasimha

Ceiling Panels

8. Indira on the elephant
9. Shiva and Parvati on Nandi
10. Vishnu with the *dikpalas* (centre)
11. Brahma
12. Varuna

Cave 3; major sculpture panels

Following Pages: Narasimha and Trivikrama

and nature. (Holes in the rock above may been for a later, adjoining timber structure.) Seven columns are raised on a plinth divided into panels filled with pairs of *ganas* in lively dancing poses, and even obscene postures. A major carved tableau at the right end of the facade illustrates the Trivikrama episode, with Vishnu shown with one leg kicked up high. (The diminutive Vamana figure, who forms part of the story, is damaged.) On the side wall at the corresponding left end of the facade is an eight-armed icon of Vishnu holding numerous weapons, with a torso of Narasimha emerging from the conical crown.

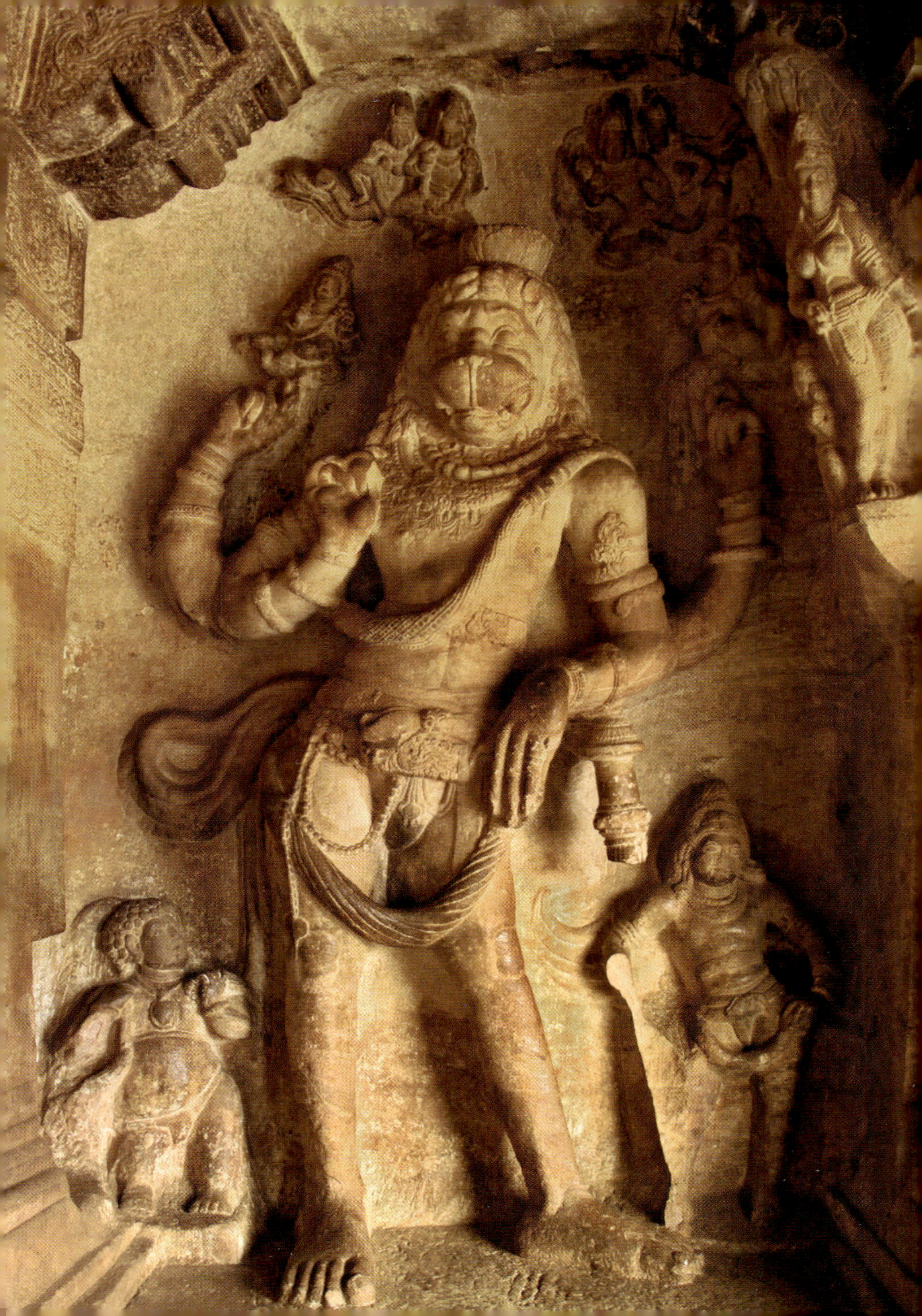

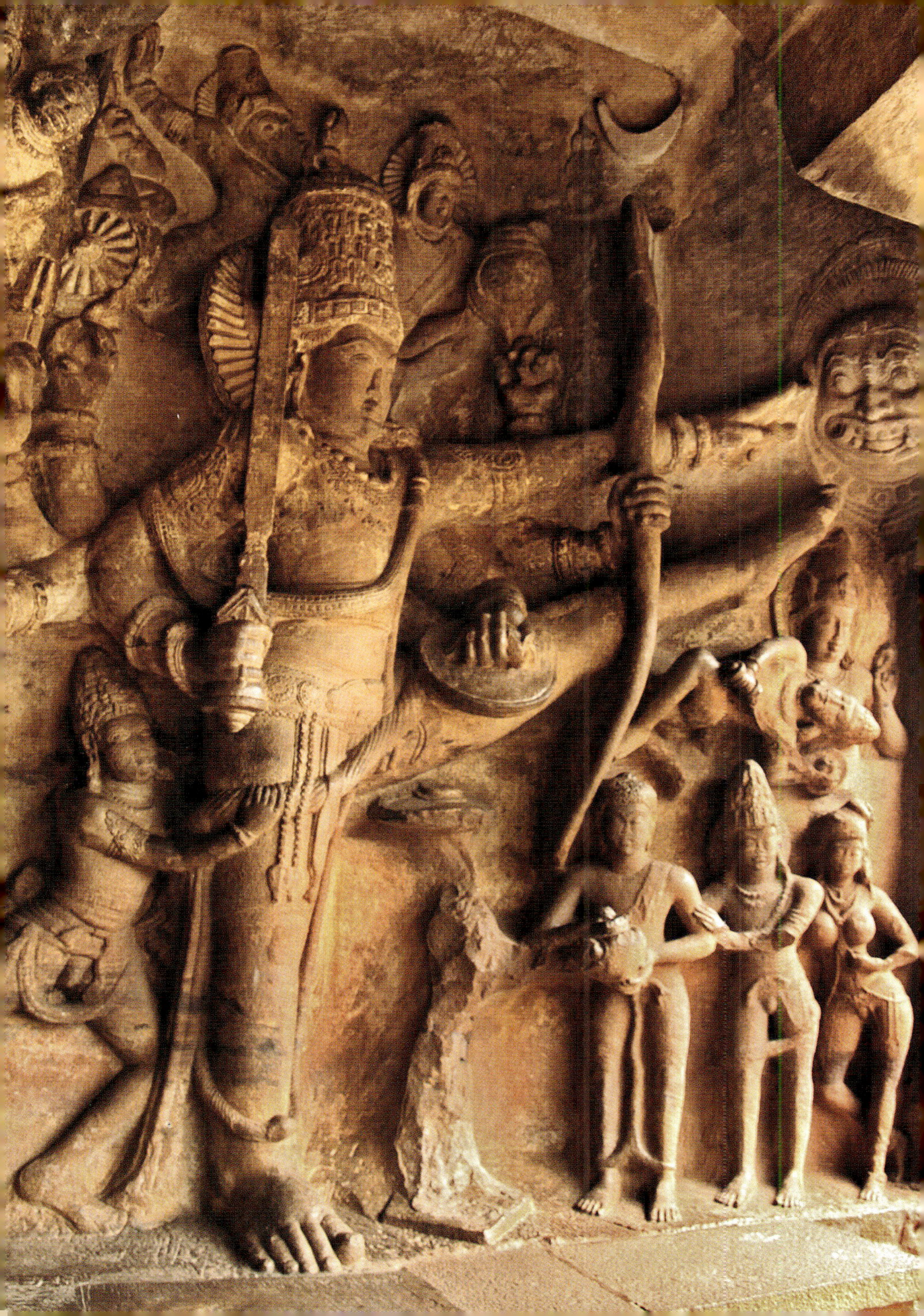

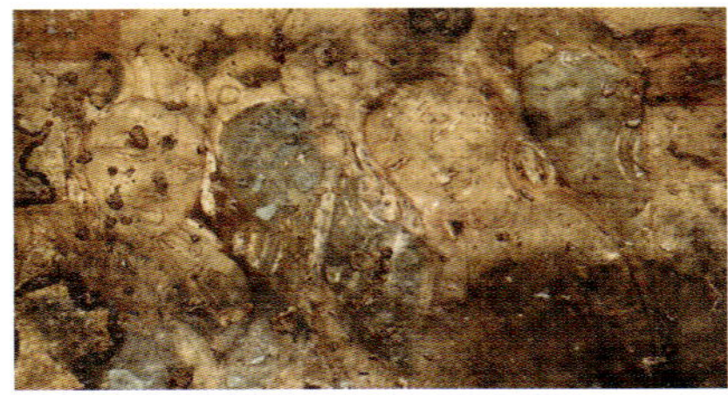
Mural fragment in Cave 3

The outer columns of Cave 3 have their shafts enhanced with full circular medallions containing figures. Brackets angling outwards above are fashioned as *yalis* in front, and as human couples in affectionate poses beneath flowering trees to the sides and within. The charm of these compositions is unsurpassed in the whole of Early Chalukya art. The brackets are partly sheltered by a deeply curved overhang, concealed within the cliff face. In the middle of this overhang (as viewed from inside the verandah) is flying Garuda, recognised by his beak-like nose and spreading wings. To the left of Garuda are traces of a mural composition with delicately painted courtly maidens. (A linear reconstruction of the scene, with male and female figures grouped within colonnaded palace buildings, is displayed in the Archaeological Museum, described below.)

The front verandah of Cave 3 is enhanced by magnificent sculptural compositions illustrating different aspects of Vishnu. At the left end of the verandah is Vishnu as Vaikuntha. The god is seated on the coils of Shesha,

Ceiling panel in Cave 3

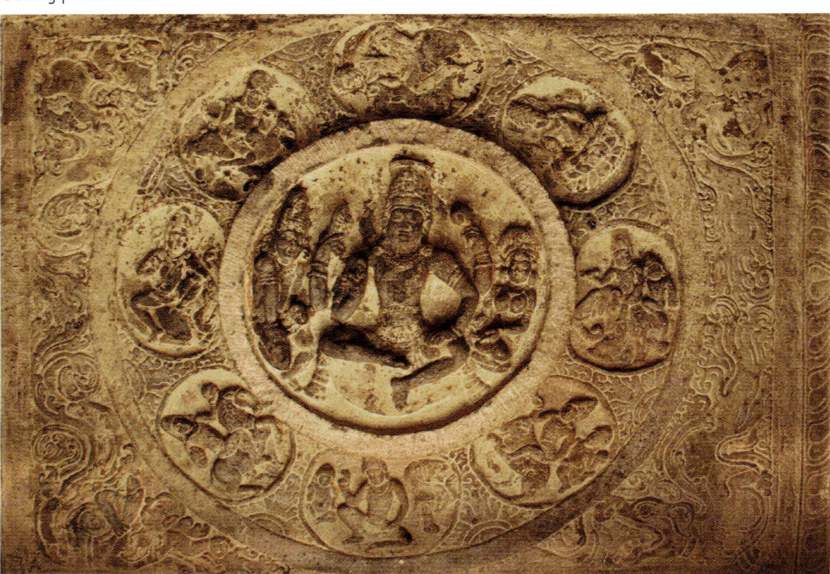

the multi-hoods of which shelter the crowned head of the god. Varaha rescuing Bhudevi is seen to one side. On the wall column next to Varaha is the inscription giving the name of the royal patron of the monument, and the precise full-moon day on 1 November 578 when the cave was consecrated. (It is worth noting that the festival sacred to Vaikuntha is generally celebrated on a full-moon day, which is considered the god's first day of wakefulness after emerging from deep cosmic sleep.) Opposite, at the right end of the verandah of Cave 3, is Narasimha with a fierce leonine head, leaning heavily on a club (broken). A representation of Harihara is carved onto the adjacent side wall. The god displays axe and conch in the rear hands; the headdress is clearly divided into the matted hair of Shiva and half-crown of Vishnu.

Ceiling panels are located over five of the bays between these compositions. From left to right: Kubera; Indra on the elephant in the company of dancers and musicians; Shiva and Parvati on Nandi surrounded by *ganas* (central bay); Brahma with guardians and *rishis*; and Varuna with *makara* and celestials. The upper portions of the walls have panels containing Vaishnava narratives: the churning of the ocean; scenes from the childhood of Krishna with village scenes with cows; Vishnu asleep on Shesha (right end); the story of Arjuna fighting Shiva as *kirata*; and Lakshmi with Narasimha (left end).

The columns in the second row of Cave 3 are remarkable for the purple veins that run through the red sandstone. Those at the ends have 16-sided shafts with circular fluted capitals; those in between display elegant, square faceted shafts. Beyond the second row of columns is a spacious, nine-bayed *mandapa* defined by 12 columns decorated with jewelled garlands, monster heads, and roundels with a seemingly inexhaustible range of fantasy foliate compositions incorporating, animals, birds and human torsos. One column preserves a record of the Vijayanagara period, dated 1554. The ceiling over the *mandapa* is divided into nine bays with Brahma on the goose in the middle, surrounded by Karttikeya (in front of the sanctuary), Agni, Indra and Varuna, interspersed with flying couples. Steps lead to the sanctuary set into the rear wall. Its doorway is flanked by couples and attendants holding conch and lotus. The central monolithic pedestal and two later pedestals are devoid of images.

From Cave 3 it is but a short distance to **Cave 4**, the last and smallest of the rock-cut monuments of the South Fort, and the only one with a Jain affiliation. The comparatively crude carving of the column details suggest that the cave-temple may be the latest of the series. As in its predecessors, the front verandah is dominated by sculpted figures at either end: on the left, the Jain saint Bahubali, with vines wrapped around his legs; on the right, Parshvanatha, with a multi-hooded cobra rising over his head. A Jina seated on a lion throne, flanked by a pair of attendants bearing *chauris*, or fly-whisks, and topped by a triple parasol and leafy tree, is carved onto the rear wall of the sanctuary within. While all these carvings are clearly the work of Early Chalukya artists, numerous smaller Tirthankara icons carved in sharp relief onto the walls and columns are later. They were added in the 11th or 12th centuries, during the Late Chalukya period, when the cave-temple was renewed, no doubt in response to a resurgence of Jainism in the Badami area.

After Cave 4, visitors must retrace their steps in order to return to the entrance gate below Cave 1 in order to continue their tour of Badami.

Interior of Cave 4

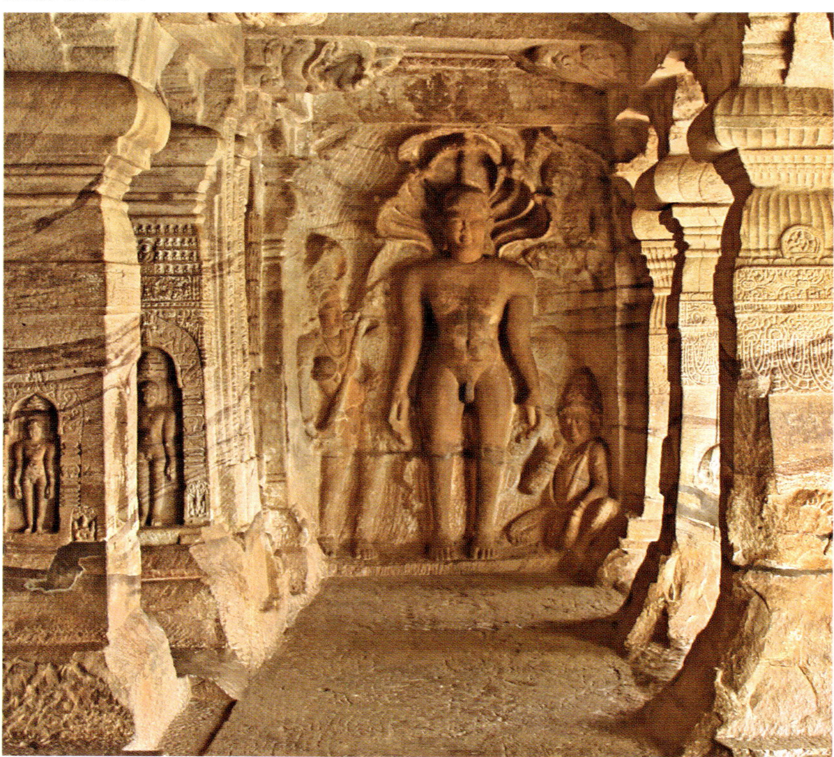

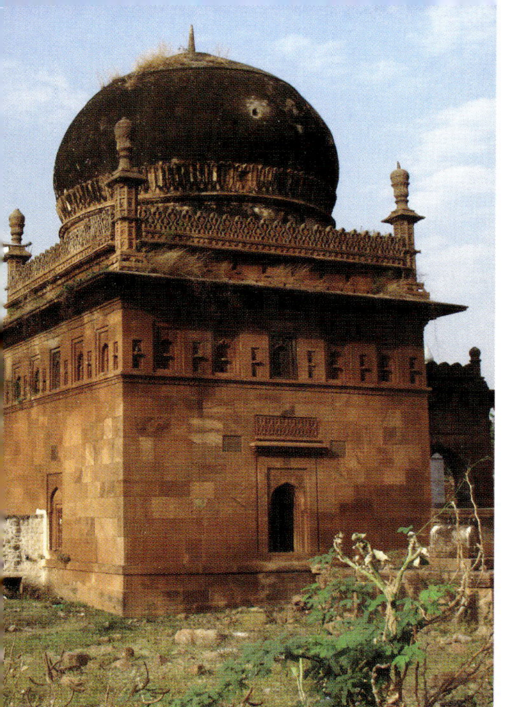

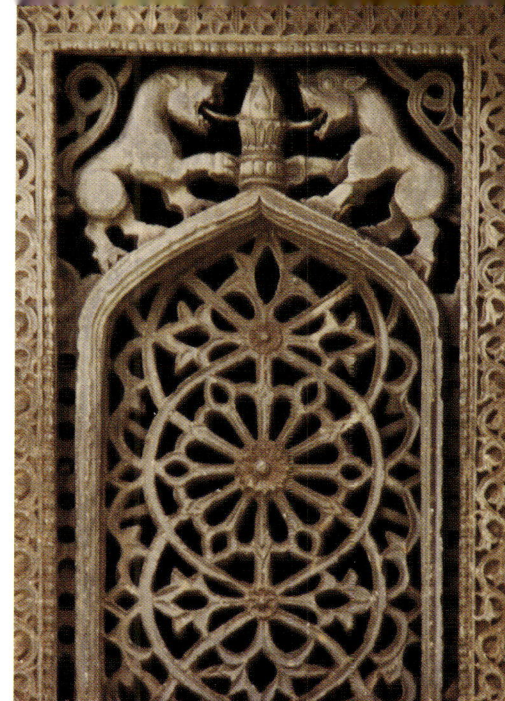

Left: Domed tomb *Right: Jali* window from the domed tomb

IN THE TOWN AND AROUND THE TANK

The first sight to be noticed by tourists as they descend from the cave-temples is the red sandstone **Domed Tomb** standing beside the car park. Dating from the 17th century, during the occupation of Badami by the Bijapur sultans, this funerary monument was erected by Malik Abdul Aziz, presumably a local governor, in memory of his wife. The finely proportioned tomb displays typical features of Adil Shahi architecture, best seen in the ornate parapet with trefoil merlon motifs and corner finials, and the imposing, slightly bulbous dome carried on a relief frieze of lotus petals. Perforated *jali* windows above the doorways on three sides, intricately worked in grey basalt, incorporate pairs of lions. Calligraphic panels around the doorways contain mostly Koranic quotations. The tomb is entered through a porch facing the tank. A whitewashed mosque and another domed tomb stand nearby.

Immediately in front of the tombs and the mosque just noticed is a broad **Dam Wall** that serves as a *bund*, trapping the ever-green waters of the tank. Well-fitted stone steps descending to the water serve as a bathing spot and clothes-washing place for Badami's inhabitants. Stone rubble walls and bastions were built on top of these steps in later times. Similarly constructed bastions and sections of walls are also found in the narrow streets of the town.

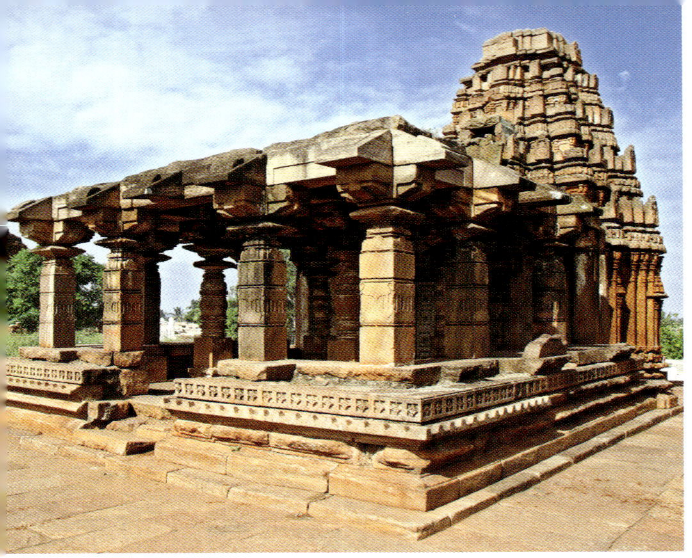

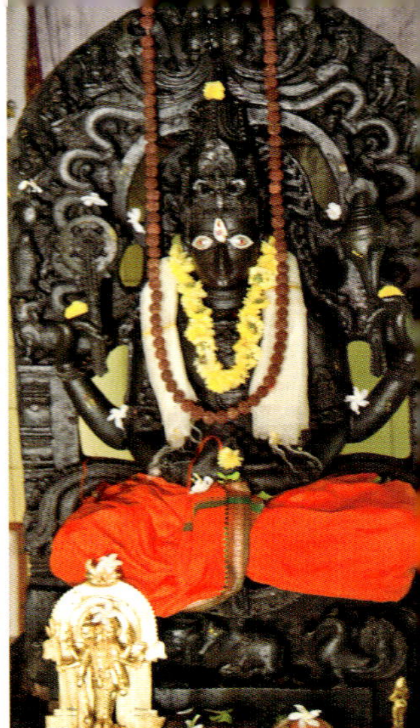

Left: Yellamma temple *Right:* Dattatreya sculpture in modern shrine opposite

Surveying the tank from an elevated spot on the dam wall a few metres north of the domed tomb is the **Yellamma Temple**. An inscription on its walls attests that it was erected in 1139 during the reign of Jagadekamalla, one of the Late Chalukya rulers of Kalyana. Originally consecrated to Vishnu, it now houses the icon of a popular goddess. The finely finished walls of its sanctuary have narrow projections defined by slender pilasters; additional pairs of pilasters carry pediments topped by relief *kutas*. The steeply pyramidal tower that rises above has four superimposed tiers of sharply modelled *kutas* and *shalas* relieved by ornate *kudus*. The temple is approached through an open *mandapa*, originally with balcony seating on three sides. Internal columns have lathe-turned shafts. From here there is an excellent view of the bastions and ramparts of the citadel that crowns the South Fort. A single cannon can even been seen protruding over the walls.

Immediately opposite the Yellamma temple, on the other side of the path, is a whitewashed walled compound containing a modern concrete shrine with cast-iron grilles. Here is worshipped a superbly worked, Late Chalukya period stone icon, probably removed from the Yellamma temple. This depicts Dattatreya, a triple-headed form of Vishnu incorporating Shiva and Brahma. A short distance from the Yellamma temple is a street that runs between flat-roofed houses to a crossing, which marks the approximate centre of Badami.

Near to the crossing stands the **Virupaksha Temple**. Its sanctuary resembles that of the Yellamma in all essential respects, except that the tower is more squatly proportioned and is fully complete with a *kuta*-roof. The *mandapa* in front, opening off the street, has its walls embellished with

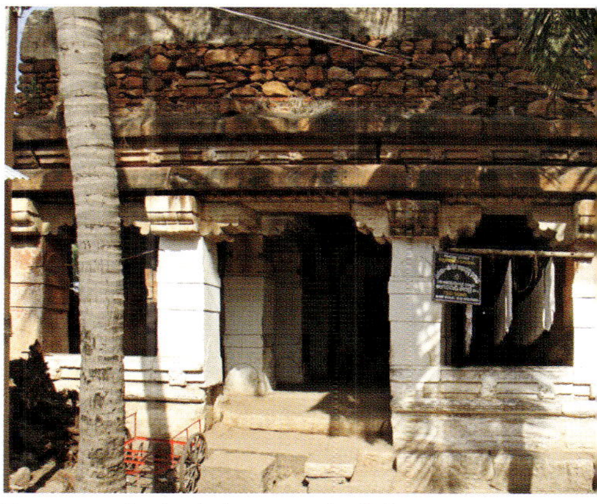

Entrance to the Jambulinga temple. *Following pages:* Bhutanatha temple at the end of the tank

similar secondary pairs of pilasters. Immediately to the rear of the Virupaksha, but reached from a narrow lane beside a spreading tamarind tree next to the crossing just noticed, is the **Jambulinga Temple.** This bears an inscription on one of the porch columns recording that it was erected in 699 by Vinayavati, a queen of Vinayaditya. The temple consists of an open porch with balcony seating that leads to a walled *mandapa*, off which open sanctuaries on three sides. The central aisle of the *mandapa* has a raised ceiling with carvings of Brahma, Vishnu and Shiva, the last accompanied by Parvati riding on Nandi. These aerial figures accord with the inscription, which specifies that the monument was dedicated to all three divinities. Even so, the northern and southern sanctuaries are now empty, but that on the west, on axis with the entrance, houses a *linga*. As in other Early Chalukya temples, the side aisles of the *mandapa* are roofed with sloping slabs. No original tower is preserved over any of the sanctuaries, though that on the north is capped with a Vijayanagara period brick tower with a hemispherical roof.

The tour described here resumes on the northern bank of the tank, which visitors can reach by wending their way through the town. A pleasant water-side path is reached immediately after passing through an arched gate at the end of the town. The gate is built on an Early Chalukya basement, as is evident from the friezes of *ganas* that flank the passageway. After passing through the gateway, in the middle of a well tended garden to the left, stands the **Archaeological Museum** (ticket required), with a colonnaded facade that imitates the cave-temples. (From a second arched gate immediately beside the museum begins the stepped path that ascends to the North Fort, described below.) The museum houses a collection of stone sculptures gathered from nearby sites. One of the most impressive is the huge, partly cut-out triangular composition with Brahma between *makaras* on both front and back faces. Dating from the 12th century, this probably served as a pediment for a portal in front of steps leading down to a pond or tank. In the same room are two 8th-century panels removed from

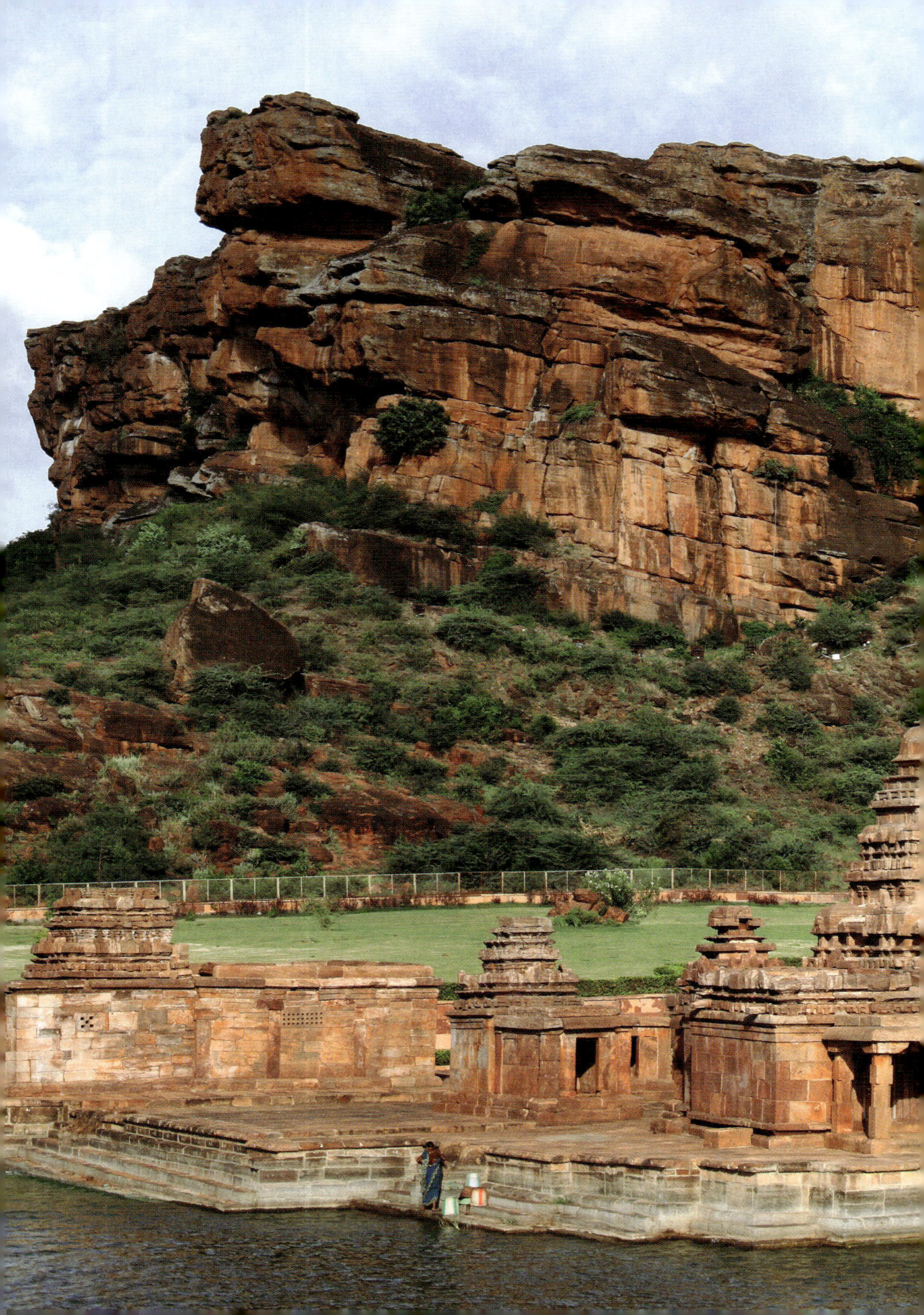

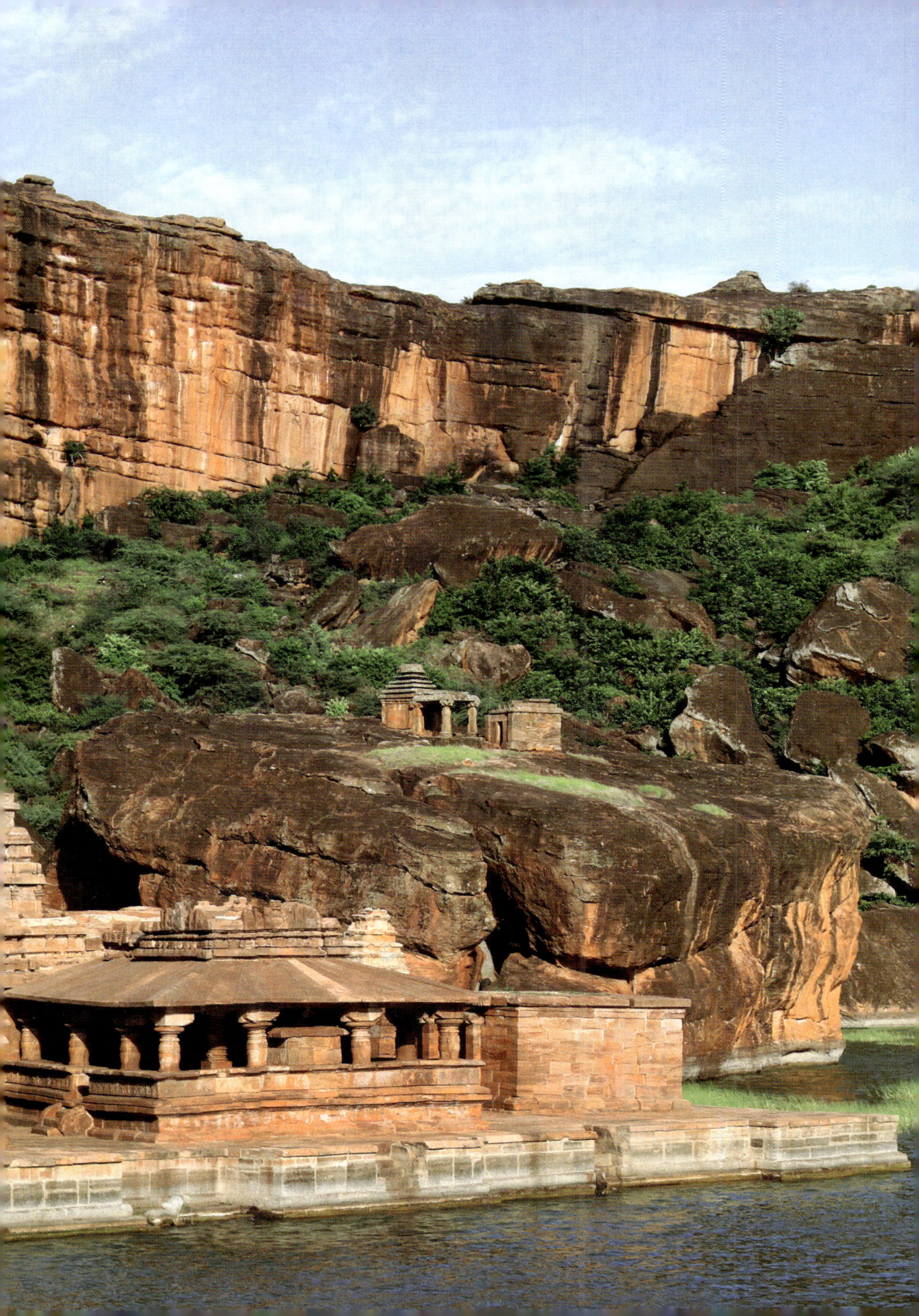

the Virupaksha temple at Pattadakal. They depict Shiva in the chariot aiming an arrow at the Tripura demons, and the same god energetically spearing Andhaka. In the room to the rear is a remarkable stone representation of the squatting lotus-headed goddess displaying her sex, known as Lajja Gauri, brought from Naganathakolla, a temple site in the vicinity (described below).

The Archaeological Museum also presents instructive translations of key inscriptions on Early Chalukya temples, and a reconstructed linear interpretation of the mural in Cave 3 (left room). There are also exhibits pertaining to prehistoric and early historical sites in the Badami area, with photographs of rock paintings, a selection of archaeological finds, and a scale model of the impressive rock-shelter at Sidilaphadi (right room, described below).

In the garden of the Archaeological Museum, to the right of its entrance, is a large boulder on the side of which is a **Pallava Inscription** sheltered by a modern portico. This records the occupation of Vatapi in 642 by Narasimhavarman I of Kanchipuram. A path nearby running away from the tank leads to Mahakuta.

Continuing along the path beside the tank, visitors will pass beside a rubble wall with a restored circular bastion that once protected Badami from the east and north. Then comes a simple stone chamber housing a collection of *nagakals* built beneath a tamarind tree, partly collapsing into the water. Immediately to the left is a garden compound housing a complex of temples, all with layered pyramidal towers characteristic of the 11th and 12th centuries. Known collectively as the **North Bhutanatha Group**, the temples all face south towards the tank. The principal monument has a porch with balcony seating sheltered by steeply sloping roof slabs; the outer walls of the *mandapa* and sanctuary have characteristic slender pilasters. An ornate part-circular projection on the frontal face of the tower fames a standing icon of Vishnu, though the sanctuary within now houses a Shiva *linga*.

A few metres beyond, at the very end of the tank, is the **Bhutanatha Temple**, with several small shrines clustering around the principal monument that faces west onto the water. While these lesser shrines are all topped with the pyramidal layered towers typical of the Late Chalukya era, the principal temple, from which the group takes its name, is much earlier. Its Dravida styled, multi-storeyed tower, capped with a prominent *kuta* is attributed to the 8th century. Its outer walls, though lacking in sculptural embellishment, are divided into regular projections and recesses by full-height pilasters, with eave and parapet above. The original, single-bayed porch to the temple accommodates a Nandi image. In later times this was encased within a larger porch with balcony seating.

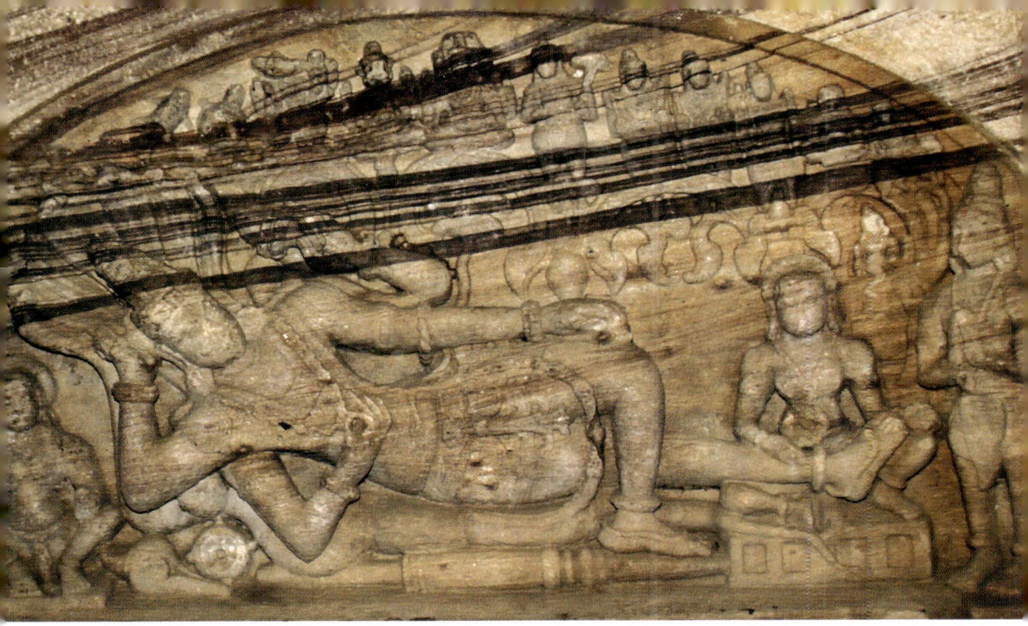

Rock-cut sleeping Vishnu

Further features dating back to Early Chalukya times are the **Rock Carvings** on the boulders to the rear of the Bhutanatha temple. The first of these to be seen are a number of miniature *linga* shrines in relief, with Nandis seated in front. Then comes a line of Hindu divinities. Notches above indicate that the figures were once sheltered by a structure, perhaps of wood. Perched on the top of the boulder, are two tiny free-standing shrines. A few metres beyond, at the edge of the water, is a cubical chamber built up to the base of the boulder. This shelters a well preserved, rock-cut icon of Vishnu on Shesha. The sleeping figure of the god is enhanced by dark veins in the sandstone.

From the Vishnu shrine it is merely a few steps to a cavern, entered beneath a low overhang. On its rear wall is a figure of Buddha, one hand held up in *abhaya-mudra*. While the cloak that Buddha wears can clearly be made out, the face has been damaged and then partly restored. Buddha is seated on an elaborate throne with lions at the base and *makaras* at the back, flanked by a pair of *chauri*-bearers. The cloak, the halo behind the head and the *pipal* tree above confirm that this indeed was a representation of Buddha.

Mutiliated Buddha figure in a cavern

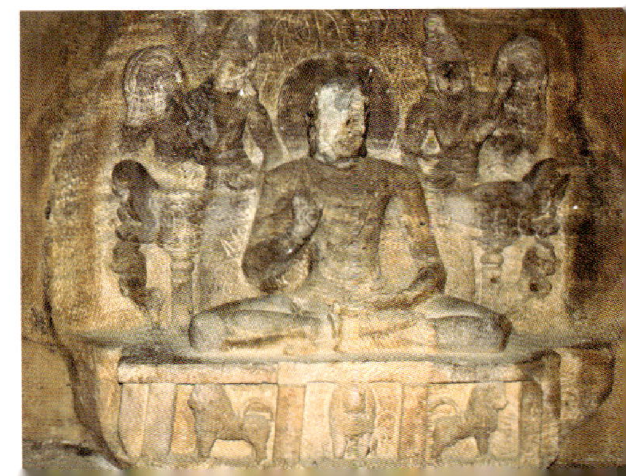

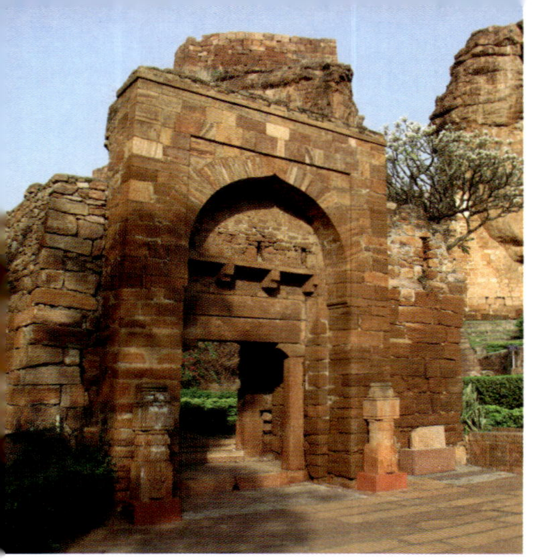

Arched gateway at the base of the North Fort

NORTH FORT

Rising almost 200 metres above the houses of Badami, the North Fort is reached via a stepped path that ascends through a spectacular ravine flanked by sheer cliffs. Gaps in the rocks are filled with fort walls, some of which descend perilously in short segments, reinforced by part-circular bastions, to the north side of the tank. The path begins immediately inside the **Arched Gateway** beside the garden compound of the Archaeological Museum. A short distance from the gateway is a flight of narrow steps to the left. This leads to a pair of **Open Mandapas** built upon a rock-cut terrace with worn elephant torsos, looking down upon the houses of the town below. The *mandapa* with two superimposed storeys adjoined some other structure, of which nothing now remains except slots cut into the bedrock. The *mandapas* seem never to have formed part of any religious monument. Possibly they are remnants of a royal, ceremonial complex used by the Early Chaluyka rulers, partly razed by the Pallavas.

Open *mandapas*, with the Upper Shivalaya in the distance

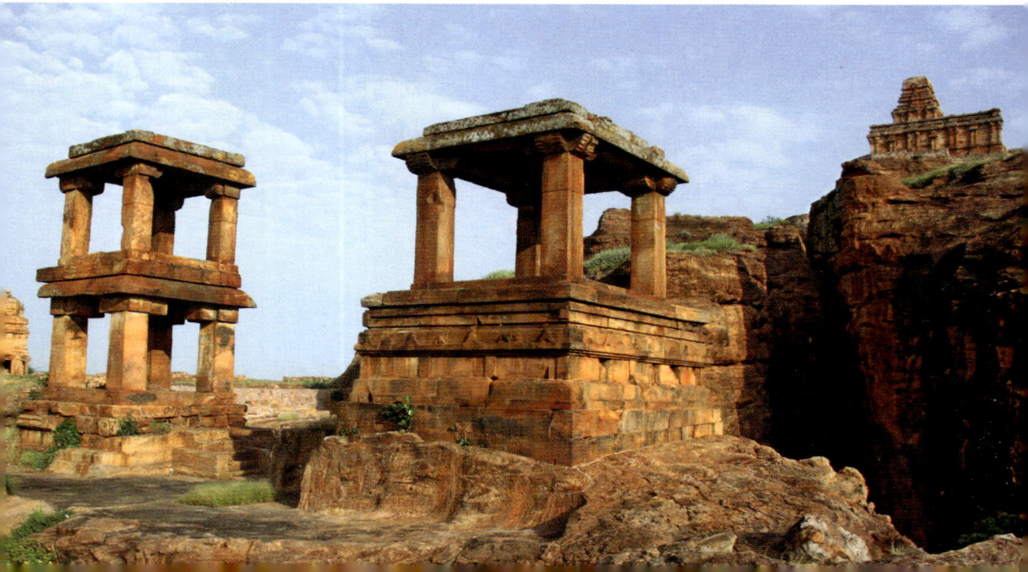

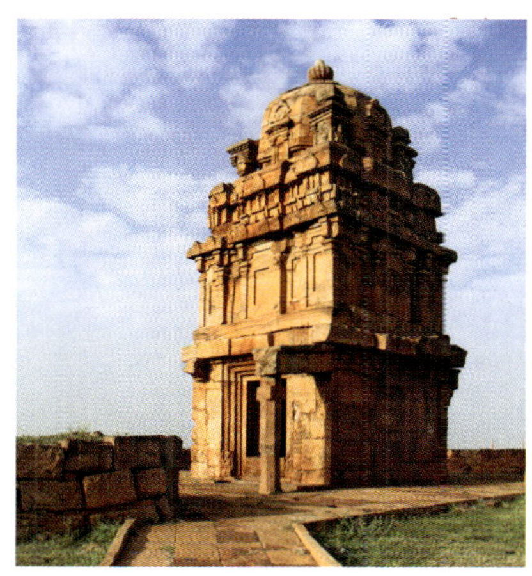

Lower Shivalaya

Returning to the main path, visitors ascend a few more steps before passing through yet another arched gateway, this example incorporating a pair of typical Early Chalukya guardian figures, removed from the ruined temple nearby. From here it is a short distance to reach a religious monument known as the **Lower Shivalaya**. The temple bears traces of having been wilfully dismantled, as only its towered sanctuary still stands. Projecting beams, however, indicate that the sanctuary was once surrounded by a passageway, and probably approached through a *mandapa* or porch. The tower over the sanctuary preserves its finely finished octagon-to-domed roof, framed by four model *kuta*-topped pavilions. The sanctuary doorway has its jambs covered with delicate foliate ornament. An oval-shaped pedestal can still be seen inside, but no votive icon is preserved. An iron canon placed next to the temple, bearing a clearly engraved date of 1550, was probably captured from the Portuguese and brought to Badami by the Marathas.

The stepped path continues upwards, passing by a ruined rubble structure with two long chambers, possibly a store or armoury. A side path to the left gives access to a **Circular Lookout**, more than 20 metres in diameter, jutting out over the edge of the cliff, looking down upon the Malegitti Shivalaya (described below). The lookout is bounded by well finished walls with angled ramparts provided with apertures for cannon, no longer extant. The European style of the ramparts suggest that they may date from Tipu Sultan's time. Just before arriving at the level top of the North Fort, the path passes by three **Circular Granaries**. Built on finely finished bases with single doorways, these granaries present conical rubble walls with projecting stone pieces that serve as steps to their summits.

At the top of the North Fort is a **Ruined Complex**, with a spacious court surrounded by a number of chambers, most likely for a Maratha garrison. On one side of the court is a plaster lined structure with pointed arches and vaults sheltering two rock-cut cisterns. The east-facing temple known as the **Upper Shivalaya** stands just a few metres away, at the highest point of the North Fort. Its prominent location and the rudimentary Dravida style of its architecture suggest

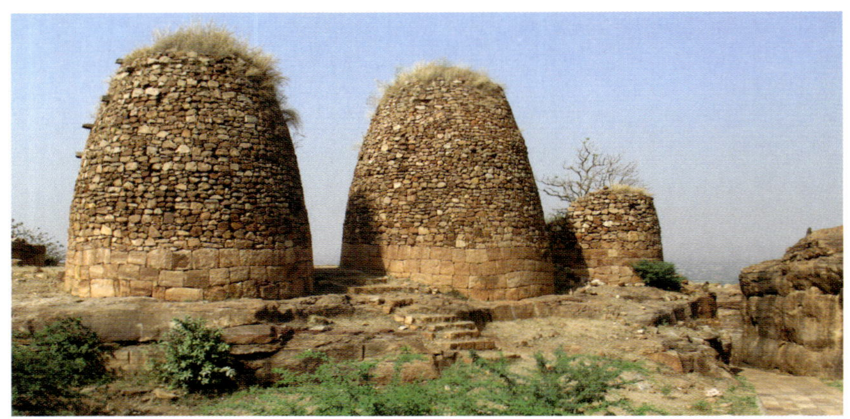

Granaries on the North Fort

that it is the earliest structural monument in Badami. Like the Lower Shivalaya already noticed, the Upper Shivalaya was partly demolished, most likely by the Pallava invaders. While the sanctuary and its tower survive, portions of the *mandapa* are now altogether missing. The outer walls of the *mandapa* and the passageway on three sides of the sanctuary are raised on a basement with a frieze of *ganas* and narrative scenes, such as the waking of Kumbhakarna from the *Ramayana* (south), and episodes from the childhood of Krishna (west). Pairs of pilasters defining the central projections on three sides frame icons of Krishna lifting Mount Govardhan flanked by herds (south), Krishna trampling the serpent demon Kaliya (west), and Narasimha disembowelling his victim (north). The walls are topped with a *kapota*-eave and a parapet with

Upper Shivalaya

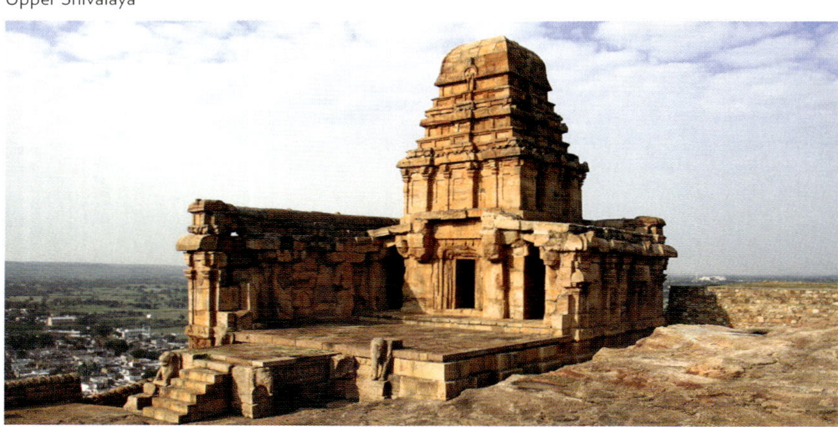

rudimentary corner *kutas* and central *shalas*. Though the sanctuary doorway appears incomplete and there is no pedestal or image within, the tower above is capped with a finely finished, enlarged *kuta*-roof with engraved *kudus* on four sides, rising upon short, pilastered walls. Elephant torsos embellish the rock-cut basement of the front portion of the *mandapa*.

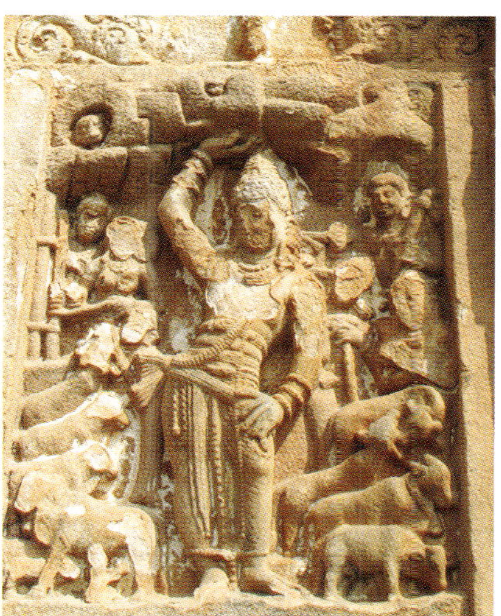

Krishna lifting Mount Govardhan; wall panel from the Upper Shivalaya

The only other feature of interest at the top of the North Fort is a *Dargah* beneath a great banyan, a short distance beyond the Upper Shivalaya. According to a painted sign, the tree shelters the modern grave of Sayyid Hazrat Badshah Pir, a popular Muslim holy figure. The annual *urs* festival marking his death anniversary attracts crowds of devotees. From here another trail descends to the northern side of the tank.

Banyan tree sheltering the *dargah*

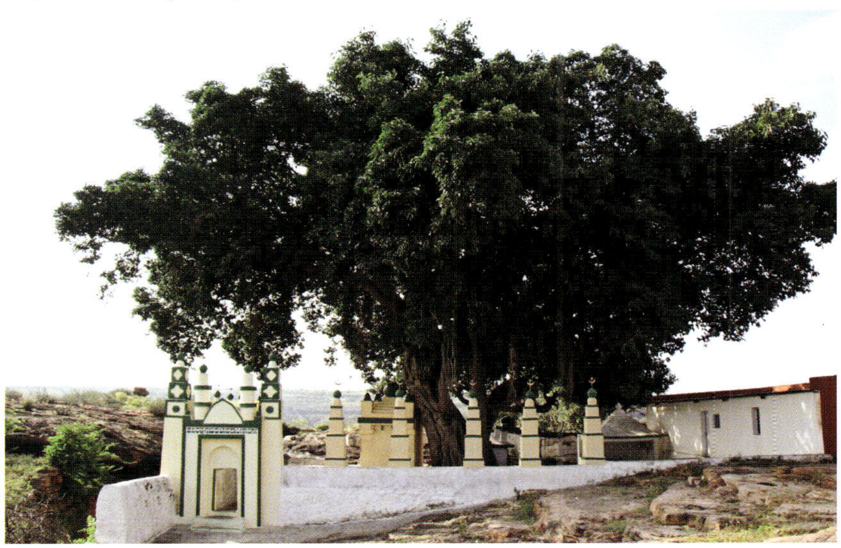

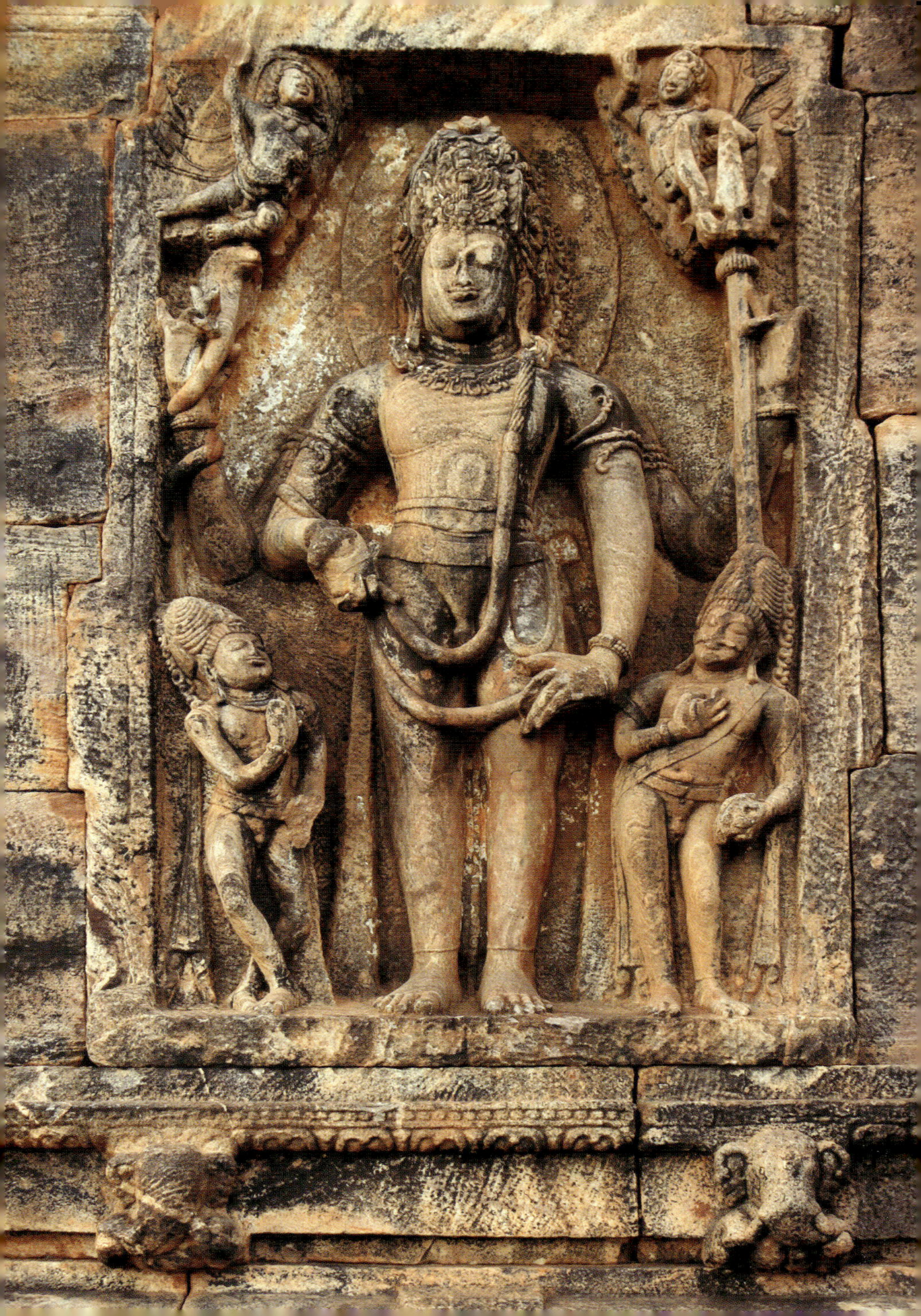

Opposite: Shiva panel on the Malegitti Shivalaya

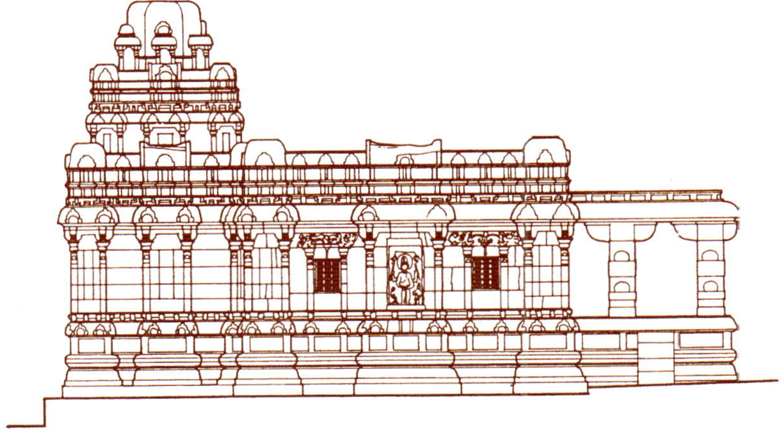

Malegetti Shivalaya

No tour of the North Fort would be complete without a visit to the Malegitti Shivalaya, the finest and most completely preserved Early Chalukya structural monument in Badami. The temple is perched dramatically on a great boulder beneath the western flank of the North Fort, reached most conveniently from a lane running away from the main road of Badami, opposite the bus station. The temple presents a sequence of open porch, triple-aisled *mandapa*, and towered sanctuary without any passageway. The *mandapa* walls are embellished with finely modelled basement mouldings and central projections framed by secondary pilasters carrying elaborate *makaras* with foliate tails in shallow relief. Magnificent carvings of Shiva bearing trident (south), and Vishnu holding conch and disc (north), are set between perforated stone windows. These icons suggest a syncretic cult affiliation for the temple, though the sanctuary within accommodates a polished, black stone *linga*. Other sculptures on the Malegitti Shivalaya are the two-armed guardians in the niches either side of the porch doorway. The walls are topped with a parapet comprising clearly articulated *shalas* and *kutas*. The tower over the sanctuary repeats the same octagon-to-domed roof noticed in the Lower Shivalaya. The inscription on one of the porch columns of the temple records the construction of a nearby bastion in 1543, when Badami was under the sway of Vijayanagara.

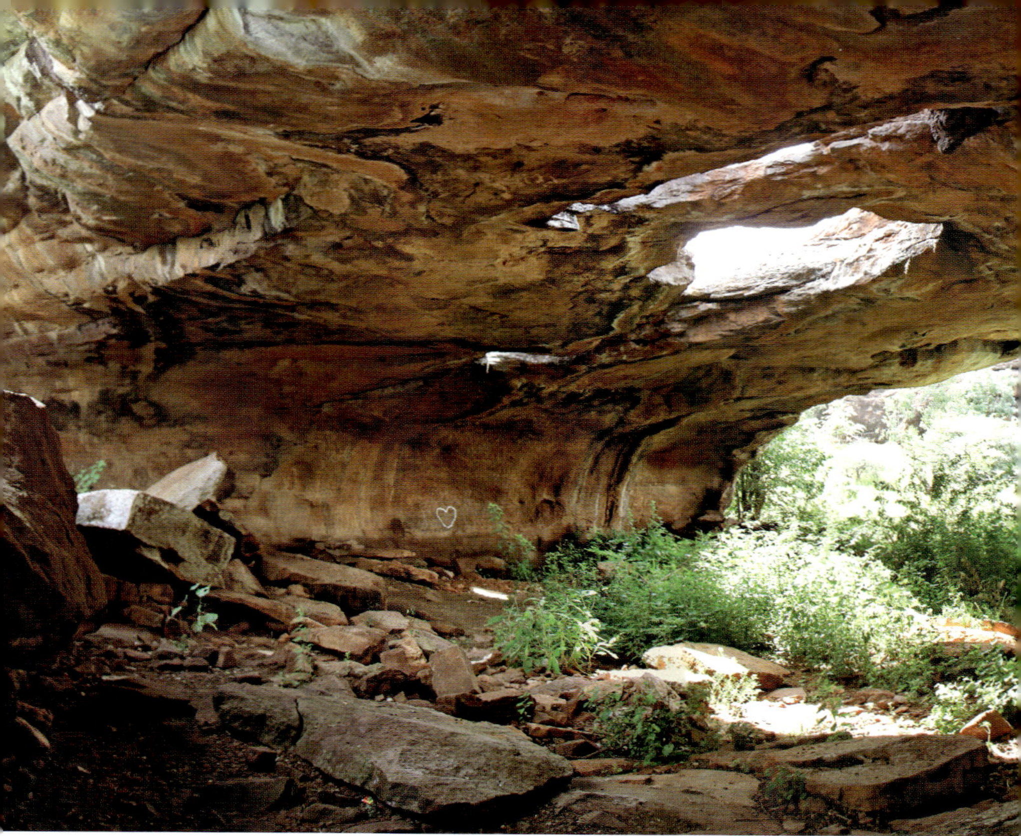

Sidilaphadi rock shelter

IN THE SURROUNDING HILLS

The rugged hinterland of Badami conceals a number of prehistoric sites with rock paintings and other artefacts. The two sites noticed here are of particular interest, well worth the walks through the arid, boulder-strewn landscape.

Sidilaphadi is reached by a path running from the main road, about 1.5 kilometres north of the town bus stand (look out for a signpost). A walk of one hour (3 kilometres) brings visitors to a spectacular natural shelter, with a rock arch spanning more than 28 metres. Holes in the roof of the arch, admitting light, are said to be the result of lightning strikes; hence the name Lightning Rock by which the site is popularly known. Traces of prehistoric paintings in white paint and red ochre can be made out in the side walls. They include a buffalo with horns, various birds and reptiles, and elongated stick-figures probably representing hunters. According to the display in the Archaeological Museum in Badami, these paintings date back to the Palaeolithic and Microlithic periods, in the 2nd and 1st millennia BCE.

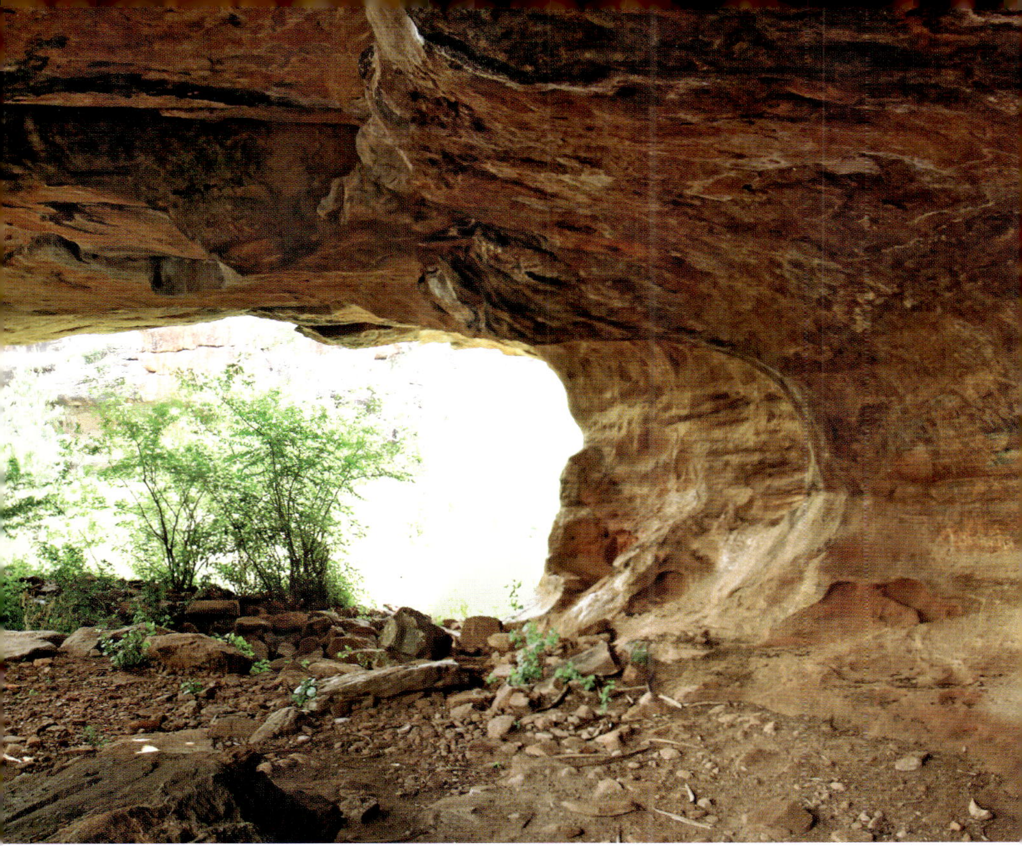

Ranganathgudda is the other prehistoric site to be described here. A partly paved path leading off the main road on the southern outskirts of Badami leads to a temple dedicated to Ranganatha, but a deviation about 1 kilometre further on gives access to a vertical rock face sheltered by an overhang. The paintings here, which were only discovered in 1993, portray wild boar together with hunters holding weapons and two curious stick-figures. Executed mostly in red ochre directly onto the rock, they have been dated to the Palaeolithic era, if not earlier.

Much more recent are the sculpted figures at **Aralitirtha**, a rock-shelter located about 1 kilometre along a strenuous track climbing into the rocky hills to the rear of the Bhutanatha group at the end of the tank. This somewhat inaccessible site comprises two curved surfaces above a natural cistern that traps rain water, looking down onto a valley below. The sides of the shelter are covered with a line of deities, including Virabhadra, Brahma, Vishnu, Shiva, Surya seated in the chariot, Durga, Nagaraja and Narasimha. A record in

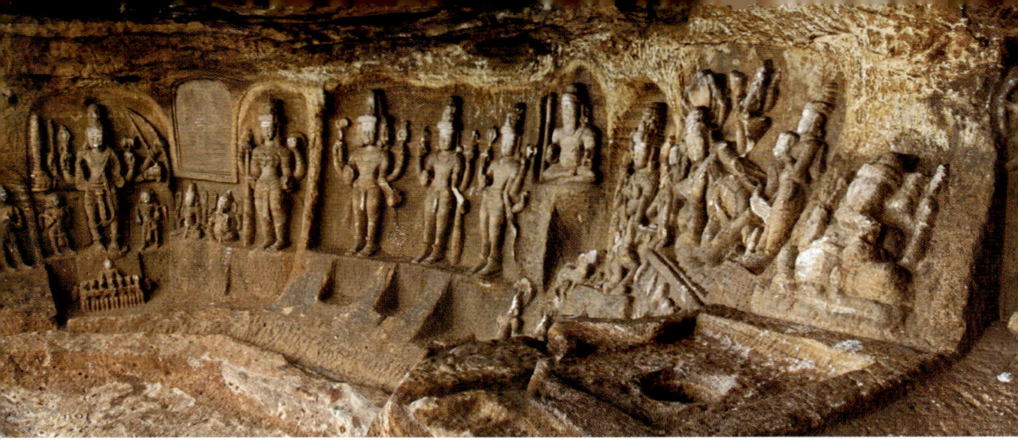

Rock carvings at Aralitirtha

Devanagari script incised onto the rock between two of the figures mentions Mahalakshmi of Kolhapur in southern Maharashtra. The temple to this goddess was substantially renewed in the early 18th century under the Kolhapur line of Maratha rulers. This suggests that the carvings at Aralitirtha may have been commissioned by a commander of the Marathas troops when they occupied Badami. Indeed, the most convenient way to reach Aralitirtha is from the South Fort, where such a garrison would have been stationed.

MAHAKUTA

Located 14 kilometres from Badami, this sacred *tirtha* can be reached by turning off the road leading to Pattadakal, or driving via the pilgrimage shrine at Banashankari. (The walk from Badami across the rocky plateau is recommended for those with extra time.) Mahakuta comprises a walled complex nestling in an attractive valley fed by a natural spring and shaded by trees, including several great banyans. The waters of the spring are trapped in a rectangular deep Tank, generally occupied with high spirited, splashing boys and young men. At water level on one side of the tank is a tiny pavilion sheltering a finely worked, four-faced *linga*. The tank is surrounded by temples and small shrines, consecrated to Shiva, the most important of which is the Mahakuteshvara Temple on the north side, after which the *tirtha* is named. Dating from latter part of the 7th century, this well proportioned monument consists of a porch contained within a later extension, a *mandapa* and a towered sanctuary surrounded by a passageway. Though now whitewashed, the outer walls preserve finely carved courtly episodes and battle scenes in the upper panels of the basement.

The walls of the Mahakuteshvara temple have central projections defined by double sets of pilasters accommodating diverse icons of Shiva, conveniently

Opposite: Tank with Sangameshvara and Mahakuteshvara temples, Mahakuta

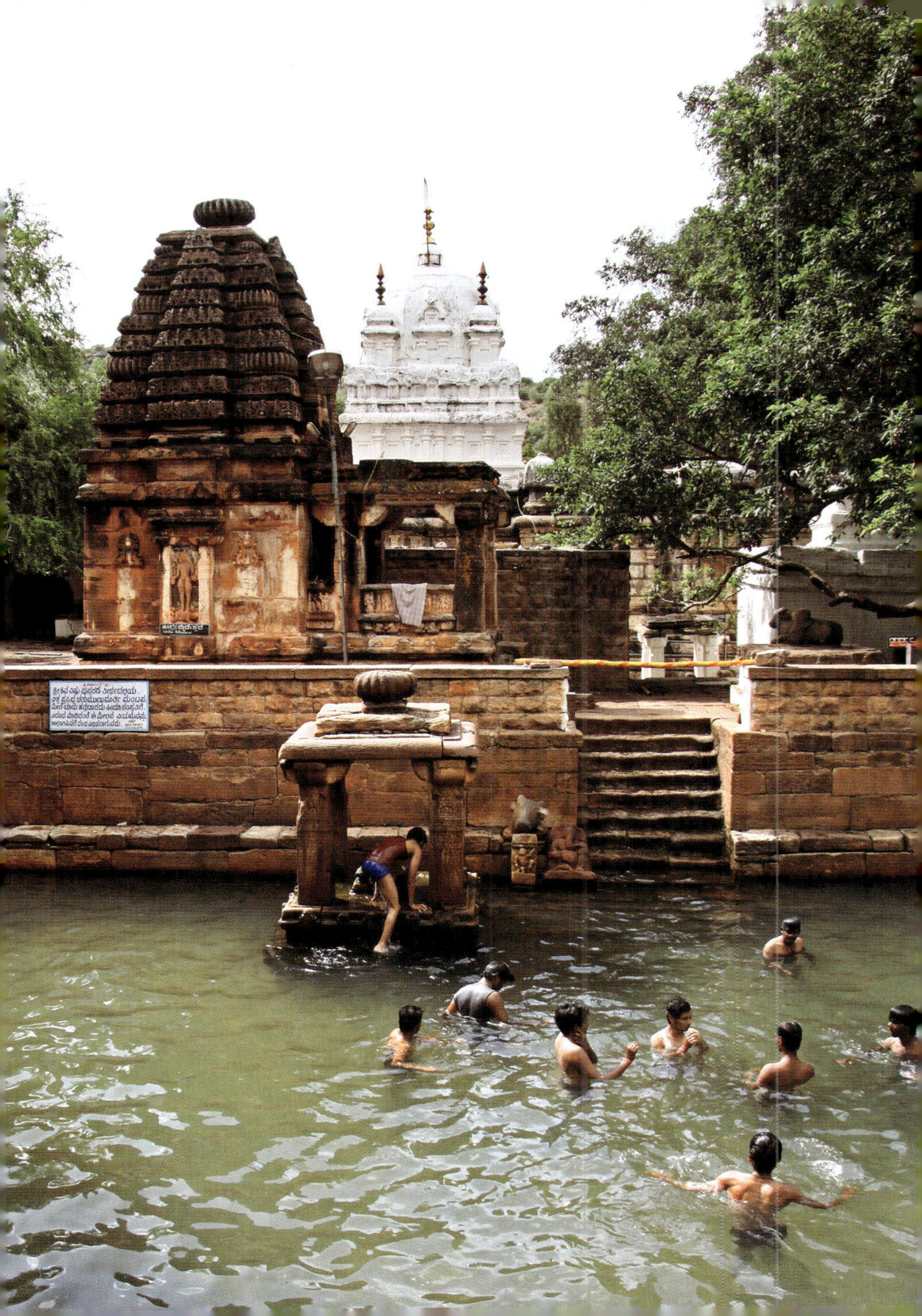

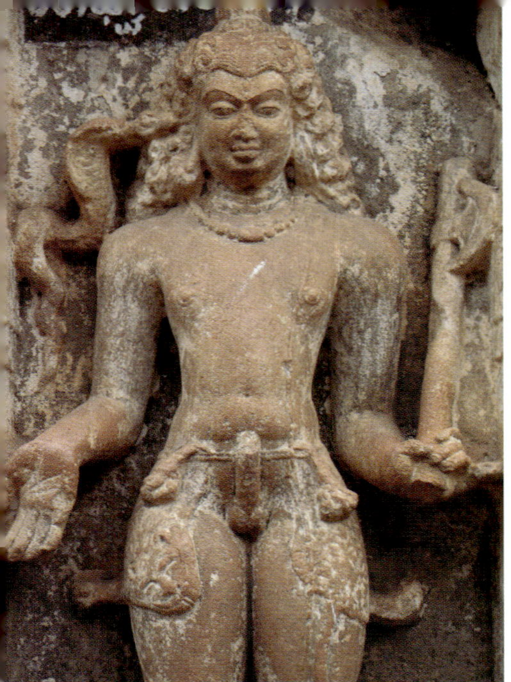
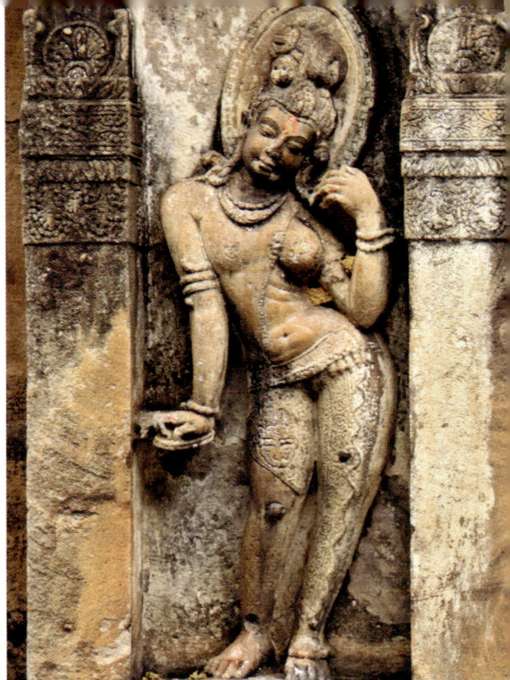

Left: Lakulisha *Right:* Ardhanarishvara; wall panels on the Sangameshvara temple, Mahakuta

supplied with modern painted Kannada and English labels. Curiously, they are all two-armed, a feature hardly found elsewhere in Early Chalukya representations of this god. Perforated stone windows admitting light to the *mandapa* passageway are headed by pediments of contrasting Dravida and Nagara designs. The walls terminate in a *kapota*-eave and a parapet with bold *kuta* and *shala* elements, now much plastered. The tower over the sanctuary is crowned by an octagon-to-dome roof framed by model corner elements with *kuta* roofs, recalling the towers of the Lower Shivalaya and Malegitti Shivalaya in Badami. A small pavilion housing a finely finished Nandi stands in front of the temple. The interior of the temple has been much remodelled and preserves little original detail.

Immediately to the south of the Mahakuteshvara, is the much smaller **Sangameshvara Temple**. Built in the contrasting Nagara manner with a characteristic curving *shikhara* tower, this dates from about the same time as the Mahakuteshvara. A small porch gives access to the sanctuary, the outer walls of which are embellished with the naked figure of Lakulisha with curling locks of hair (south), gracefully posed Ardhanarishvara (west), and Harihara (north, partly obscured), all in pilastered niches. A few metres to the rear stands the **Virupaksheshvara Temple**, built in a similar Nagara style, but with icons of Varaha (south), Vishnu (west) and Narasimha (north). Lesser shrines in the walled complex with stepped pyramidal towers are probably later additions.

The southern periphery of the Mahakuta complex is partly occupied by the **Mallikarjuna Temple,** which may be considered a slightly later copy of the Mahakuteshvara. Lacking disfiguring whitewash, its outer walls preserve much of the original detail, best seen in the friezes of *ganas* on the basement, the four-armed icons of Shiva in the niches, and the pediments over the windows. A curious moustachioed guardian figure clutching a staff is carved onto one of the porch columns. The interior has two ceiling panels: one with Brahma and the Dikpalas, the other with Shiva and Parvati riding on Nandi.

Outside the south-east corner of the walled complex stands a **Gateway.** Its south-facing doorway is flanked by skeletal male and female guardians, identified as Kala and Kali, possibly removed from an earlier structure. (From here commences the footpath to Badami.) Found fallen nearby to the gateway was a 6.8 metre-high sandstone fluted column with an inscription dated 601 recording a grant of ten villages to the god Mahakuteshvaranatha. The column was removed many years ago to the Archaeological Museum in Bijapur, where it can still be seen.

Another feature of interest at Mahakuta is the lofty wooden **Chariot,** generally kept near the modern car park outside the complex. Though of no great antiquity, it is covered with lively carvings.

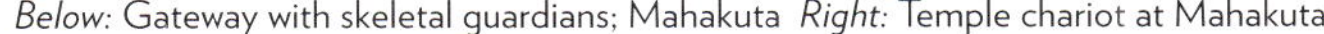

Below: Gateway with skeletal guardians; Mahakuta *Right:* Temple chariot at Mahakuta

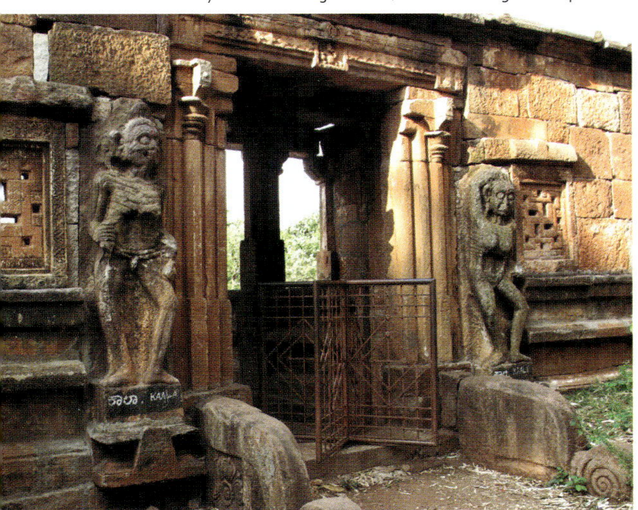

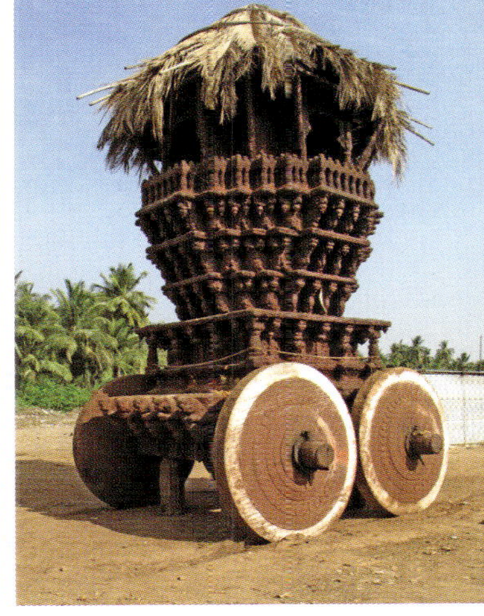

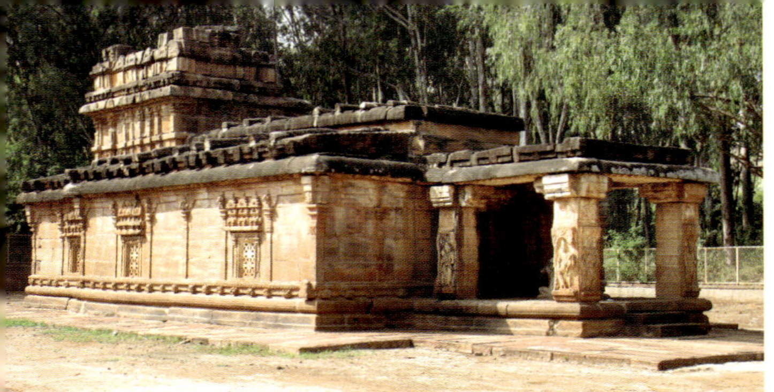

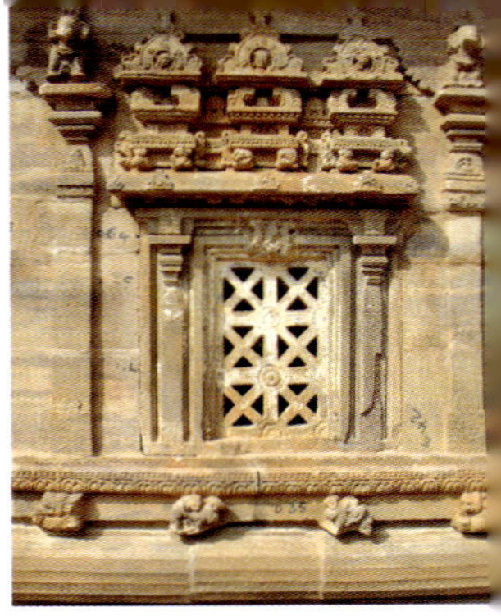

Left: Naganatha temple at Naganathakolla *Right:* Window detail

NAGANATHAKOLLA

Approximately midway along the road running between Mahakuta and Banashankari is a turnoff leading to a secluded forested spot where stands the isolated Naganatha Temple. This fine Early Chalukya monument is laid out in a manner similar to temples in Aihole, with a *mandapa*, sanctuary and passageway contained within a rectangle of walls. The small porch at the east has columns with charming carvings of couples beneath trees. A Nandi sculpture is placed here, with a *nagaraja* composition on the ceiling above.

The outer walls of the temple are of interest for the narrow pilasters topped by cut-out, upright yalis. Windows with crisscross perforated designs are topped by ornate pediments, mostly of the Dravida type, but there is one example with interlocking *gavaksha* motifs, in the typical Nagara manner. The tower that rises above had an octagon-to-dome roof, as in the two large temples at Mahakuta, but this has mostly fallen. Somewhat damaged ceiling panels can be made out on the *mandapa* ceiling. They illustrate (from the entrance) Vishnu on Garuda; Brahma with Dikpalas and flying celestials; and Shiva and Parvati on Nandi. The sanctuary is now empty.

BANASHANKARI

The most popular pilgrimage destination in the Badami area is the Banashankari Temple, 5 kilometres south-east of the town. The temple is an 18th-century Maratha period foundation, but no particular patron is known. That there was a shrine here in earlier times is evident from the incomplete, Late Chalukya period sanctuary that stands outside its walled compound.

Visitors approach the Banashankari temple from the east, passing through a lofty gateway with an arched profile. The walkway within is lined with reused, 11th-century columns. Immediately inside the compound stand three tall, tapering octagonal *dipa-stambhas* with multiple curved stone brackets for oil lamps that are lit on special occasions. The temple itself is of little architectural merit, having plain outer walls, but the brightly painted multi-stage tower is crowned with a small bulbous dome on a frieze of petals. The goddess venerated within the sanctuary is a form of Devi, gorgeously dressed and framed by an ornate gilded frame. Arcades surround the temple on three sides.

In front of the temple gateway is a huge square Tank surrounded by colonnades. At the edge of the water, on axis with the temple gateway, is a *mandapa* with reused, Late Chalukya columns. A few metres away, near to the south-west corner of the tank, stands a remarkable Lamp Tower. This unique triple-storeyed structure, with decorated arched openings at each level, accommodates an octagonal masonry column that protrudes above the roof as a tapering *dipa-stambha*. Curved brackets for lamps are seen beside the arched openings of the tower, as well as on the lamp-column itself. Donor figures are carved in relief on the column shaft inside.

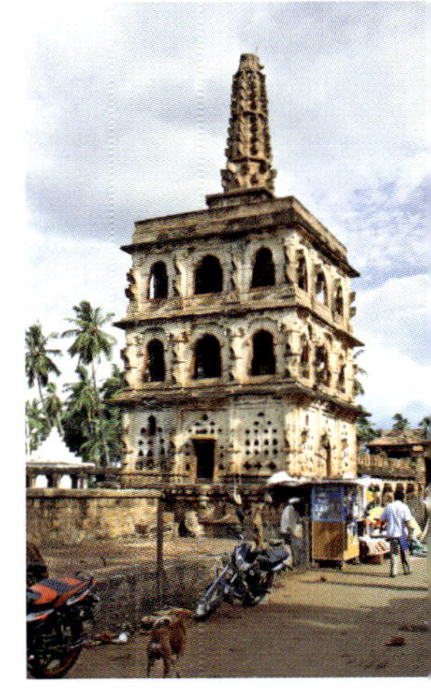

Above: Lamp tower at Banashankari

Below: Market stall at Banashankari

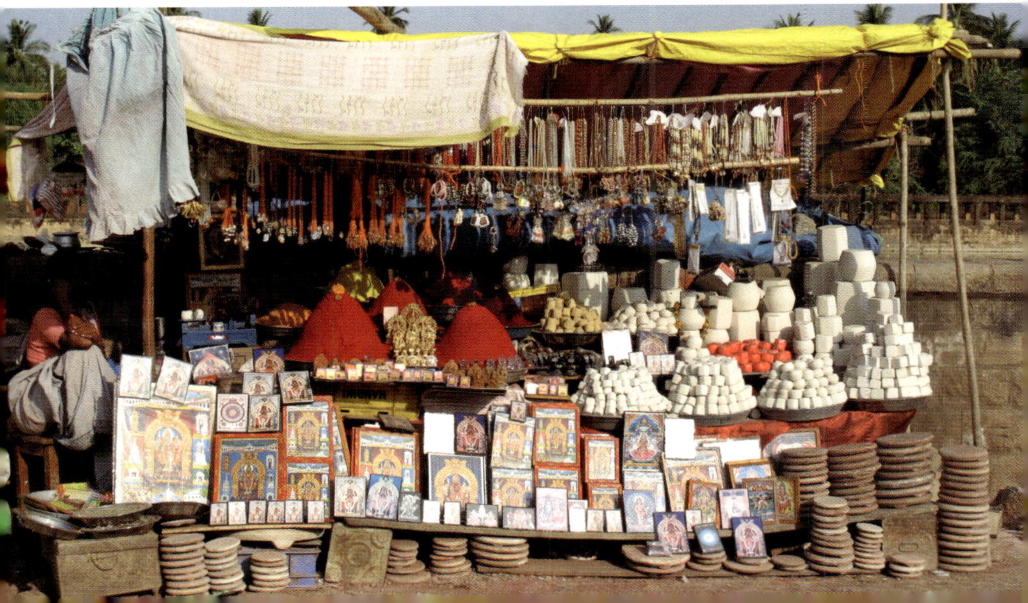

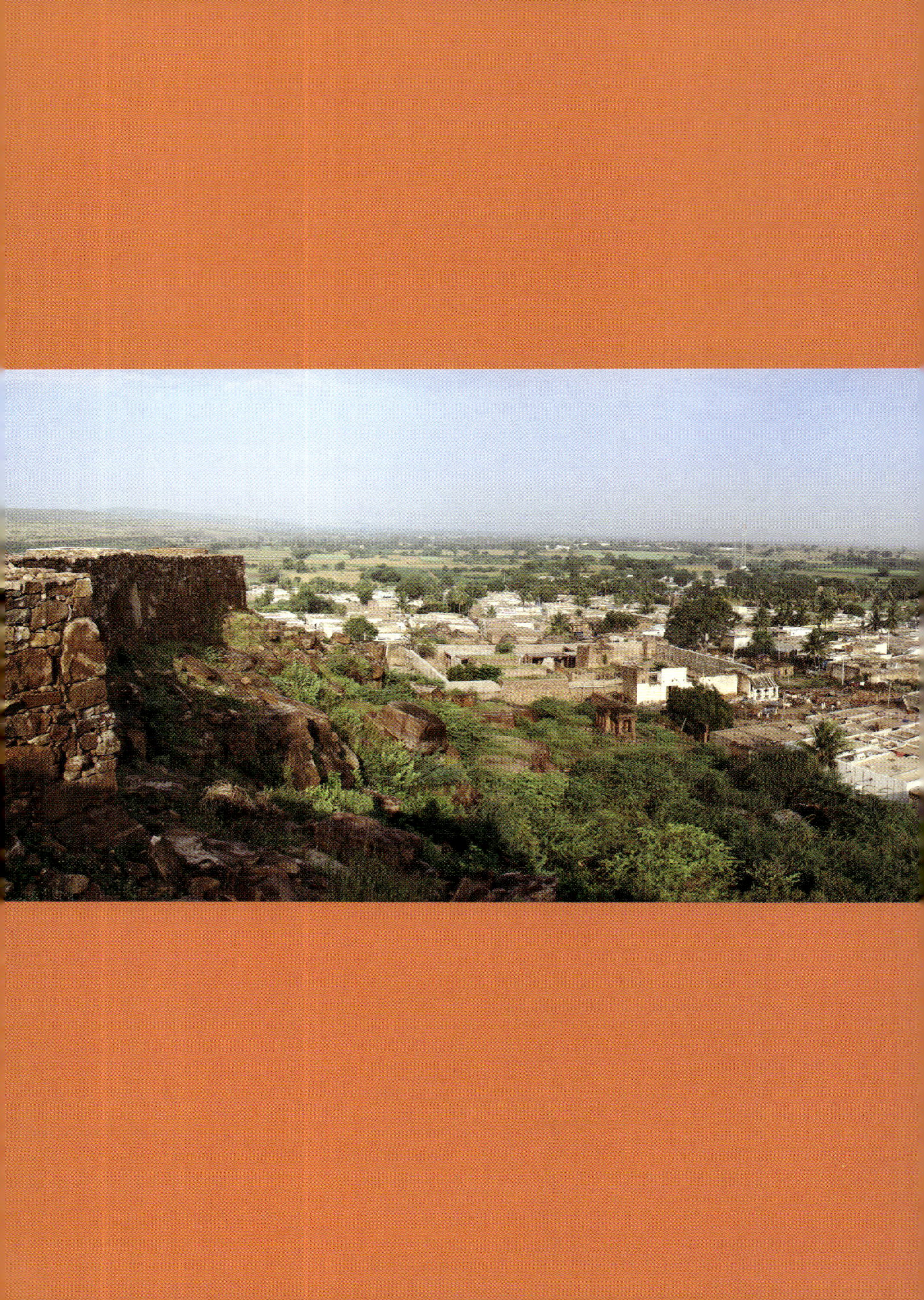

AIHOLE

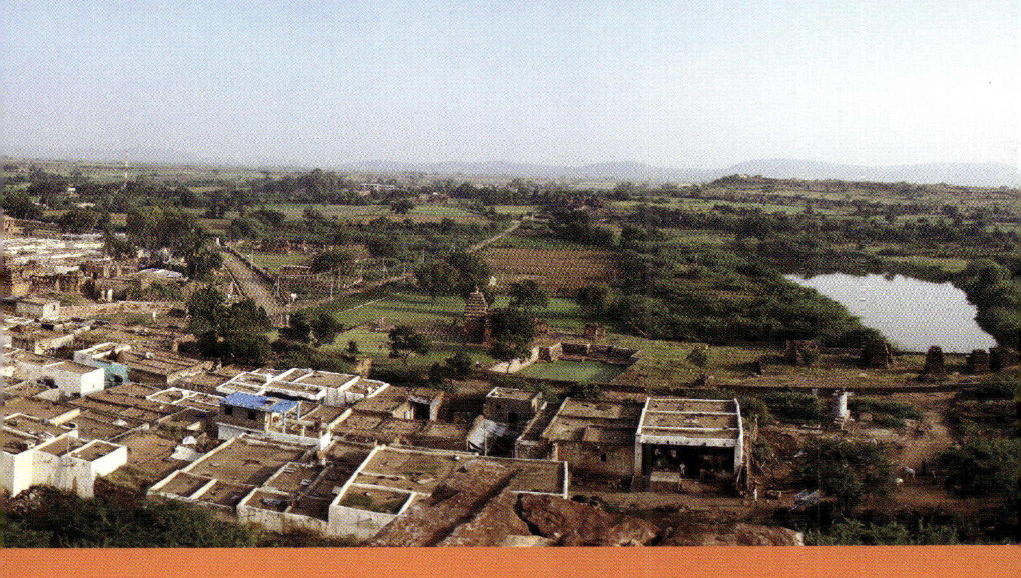

Preceding pages: Panorama of Aihole from Meguti hill

Located near to the right bank of the Malprabha river, about 35 kilometres from Badami via Pattadakal, this town preserves a large number of Hindu and Jain temples built out of, and even occasionally excavated into, golden yellow sandstone. There is even a single Buddhist structure. These religious monuments are mostly assigned to two distinct eras: that of the Early Chalukyas and Rashtrakutas, extending from the late 6th to the 8th centuries, and that of the Late Chalukyas, spanning the 11th-12th centuries. Until the recent clearing work by the archaeological authorities, Aihole had the appearance of an ancient settlement untouched by time, with houses built up to, and even extending into, historical edifices. In consequence, many temples bear the names of their past inhabitants! Today the most important monuments are contained within fenced garden enclosures, separated from houses with their characteristic timber columned facades, whitewashed masonry walls and mud-coated flat roofs. Evidence of continuous habitation in Aihole is borne out by the changes in level between the streets and houses of the town and the temples themselves, of which only the most architecturally important and artistically distinguished are described here.

Fortifications contain Aihole in an approximate circle, about 500 metres from north to south and somewhat less from east to west. (The walls are mostly missing on the west). Partly rebuilt, the fortifications employ huge sandstone blocks with tapering profiles, reinforced at regular intervals by sloping square bastions. Gateways with one or more turns give access to the streets within the town. Some wall blocks are inscribed with letters in the style of the 11th-12th centuries, suggesting that the fortifications should be attributed to the Late Chalukyas, perhaps replacing earlier earthen ramparts. This would accord with the history of the town, which underwent considerable development in Late Chalukya times. It was during this period that a federation of wealthy merchants based in Aihole, known as the "Ayyavole 500", became celebrated throughout much of the Deccan and Southern India.

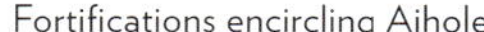

Fortifications encircling Aihole

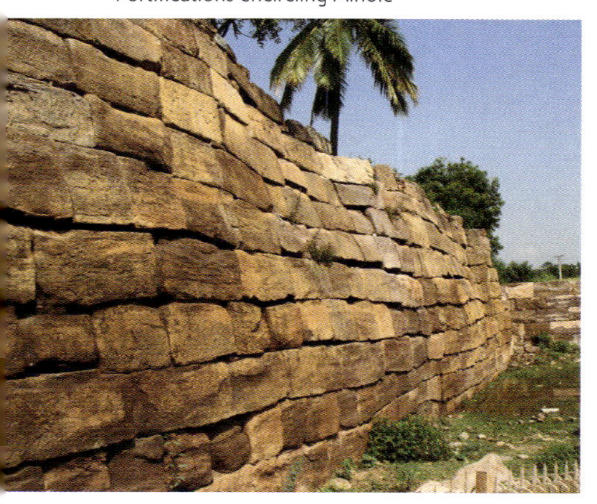

The tour of Aihole described here begins at Meguti hill south-east of the town, from where fine aerial view made be had of the streets and houses, and indeed of the whole Malprabha valley as far as Pattadakal. It then proceeds to the Durga temple complex in the middle of Aihole (ticket required), where many of the larger and more interesting religious monuments are clustered, in the vicinity of the Archaeological Museum. For visitors with greater interest the tour continues with the temples to the north of the town, including the Ravanaphadi cave-temple with its splendid carvings, and the temples both within the town and to the south of the ramparts.

Also described here is the site of Siddanakolla, with its natural spring hidden in the sandstone bluffs at the edge of the Malprabha valley, a short distance from Aihole.

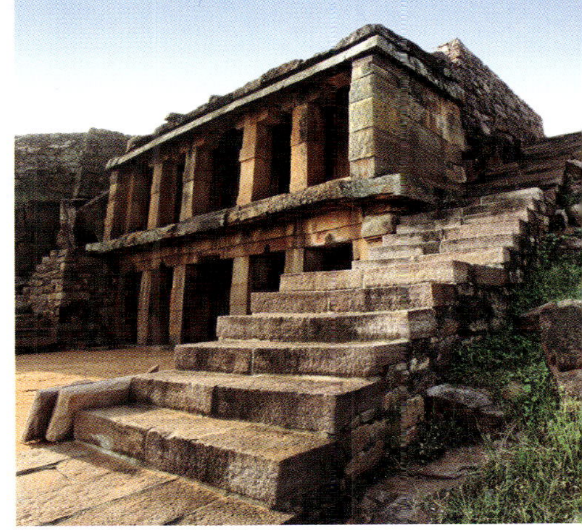

Two-storeyed Buddhist temple beneath Meguti hill

MEGUTI HILL

An early morning climb to the top of this hill is a recommended introduction to any visit of Aihole. The flight of steps that ascends the hill is accessed from a lane running from beside the Mallikarjuna complex of temples beside the main road, passing through a farm compound dotted with cattle and carts. Just below the crest of the hill is a **Two-Storeyed Buddhist Temple**. In front is placed a headless statue of Buddha, presumably removed from the inner shrine. The temple presents two superimposed colonnades, each of which gives access to a small chamber cut into the cliff face. The doorway to the lower chamber, now empty, has delicately worked foliate ornament which suggests an early date, perhaps towards the end of the 6th century. A relief carving of Buddha seated beneath a parasol in seen in the central ceiling bay of the upper colonnade.

Only a few more steps are required to reach the summit of the level-topped Meguti hill. Here, facing north towards the town, stands the **Jain Temple**, of considerable importance both historically and architecturally.

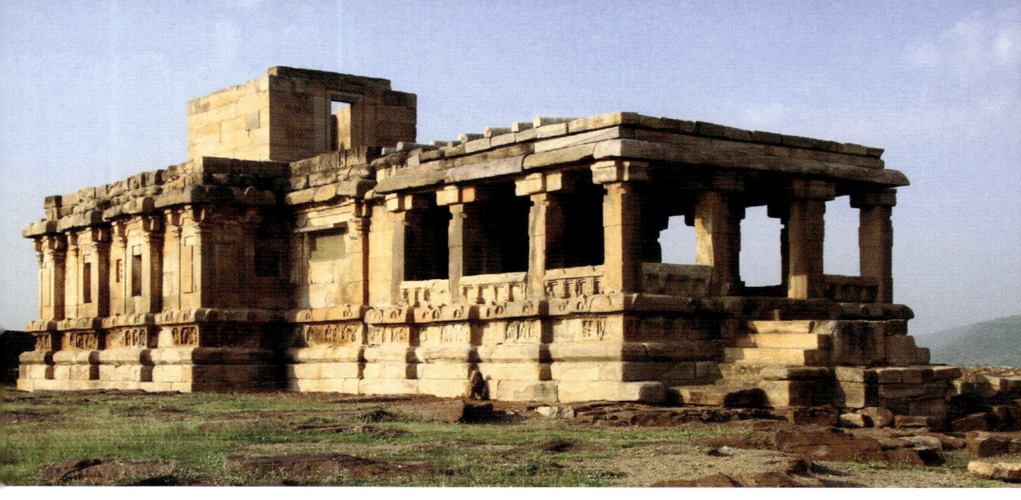

Jain temple on Meguti hill

Set into its side wall is a grey stone slab with an inscription (sheltered by a modern overhang). Dated to 634, this consists of poem employing different metres in Sanskrit composed by Ravikirti, the court author of Pulakeshin II. The composition gives an account of the Chalukya family and the exploits of his royal patron. The temple consists of an open porch adjoining a closed *mandapa* and a sanctuary surrounded by a passageway. The outer walls are raised on basement mouldings that rhythmically project and recess in accordance with the pilastered walls above. Empty niches as well as uncut, raised blocks indicate that the sculptural portions of the temple were never completed. While the *kapota*-eave and portions of the parapet with model roof forms can still be seen, the original tower is lost. (The small rooftop chamber is a later replacement.)

The Jain affiliation of the Meguti temple is evident from the image placed within the sanctuary. Now defaced, the naked meditating figure of a Tirthankara is depicted seated on a throne with lions at the base and *makara* heads at the sides. Richly dressed, *chauri*-bearing attendants are seen at either side. The remarkable icon of the Jain goddess Ambika, seated beneath a flowering tree, that was once placed within the vestibule in front is now displayed in the Archaeological Museum in the town.

Inscription on the wall of the Jain temple

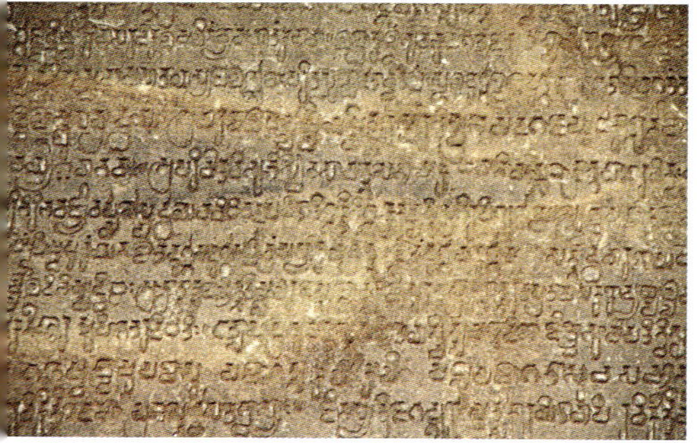

The Meguti temple stands in the middle of a spacious enclosure

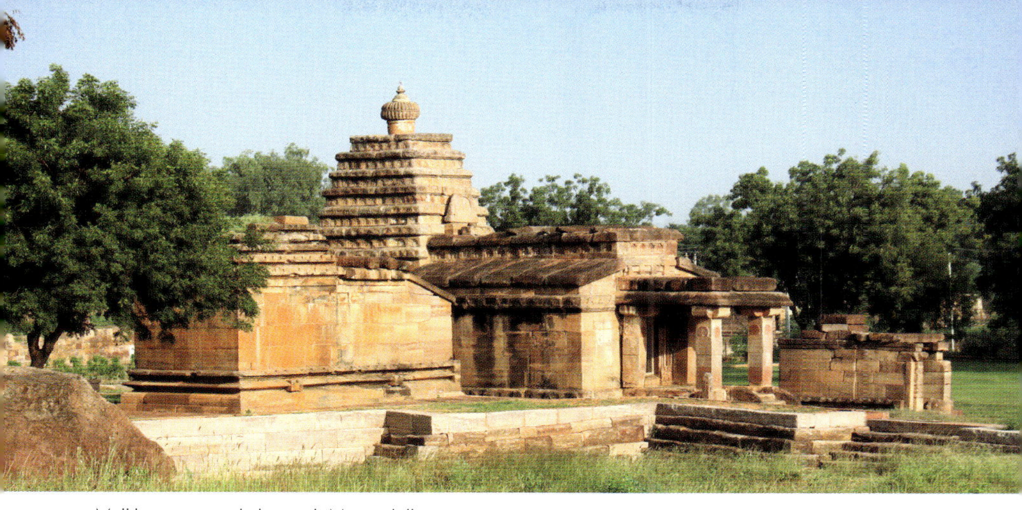

Mallikarjuna temple beneath Meguti hill

defined by rubble **Walls** that run up the sides of the hill, with a prominent circular bastion at the south-west corner. The occasional reused Jain memorial stone from the 10th-11th centuries set into the walls indicate that the hill continued to be sacred to followers of this religion in Late Chalukya times. On the boulder-strewn top of the hill beyond the walls can be seen a number of **Dolmens**, many now collapsed. Those that survive in a comparatively complete condition consists of four upright stone slabs creating a quadrangular chamber, topped by a much larger, unshaped horizontal slab. These megalithic remains date back to the 2nd-1st millennia BCE.

Visitors must now retrace their steps and descend the hill by the same stepped path in order to continue their tour of Aihole. Next to the main road they will notice the **Mallikarjuna Complex**. The main temple here is assigned to the Early Chalukya period, its pyramidal tower consisting of diminishing tiers of eave-like mouldings. The outer walls are plain, and the interior is of little interest except for a Nandi placed in front of the sanctuary. The temple faces towards a portal with a decorated lintel near to a stepped tank. The lesser shrines of the complex, all with stepped pyramidal towers, are Late Chalukya structures.

The last feature to be noticed in this part of the itinerary of Aihole is the **Jain Cave-Temple** cut into the southern flank of Meguti hill. It, too may be considered one of the earlier monuments of Aihole, having been excavated towards the end of the 6th or early in the 7th century. The cave-temple is most conveniently reached by a side road, about 1 kilometre to the south of the town. Though presenting an unadorned, severe exterior, the interior is richly embellished with carvings, though these seem to have been left uncompleted. The long transverse vestibule, which is reached after passing through a

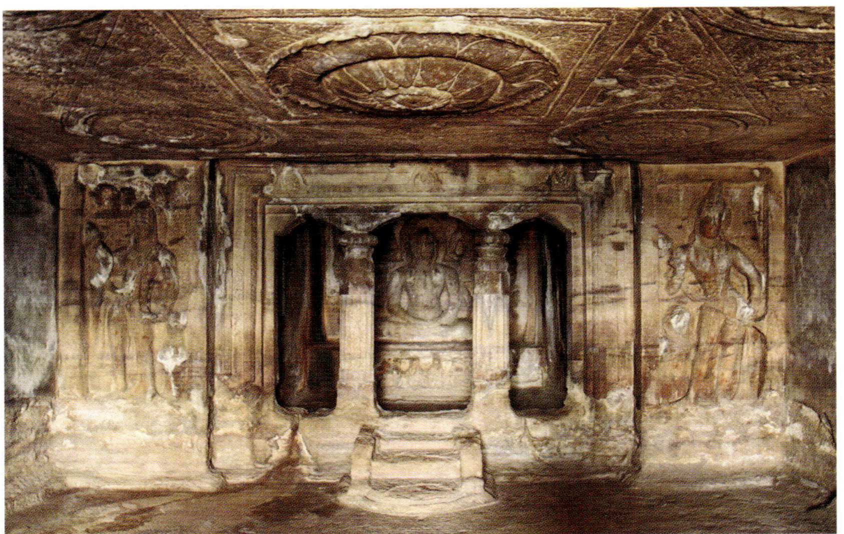

Interior of the Jain cave-temple

plaidoorway, has its ceiling entirely covered with delicate relief patterns of lotus petals, separated by panels with *makaras* disgorging tiny human figures. At either end of the vestibule are deeply sculpted figures of Parshvanatha (left) and Bahubali (right), both with female attendants. A triple-bayed opening within the vestibule leads to a spacious square hall. This, too has its ceiling covered with relief designs, especially lotus medallions with imaginative designs in between incorporating *makaras*, fish and even human torsos. Triple-bayed openings on three sides give access to small chambers. That on axis with the entrance is flanked by two-armed guardians holding small lotuses; an enthroned Jina is seated within. The chamber on the left contains a similar figure, but this is flanked by a host of worshippers, mostly of women, others riding on an elephant. The corresponding chamber of the right was never finished. A path to the left of the Jain cave-temple ascends to the dolmens at the top of Meguti hill.

DURGA TEMPLE COMPLEX

The principal attraction for most visitors to Aihole is the complex containing the **Durga Temple**, by far the largest and most richly embellished Hindu monument in the town. Its name is misleading, since the temple was originally dedicated to Surya when constructed in the early 8th century; only later did it come to be known as the Durga when a stone rubble *durg*, or fortified lookout,

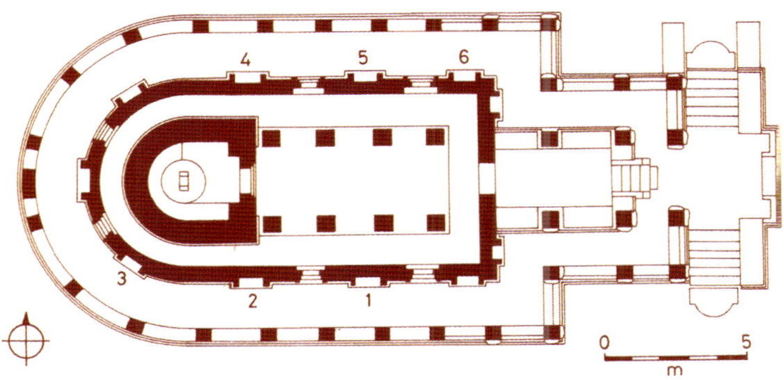

1. Shiva with Nandi
2. Narasimha
3. Vishnu on Garuda
4. Varaha
5. Durga spearing Mahisha
6. Harihara

Durga temple; major sculpture panels

was raised upon its roof (now removed). Visitors approach the Durga temple from the west, giving them a full view of the building's semicircular end. This apsidal-ended layout derives from rock-cut Buddhist *chaitya* halls going back to the 2nd-1st centuries BCE, but is virtually unique within the context of Early Chalukya architecture. The Durga temple comprises an outer colonnaded verandah with an entrance porch on the east that wraps around a complete unit comprising a porch, rectangular *mandapa* and semicircular sanctuary surrounded by a narrow passageway. The outer verandah is raised on a high basement with

Durga temple

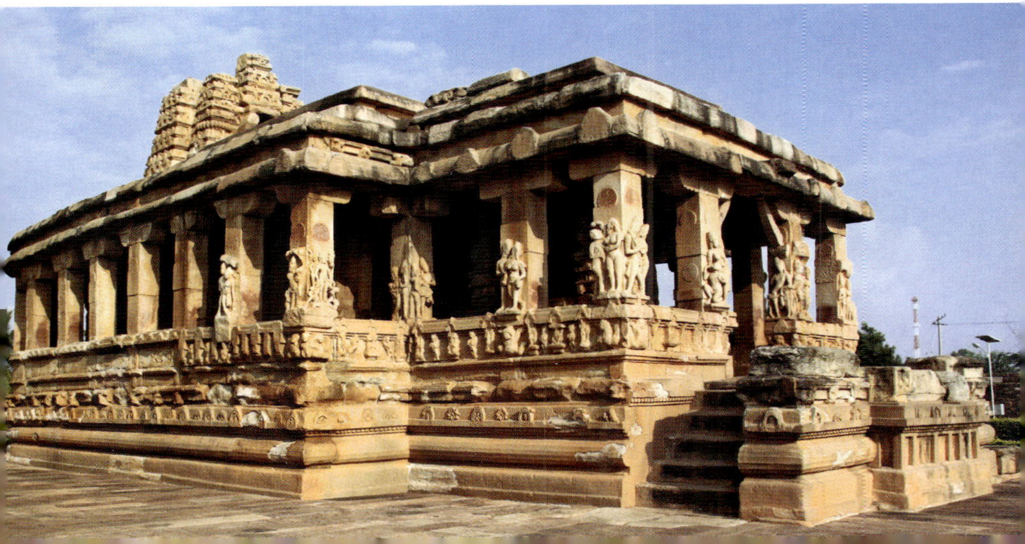

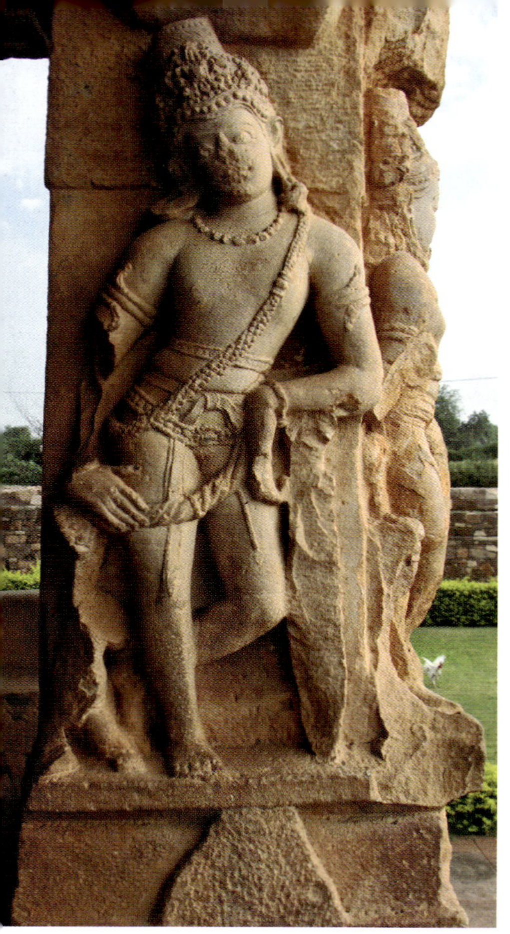

Guardian figure on a porch column of the Durga temple

a faceted rounded moulding that is somewhat crudely restored. The verandah columns are mostly plain, except for one example with a worn icon of Shiva inserted at the western end to prop up a failing beam. At the eastern entrance to the temple, however, the columns are enhanced with guardian figures and human couples in animated and affectionate postures. One composition even shows a male embracing a horse-headed woman. Rising upon the roof is an incomplete Nagara styled tower; its crowning *amalaka* finial now seen fallen on the ground nearby. The tower's square plan, with central projections, sits somewhat uncomfortably on the semicircular sanctuary roof. Elsewhere, the roof consists of tiers of sloping slabs that continue around the apsidal end of the building.

On climbing the somewhat steep steps to the Durga temple visitors arrive at an internal porch, complete with basement, balcony seating and sculpted columns, preceding the *mandapa* doorway. However, before entering the temple visitors should make a round of the colonnaded verandah. En route they will notice the carved reliefs on the basement of the internal porch, some with narratives that depict episodes from the *Ramayana*, as well as scenes from everyday life. The outer walls of the *mandapa* and semicircular sanctuary as viewed within the verandah are also raised on a basement with panels filled with elegantly carved foliation and scrollwork. The walls above have regularly spaced niches alternating with perforated windows, some conceived as wheels with fish-spokes. The niches are headed with pediments displaying diverse Dravida and Nagara elements. The carved panels set into many of these niches are among the greatest masterpieces of Early Chalukya art. In clockwise sequence these portray Shiva with Nandi;

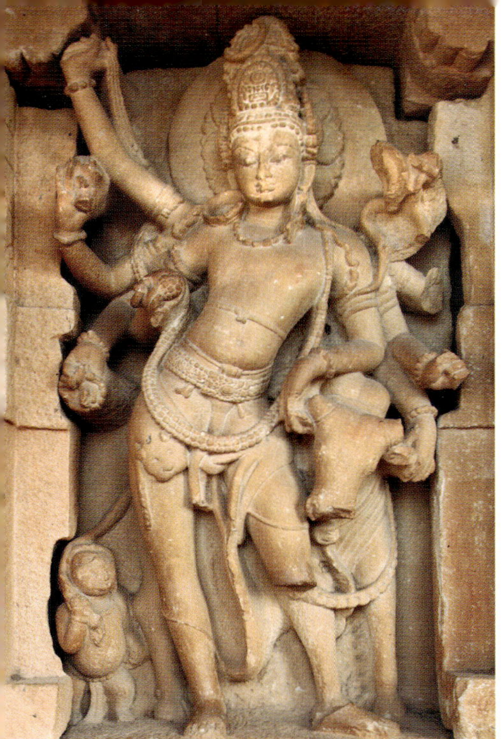
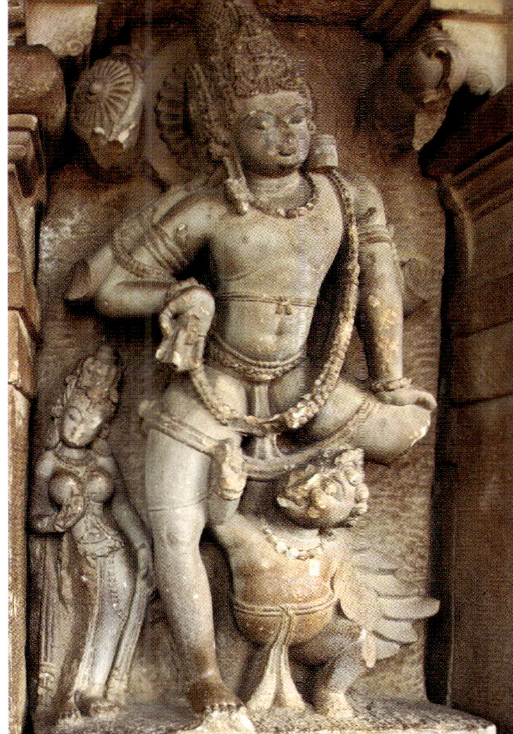

Left: Shiva with Nandi *Right:* Vishnu on Garuda; panels on the Durga temple

lion-headed Narasimha leaning on the club; Vishnu flying on Garuda, with the eagle's spread-out wings clearly delineated; Varaha, with the god's boar head nuzzling the diminutive figure of Bhudevi; Durga energetically spearing Mahisha; and the somewhat stiff, symmetrical figure of Harihara. The range of these icons and the fact that the backs of several panels have been cut so as to fit them into the niches suggest that some carvings may have been brought from other monuments and inserted here at some later date. Indeed, not all the icons would have been considered suitable in a temple originally dedicated to Surya. Aerial couples, their legs kicked up in the act of flying through the clouds, once graced the sloping ceiling slabs above the colonnade, but only a few worn figures of this type can now be seen (east end of the verandah). As already mentioned, the two best preserved of these slabs are now in New Delhi.

The inner porch of the Durga temple is elaborately treated. Column shafts here are adorned with medallions containing garlands and jewels; fully modelled couples and guardians are carved onto the outermost supports. The porch interior is roofed with ceiling panels representing a *nagaraja* with a coiled serpent body, and a wheel with fish-pokes surrounded by luxuriant lotus ornament, two themes familiar from the cave-temples in Badami. (The tusk-like struts carrying the transverse beam are modern reinforcements.) The *mandapa* doorway is the most elaborate in Aihole, with river goddesses, male guardians and female attendants beneath at either side, and decorated jambs and slender fluted pilasters above. The pediment over the doorway lintel has miniature niches containing figures, that in the middle portraying two-armed Surya. Compared with the sculptural exuberance of the colonnaded verandah and entrance porch, the *mandapa* interior is strikingly plain, with a circular pedestal devoid of any image within the sanctuary.

Standing a few metres to the south of the Durga temple is a gateway with a central passageway, curiously out of alignment with the entrance to the temple itself, but probably built at about the same time. An icon of Surya is carved onto one of the parapet elements over the passageway, confirming the original dedication of the temple itself.

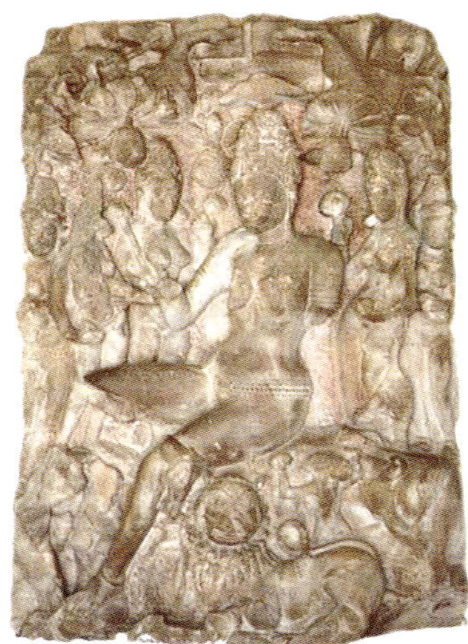

Ambika from the Jain temple on Meguti hill, now in the Archaeological Museum, Aihole

Further to the east is the **Archaeological Museum,** which is of interest, especially for its large-scale model of Aihole and its monuments displayed in an open-air inner court. The garden in front of the museum is dotted with hero memorials and *sati* stones dating from the 12th century and later. The chief exhibit within the museum is a deeply carved panel portraying Ambika seated beneath a flowering tree, removed from the Jain temple on Meguti hill. The Jain goddess is portrayed seated on a lion beneath a fruit tree, in the company of female attendants, one of whom carries a small infant. Here, too can be seen a gigantic representation of evil-looking Bhairava, and a complete set of the Saptamatrikas, now missing their heads.

From the Archaeological Museum visitors should proceed to the other temples within the complex, noting the many smaller shrines with pyramidal

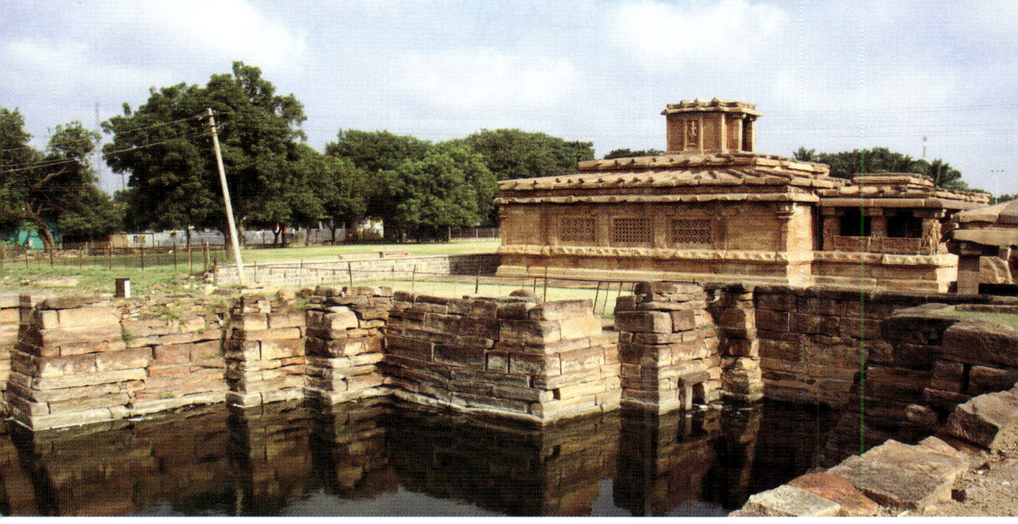

Tank with Ladkhan temple

stepped towers dating from later to times. The first monument to be described here is the **Suryanarayana Temple**, which takes its name from a finely worked, Late Chalukya icon placed in its sanctuary. The sculpture portrays the god with two hands bearing lotuses, standing within an ornate, cut-out frame. This piece, however, is a later insert as the building itself dates from the 8th century. This is evident from its Nagara style tower, with a noticeable curved profile, now missing its upper tiers and capping *amalaka*. Most of the detail of the outer walls is now lost.

Of greater interest is the **Ladkhan Temple**, which curiously retains the name of a Muslim inhabitant in former times. This early-8th-century monument is laid out as a spacious square *mandapa*, with a central bay topped by a small rooftop shrine surrounded on four sides by sloping roof slabs in two tiers. The joints of the roof slabs are protected by log-like stone strips that recall timber construction. The entrance to the *mandapa* is through a rectangular porch on the east, the outer columns of which have carvings of river goddesses, and of human couples embracing beneath trees, including one showing a horse-headed woman with male companion. The fluid postures of the figures communicate an unmistakable charm that represents a highpoint in Early Chalukya art. Inclined seating slabs placed in between the columns, embellished with auspicious pots and knot motifs, are probably inserts of the Rashtrakuta era. A full range of decorative motifs embellish the columns within the porch. An inclined stone ladder set up here once gave access to the rooftop shrine. This has worn carvings of Vishnu, Surya and Ardhanarishvara on the central projections, but lacks any tower.

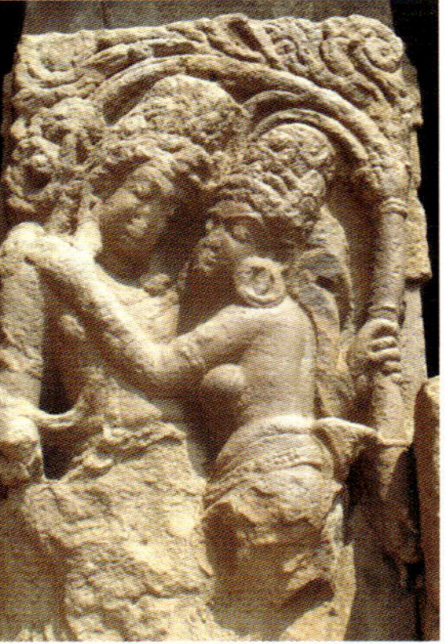

Couple beneath a tree; column detail from the Ladkhan temple

Large perforated screens with geometric designs admit light into the interior of the Ladkhan temple. Within, majestic columns with rolled brackets carry the sloping roof slabs on four sides. A large Nandi is placed in the middle of the *mandapa*, facing towards a small *linga* shrine built up to the rear wall. Quite possibly the Nandi and *linga* shrine did not form part of the original scheme, and that the *mandapa* was intended to function as some sort of meeting hall, with a sanctuary unusually positioned on the roof above.

A few metres away stands the **Gaudargudi**, located at a noticeably lower level, and presumably earlier date, than the Ladkhan temple. The Gaudargudi is conceived as an open rectangular structure, with a colonnaded verandah on four sides roofed with sloping slabs, also with log-like strips. Angled seating slabs decorated with pot motifs are placed between the outer columns. In the middle of the temple is a rectangular sanctuary entered from the east through a doorway embellished with delicately worked foliate ornament. Equally elegant designs decorate the beams over the *mandapa* in front. Trefoil niches above the lintel of the doorway accommodate Gajalakshmi and female attendants. A long inscription engraved on a lintel in front of the sanctuary indicates that the

Gaudargudi

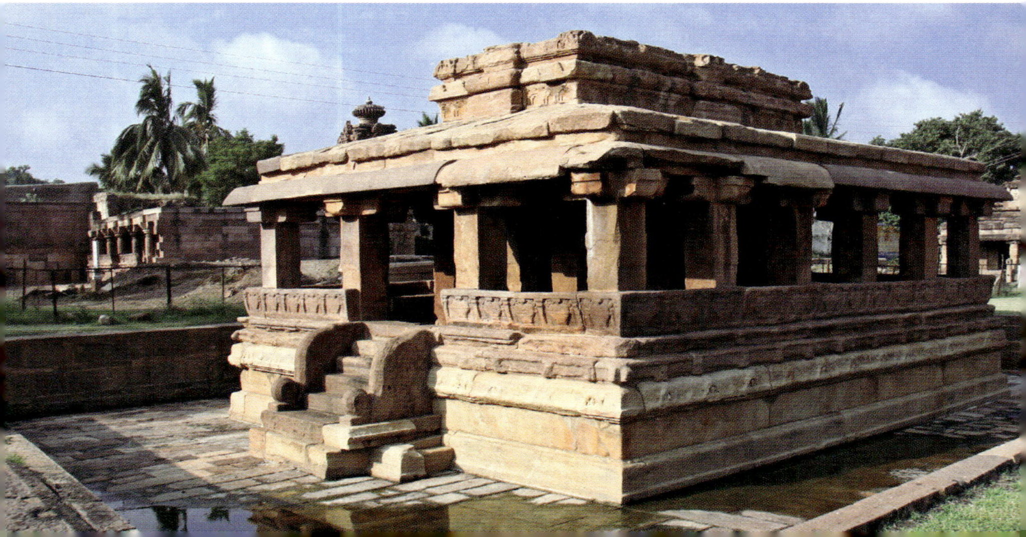

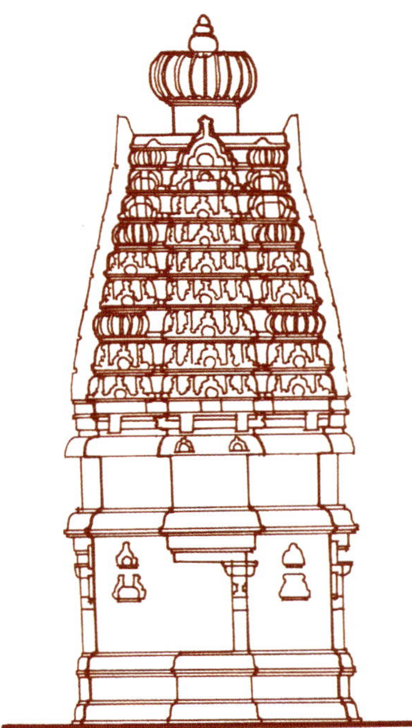

Towered shrine of the Chakragudi

temple was originally dedicated to the goddess Gauri. However, the sanctuary interior and the niches on the outer walls on three sides, topped by elaborate *gavaksha* pediments, are all empty.

A large tank with several ancient sculptures inserted into side walls separates the Gaudargudi from the **Chakragudi**, of interest for its fully preserved Nagara styled tower. Complete with all of its *gavaksha* elements in diminishing tiers, the tower is crowned with a prominent *amalaka* and vase finial. The adjoining *mandapa*, however, is a Rashtrakuta addition of about the 9th century, as can be seen from the style of the columns. Also attributed to the Rashtrakuta period is the **Badigargudi**, in the extreme south-west corner of the complex. Over the sanctuary of this temple rises a pyramidal tower of squat proportions, with ornate *kudus* in the middle of the diminishing eave-like tiers. On the front of the tower is a cubical projection with a finely sculpted Suryanarayana icon. The temple is otherwise plain except for the porch, the columns of which have circular designs incised onto their shafts. Worn pot motifs are seen on the inclined balcony slabs placed in between the columns.

NORTH OF THE TOWN

Among the temples outside the fortification walls on the northern side of Aihole are several interesting examples. The first to be seen, opposite the entrance to the Durga temple complex, is the **Ambigergudi Complex**. This comprises three separate structures aligned on an east-west axis. The easternmost is a square building open on the west, but walled on the other three sides. It lacks a tower and seems to have served as a subsidiary building to the temple in the middle, which is surrounded on three sides by an open verandah roofed by sloping slabs.

The sanctuary towards the rear of its interior accommodates a damaged icon of Suryanarayana, wearing a crown and fluted headdress. The treatment of the columns of the central aisle leading to the sanctuary is typically Early Chalukya in style. No tower is preserved above, but there are remnants of bricks inserted beneath the foundation slabs on the west, possibly from an earlier structure.

Immediately to the west, at a level about 2.5 metres above the two structures just described, stands a Late Chalukya temple of unknown dedication. This 11th-century structure has a *mandapa* entered from the north and south through doorways flanked by part-circular pilasters. The *mandapa* walls and those of the adjoining sanctuary are relieved by shallow, but these are cubical. The parapet above the sanctuary walls has sharply modelled Dravida elements, repeated in the single storey of the tower that rises above. There is no capping roof.

Of greater artistic interest is the **Chikkigudi,** located a few metres to the north of the Ambigergudi complex, on the other side of the road running north from Aihole. The comparatively modest scale and plain exterior of the Chikkigudi, with sloping roof slabs on four sides and a flat roof over the sanctuary and *mandapa*, give little hint of the sculptural exuberance of the interior. The *mandapa* columns are notable for the exquisitely carved jewelled garlands, monster masks, birds and other motifs; the capitals are enhanced by petal-like curved flutings. Similarly refined foliate decoration adorns the beams above. The two ceiling panels over the central bays have lotus medallions framed by finely carved pairs of divinities: Trivikrama, and Vishnu on Shesha; and Shiva spearing Andhaka, and dancing Shiva. Lobed niches over the sanctuary doorway accommodate icons of Shiva flanked by those of Vishnu and Brahma. The sanctuary is now empty.

Column detail from the Chikkigudi

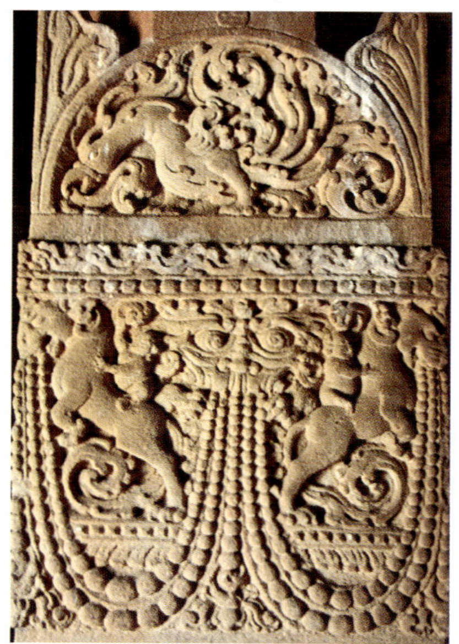

Opposite: Ceiling panels in the Chikkigudi

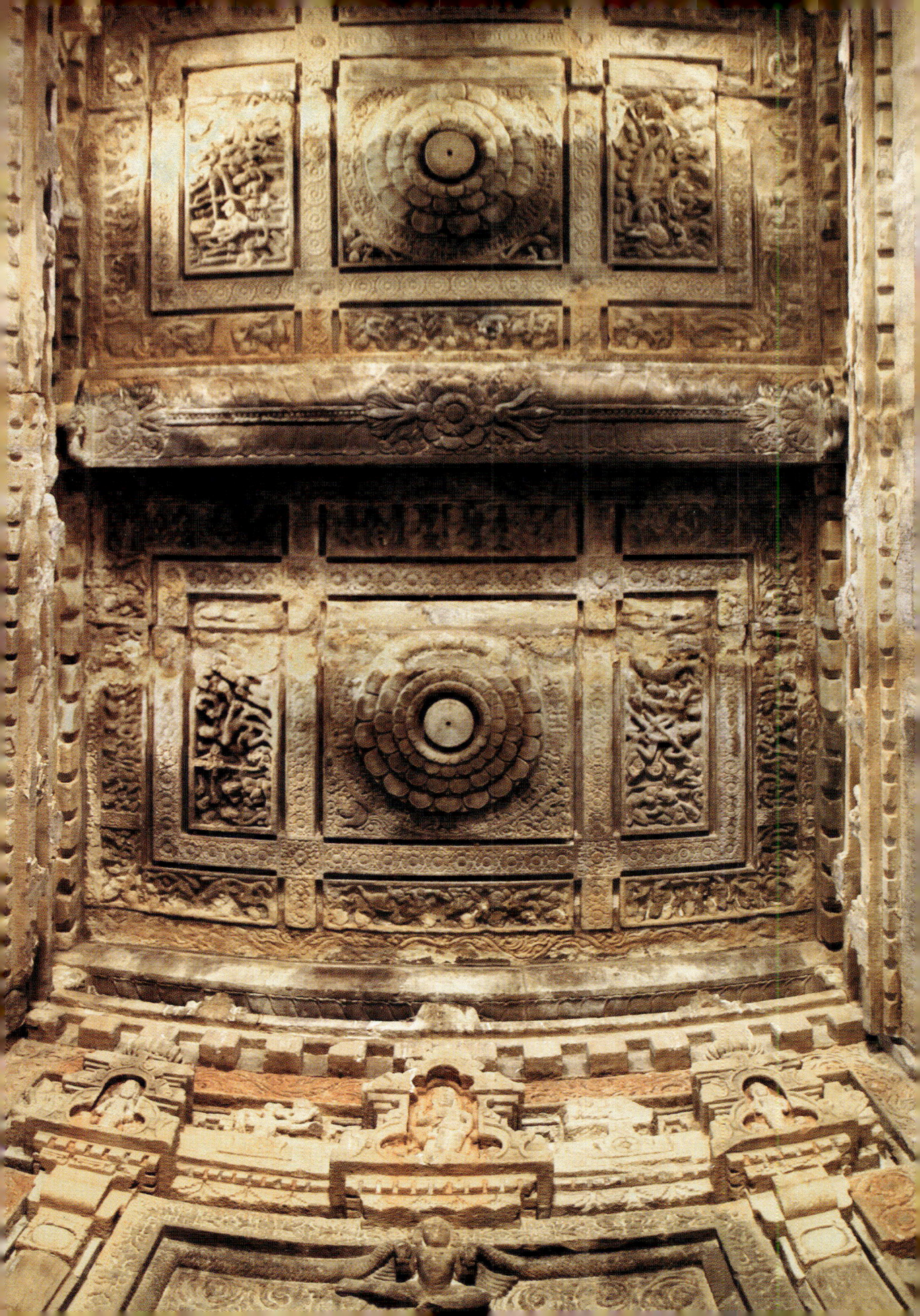

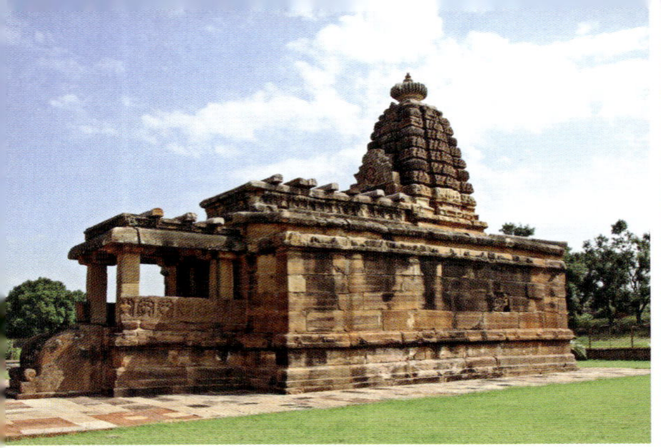

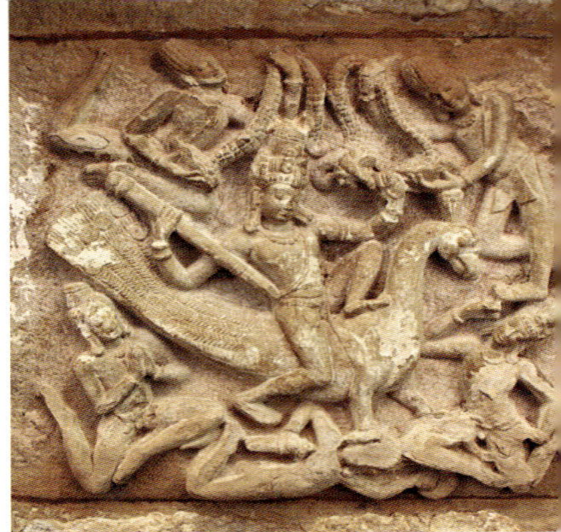

Left: Hucchimalligudi *Right:* Karttikeya on the peacock; ceiling panel from the Hucchimalligudi

Immediately north of the Chikkigudi, but within the same compound, are the remains of a small, apsidal-ended shrine, of which only the basement survives, as well as a *linga* set up on a circular pedestal. A reconstructed portal in front has finely decorated columns, brackets and lintel. A Nandi is placed on a small pedestal nearby.

From the Chikkigudi visitors must proceed along the road running north away from the town, and then take a lesser road to the right in order to reach the Hucchimalligudi. This temple faces west towards a stepped tank, the sides of which incorporate sculpted divinities, evidently removed from some other Early Chalukya monument. The **Hucchimalligudi** consists of a *mandapa* and sanctuary with passageway contained within a rectangle of walls, with sloping roof slabs on four sides. Its plain exterior, with small perforated windows, contrasts with the comparatively well preserved Nagara style tower that rises above the sanctuary. The temple is entered through a small porch, of interest for its ceiling, carved with a unique image of Karttikeya flying through the air on a peacock. A later inserted screen wall within the temple creates small square vestibule in front of the *linga* sanctuary. The ceiling over the central aisle shows divinities around a lotus (now worn).

A short walk from the Hucchimalligudi brings visitors to the **Ravanaphadi**, a cave-temple that belongs to the first phase of Early Chalukya architecture, towards the end of the 6th century. In front of the cave stands a worn fluted column with an *amalaka* capital fallen to one side, a Nandi image, and three small shrines, each with a porch leading to a chamber, one topped with rudimentary *kuta*-type roof.

The entrance to the Ravanaphadi is flanked by worn, relief images of pot-bellied *nidhis* seated within Dravida-styled pavilions, and guardians wearing skirt-like costumes, bearing spears. The latter figures are sometimes identified as foreigners, possibly Scythian mercenaries, at the Early Chalukya court. The entrance to the cave leads to a rock-cut *mandapa* with chambers on three sides,

Ravanaphadi: major sculpture panels

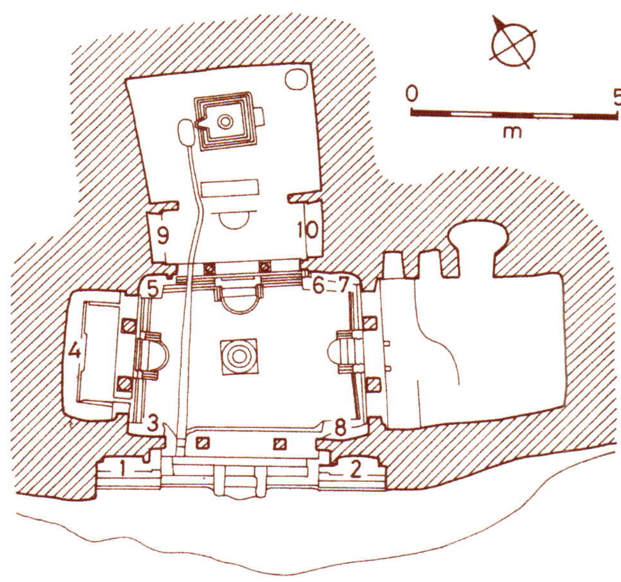

1. *Nidhi* and guardian
2. *Nidhi* and guardian
3. Ardhanarishvara
4. Dancing Shiva with Parvati and the Saptamatrikas, Ganesha and Kartikeya
5. Shaiva guardian
6. Shaiva guardian
7. Harihara
8. Shiva with three river goddesses, together with Parvati and Bhringi
9. Varaha
10. Durga spearing Mahisha

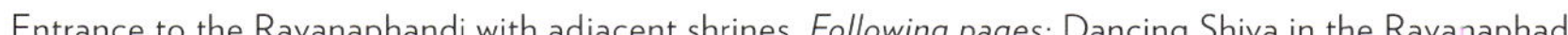

Entrance to the Ravanaphandi with adjacent shrines *Following pages:* Dancing Shiva in the Ravanaphadi

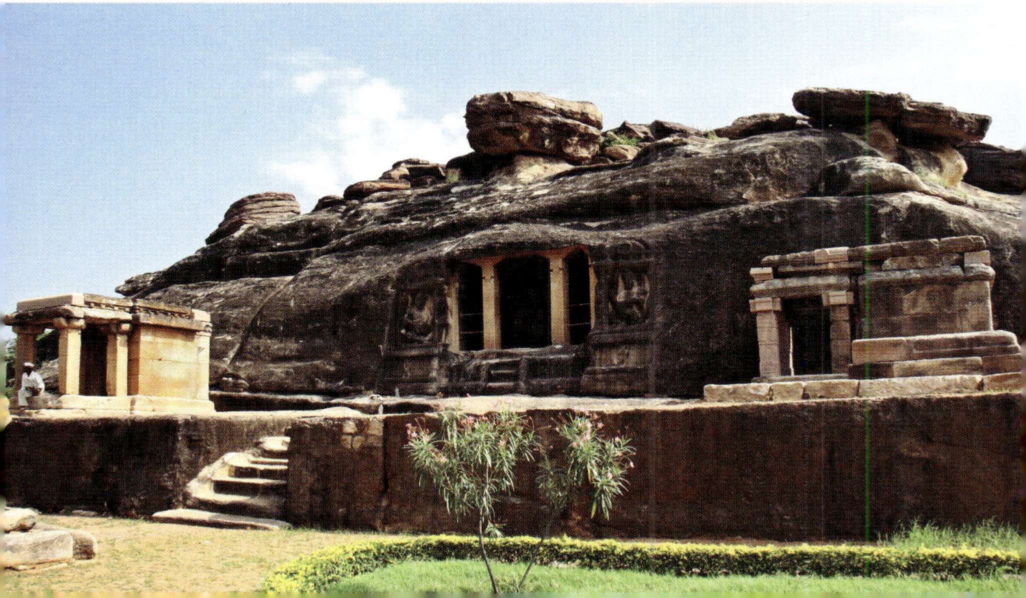

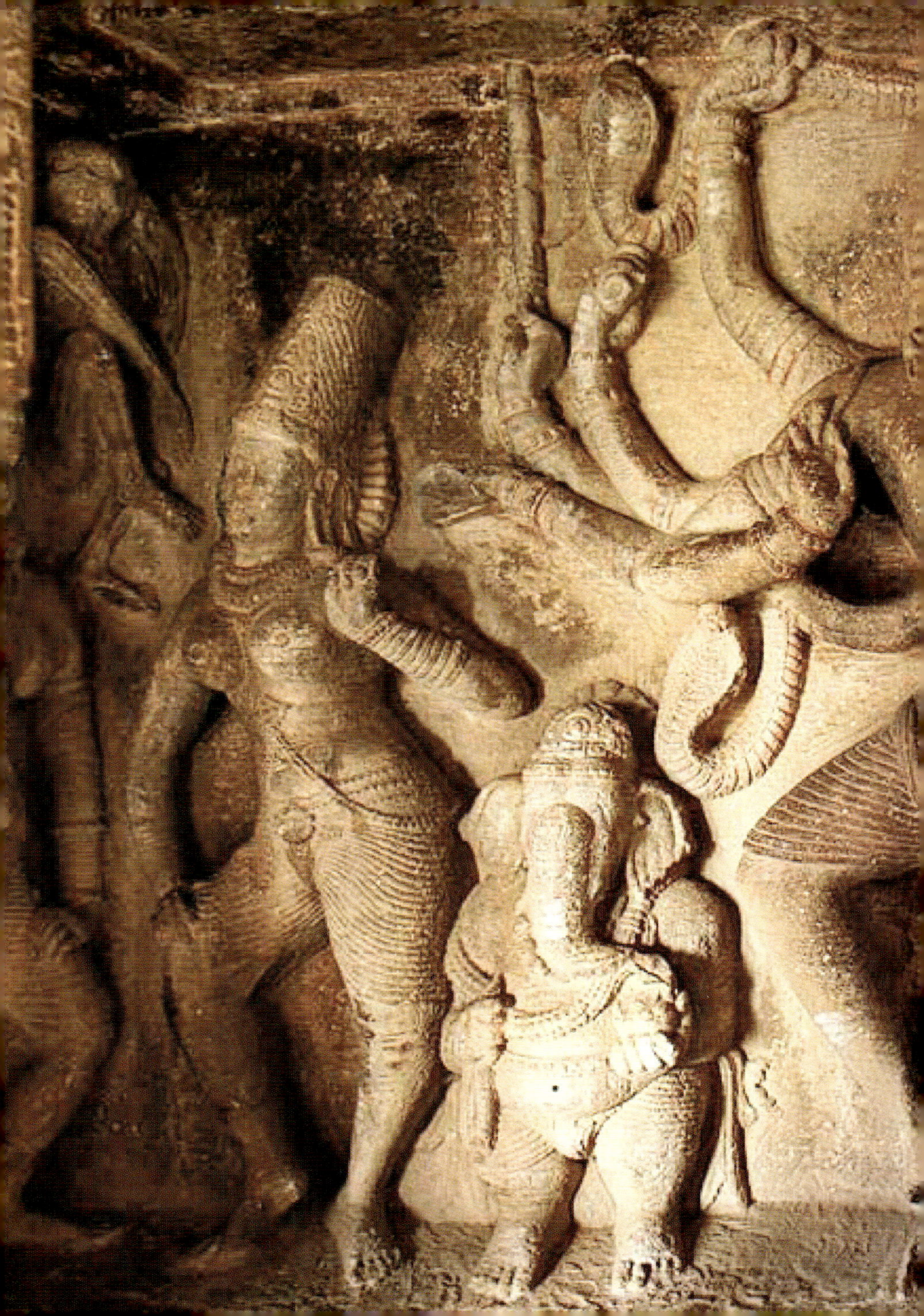

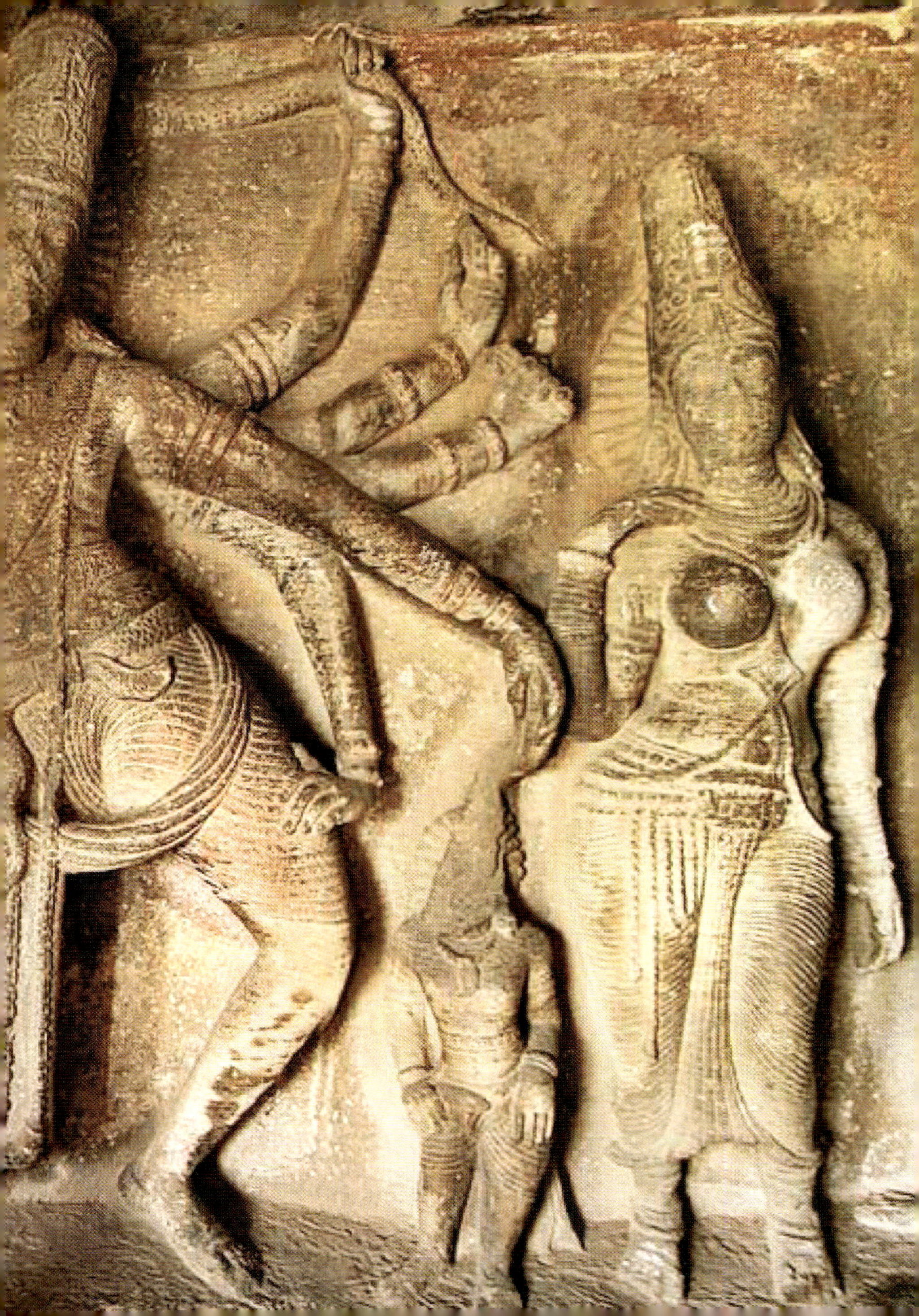

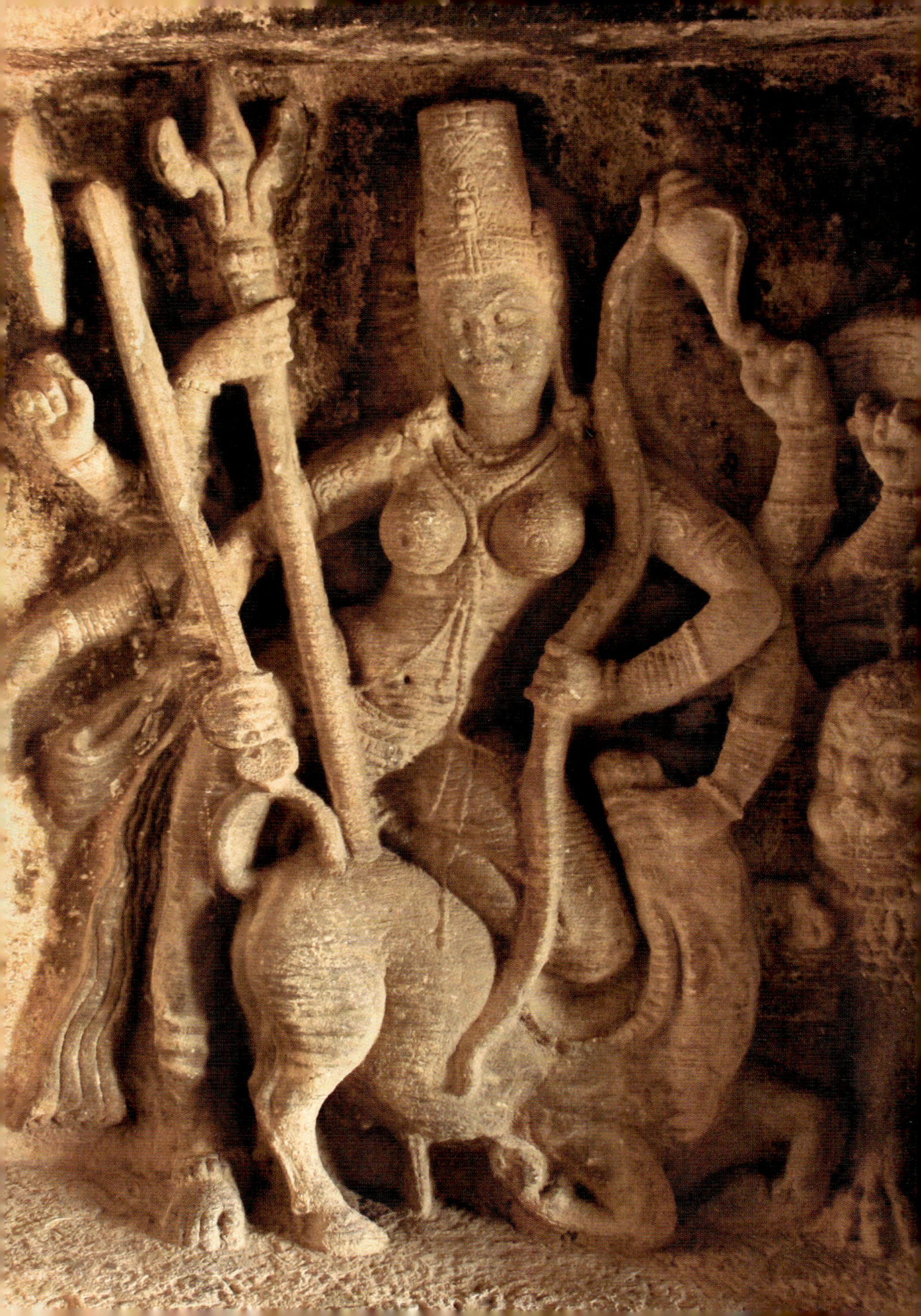

Opposite: Durga spearing Mahisha in the Ravanaphadi

each with a triple-bayed opening defined by a pair of monolithic columns. Figures are carved in relief on the wall surfaces in between. From the left of the entrance these depict (in clockwise sequence): Ardhanarishvara clutching a trident; two-armed Shaiva guardians holding weapons (at either side of the triple-bayed opening leading to the *linga* chamber); and Harihara displaying snake and conch in two of his four hands; Shiva with triple river goddesses above his head, accompanied by Parvati and Bhringi, the latter standing on one leg (to the right of the entrance). The *mandapa* ceiling is treated like a textile canopy, with a central lotus medallion in shallow relief surrounded by bands of ornament incorporating human torsos, *makaras* and fish.

The left side-chamber of the Ravanaphadi accommodates an elaborate tableau dominated by ten-armed Shiva, energetically pacing out the rhythm of the cosmic dance. The head of the god is angled sharply to the torso, while in his rear hands he holds up a sinuous cobra. Shiva is accompanied by Parvati and a complete set of the Saptamatrikas, including boar-headed Varahi and triple-headed Brahmi, as well as Ganesha and Karttikeya. All these figures, as well as those on the *mandapa* walls just noticed, are remarkable for their slender proportions, pleated costumes, intricately worked jewellery, and conical crowns with circular, fluted head-pieces behind. Traces of colour indicate that these figures were once painted.

The triple-bayed opening within the *mandapa* of the Ravanaphadi, directly opposite the entrance, leads to a small vestibule, the side walls of which have deeply carved images of Varaha rescuing Bhudevi (left), and Durga spearing Mahisha (right). Two ceiling panels here show flying Shiva and Parvati on Nandi (in front of Varaha), and Vishnu and Lakshmi on Garuda (in front of Durga). A pedestal with a monolithic *linga* can be seen within the sanctuary, but the doorway jambs, carved from separate stone blocks, lie fallen nearby. That the cave was never fully completed is evident from the bare, scooped notches in the right side-chamber.

IN THE TOWN

By continuing for a short distance along the road that runs past the Ravanaphadi cave-temple visitors will soon return to the main road that skirts Aihole's fortifications. Opposite, on the other side of this road, is a gateway in the fortifications that leads directly into the town.

A group of temples is seen immediately on passing through the entryway. The 12th-century example on the right, known as the **Gauri Temple**, is the

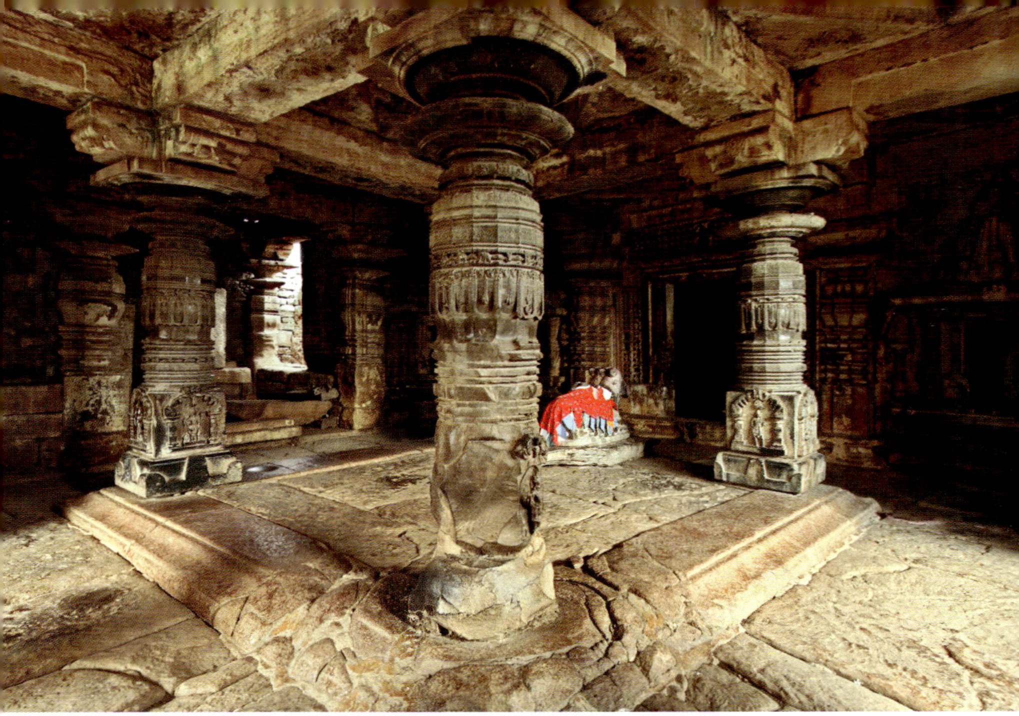

Interior of the Gauri temple

largest and most elaborate Late Chalukya monument in Aihole. Though partly obscured by houses that crowd up to its outer walls, the temple incorporates a spacious *mandapa* with porch projections on three sides, each with balcony seating, though now partly filled in. The four columns in the middle of the *mandapa* are ornate compositions with 16-sided shafts adorned with hanging jewelled garlands, topped by sharply modelled double capitals. The ceiling above has a design of rotated squares crowned with a dome-like roof. Set into the *mandapa* walls between the balconies are deep niches topped by Nagara-styled towers in shallow relief. A screen-wall divides the *mandapa* from a vestibule where is placed a finely carved icon of Durga bearing different weapons in her eight arms. Guardians holding disc and conch flanking the sanctuary doorway indicate that the temple was once consecrated to Vishnu. Yet, a *linga* is now installed here, towards which a Nandi placed in the middle of the *mandapa* faces. Pilastered niches on the sanctuary's external walls, now empty, are topped by Dravida-styled pediments. No tower is preserved above.

A few metres south of the Gauri temple is an 11th-century Jain Complex consisting of two temples linked by an open porch with balcony seating, approached by steps from the north and south. The western temple of the complex has a trio of sanctuaries facing into a common *mandapa*. Installed in

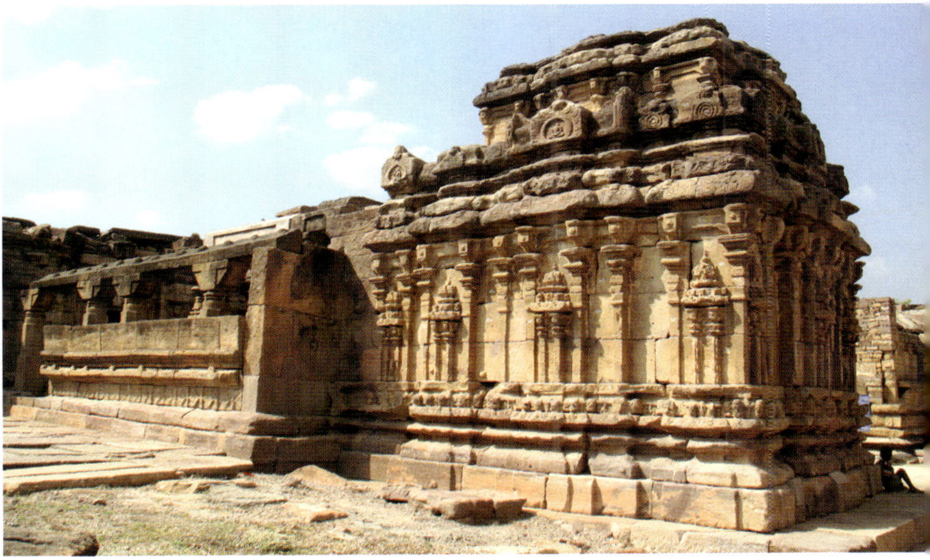

Jain Complex near the Gauri temple

the principal (western) sanctuary is an imposing, polished basalt image of Parshvanatha seated on a lion throne. The outer walls of this sanctuary are treated in characteristic Late Chalukya fashion with slender pilasters, in contrast to the walls of the other two sanctuaries which are quite plain. Only the southern sanctuary preserves a portion of its Dravida styled tower. The single sanctuary of the eastern temple of the complex also housed a seated Jina icon, but this has now been removed to the Archaeological Museum. However, the superbly fashioned throne on which this icon was placed is still in its original position. This shows a throne with a naturalistic bolster mounted on a seat carried by lions and framed by leaping *yalis*, with a back-rest terminating in *makara* heads. *Chauri*-bearing attendants in symmetrical, swaying postures flank a triple-tiered parasol above.

Seated Parshvanatha in the Jain complex

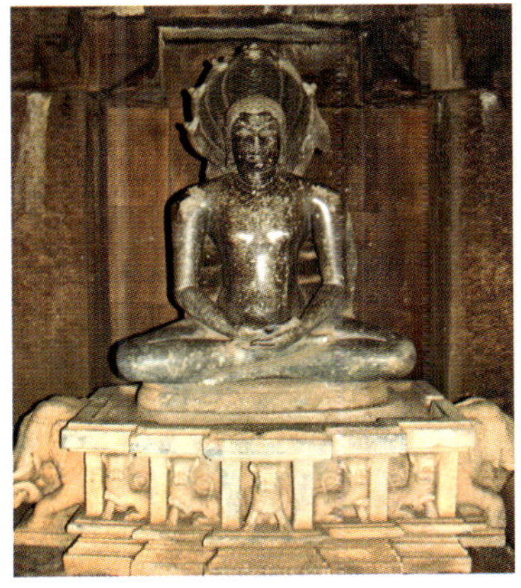

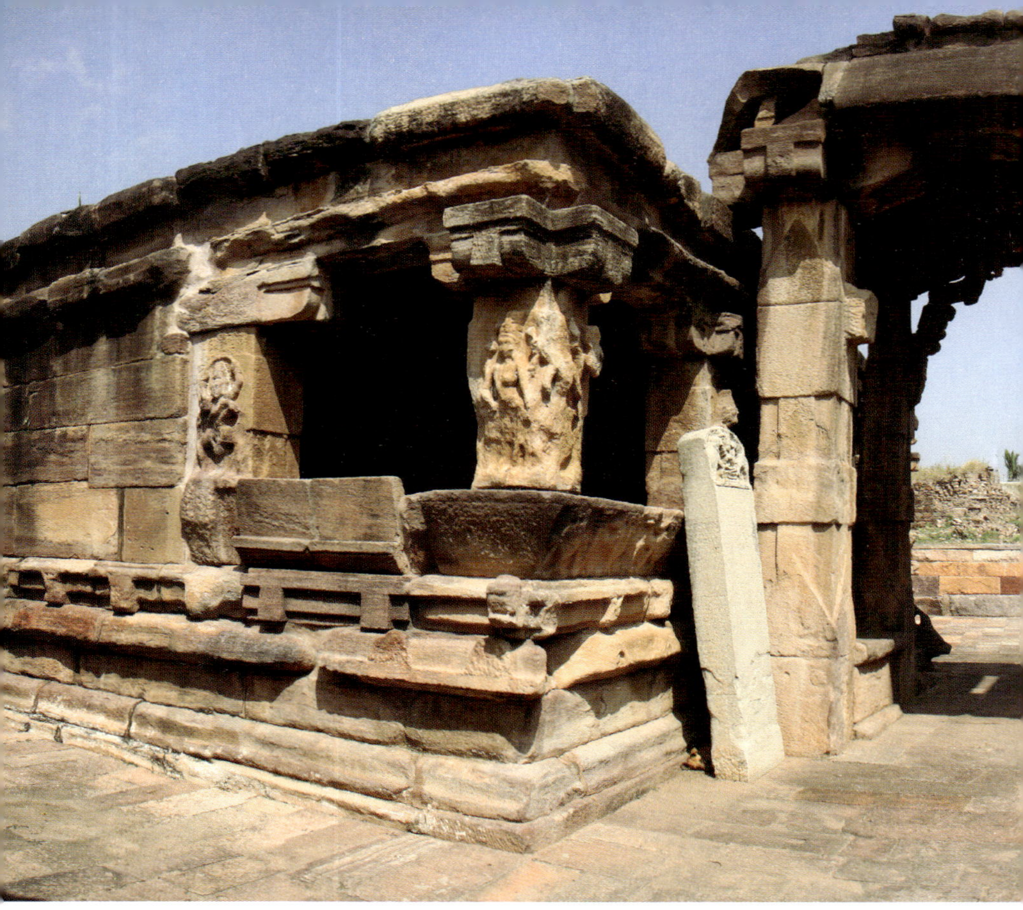

Kunti group

An additional cluster of Jain Temples is encountered further to the south, arrayed on either side of the main road that winds its way through Aihole. One example known as Charantimatha, dating from the early 12th century, has twin sanctuaries arranged unusually one beside the other. The sanctuaries are preceded by a six-bayed verandah with columns exhibiting sharply-cut flattish ornament typical of Late Chalukya architecture. The underside of the eave that shelters these columns has timber-like ribs, deeply cut scrollwork and miniature figures. Set into the rear wall of the verandah is a pair of matching doorways with cut-out *yalis* beside part-circular pilasters; rows of tiny Jina figures are carved above the lintels. The doorways give access to identical *mandapas* and sanctuaries, neither with any tower. Beside the road a short distance from this monument is a Wada, or fortified mansion, being the residence of a family which acted as tax collectors for the British. Part of the timber colonnade

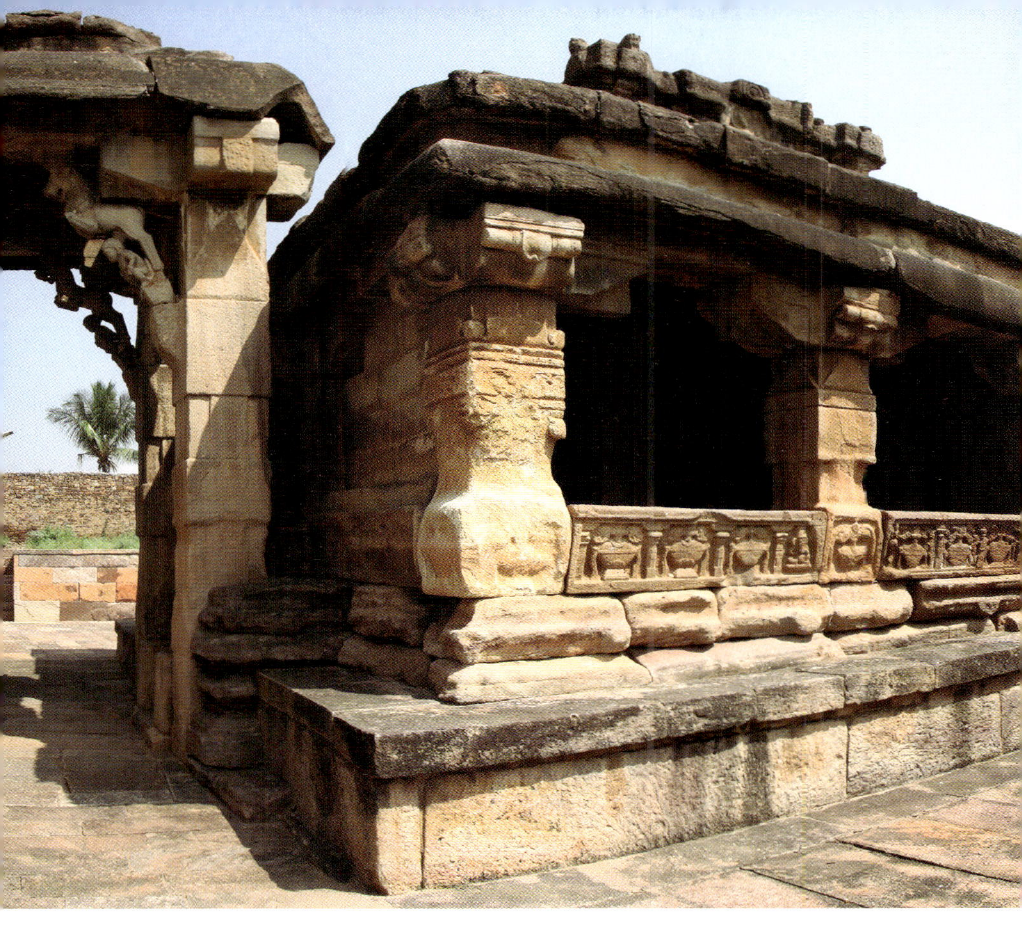

facing into an internal court can still be seen, together with a corner lookout tower constructed of massive stone blocks.

By following along the main east-west bazaar street that runs through the middle of Aihole visitors will eventually reach a quartet of shrines still partly embedded in local houses, known collectively as the Kunti Group. The north-west shrine, assigned to the 8th-century Early Chalukya era, has an east-facing colonnade with worn figures, including amorous couples, carved onto its entrance porch. The rectangular *mandapa* within has raised ceiling slabs with a trio of divinities: from right to left, Vishnu asleep on Shesha; Shiva with Parvati; and Brahma seated on the lotus. A small empty sanctuary, its doorway flanked by four-armed guardians, is placed against the rear wall. This temple is linked to the one opposite by a free-standing porch with four lofty columns with angled, cut-out brackets fashioned as *yalis* with male attendants.

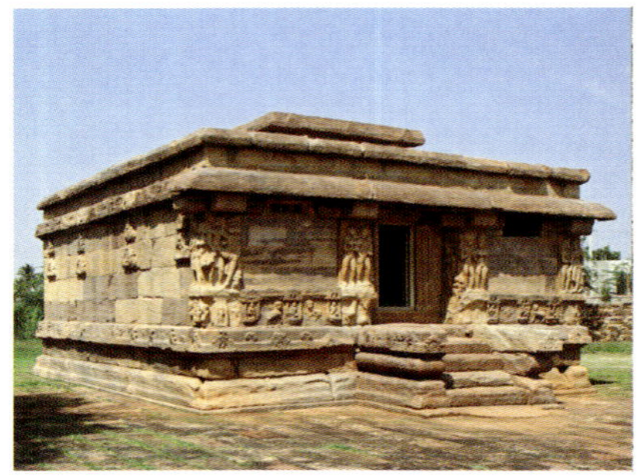

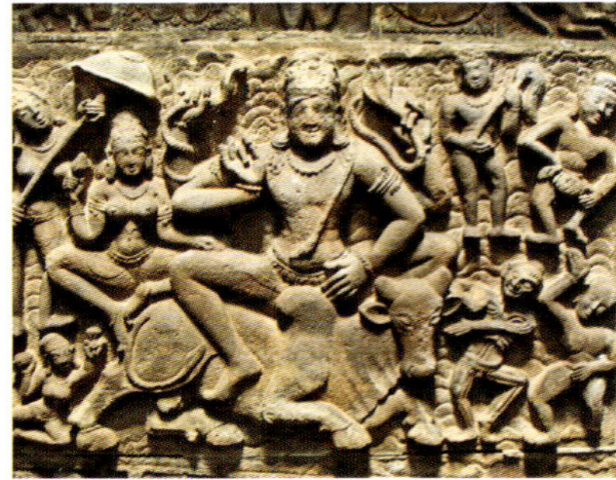

Left: Hucchappayyamatha *Right:* Shiva on Nandi; ceiling panel in the Hucchappayyamatha

The north-east shrine is laid out as a square. Its four central supports have evolved foliate decoration on the shafts, and exaggerated circular and square capitals, typical features of the 9th-century Rashtrakuta style. The central ceiling panel shows Brahma together with a complete set of the Dikpalas.

The rectangular, south-east shrine of the Kunti Group is another Early Chalukya structure, also with human couples carved onto its outer four columns. The interior, partly blocked up, has a small sanctuary at the rear with an ornate doorway. The south-west shrine, also rectangular, is a Rashtrakuta period structure. It outer columns have fluted shafts, while part-circular colonettes flank the doorway of the sanctuary set against its rear wall.

Standing in a walled compound a short distance south of the Kunti Group is a temple known as the **Hucchappayamatha**. The four columns of its frontal east facade, which originally framed an open porch (later filled in), are graced with human couples, including one showing a horse-headed woman in the company of a man with a fierce expression. The *mandapa* interior has three fine ceiling panels: from the entrance, they depict Vishnu on Shesha in the company of flying celestials; Shiva and Parvati on Nandi; and Brahma on the goose. Delicate lotus ornament embellishes the beams and the surrounds of the ceiling compositions just described. A Nandi placed in the middle of the *mandapa* faces towards the *linga* installed in the sanctuary that projects beyond the *mandapa* walls.

Rachigudi

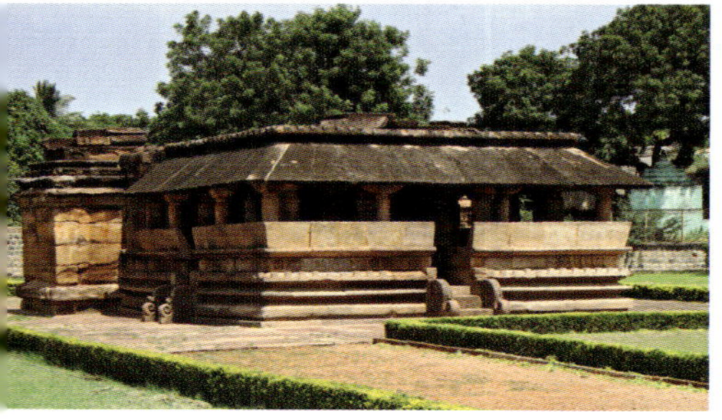

SOUTH OF THE TOWN

The road running southwards from the entrance to the Durga temple complex passes by **Rachigudi**, a temple that bridges the Rashtrakuta and Late Chalukya periods. Dating

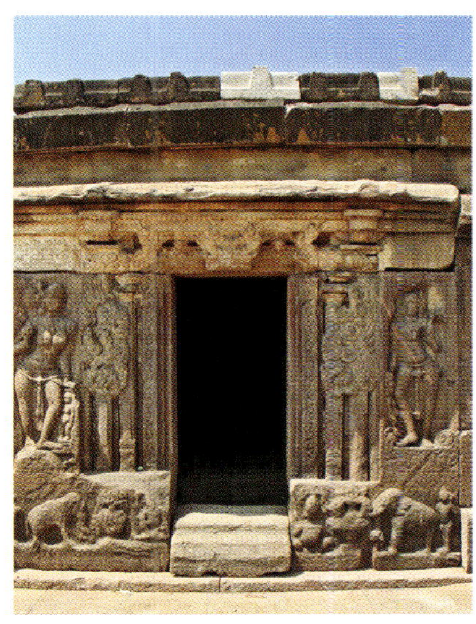

Doorway of the Aralibasappa temple

from the 10th century is a trio of *linga* sanctuaries, one with pilastered walls and the lower portions of a Dravida styled tower, facing into a common *mandapa*. A spacious porch with balcony seating on three sides sheltered by steeply angled roof slabs was added to this scheme in the 11th century. Interior columns have massive, bell-shaped shafts and prominent double capitals. A short distance further on is the **Veniyavur Complex**. The largest temple of this group, dating from the early 11th century, is recognised by its pilastered walls, with secondary pilasters carrying miniature Dravida pediments. Only a single tier of its tower is preserved. In one corner of the complex is a deep tank approached by steps. At the top of the steps stands a portal with octagonal columns and an ornate lintel embellished with *makaras*. Triple divinities framed by garlands are carved in between.

A path running through the Veniyavur complex exits the town through a nearby break in the fortifications. Immediately after leaving the town a small whitewashed **Hanuman Shrine** is seen on the right. This is entered through a porch with reused columns. A Vijayanagara period icon of the popular monkey hero is worshipped within. A few metres further on stands the **Aralibasappa Temple**. This 9th-century, Rashtrakuta period structure is of interest for its ornate doorway flanked by *makaras* with extravagant, ornate tails carried on shallow pilasters, and enlarged river goddesses standing on the tortoise (left) and *makara* (right, somewhat worn). The four central columns within the *mandapa* carry an independent eave, as if this was once belonged to a free-sanding feature. A *linga* is preserved in the sanctuary that protrudes from the rear walls, but there is no tower.

Continuing southwards, a small stream is soon reached. Visitors are encouraged to ford the water and follow a path that winds pleasantly through the fields in order to reach the **Hucchappayyagudi** (not to be confused with the Hucchappayyamatha, described above). This Early Chalukya temple is of interest for its fine carvings, best seen in the naked, horse-headed women embracing bearded males carved onto the porch columns beside the east

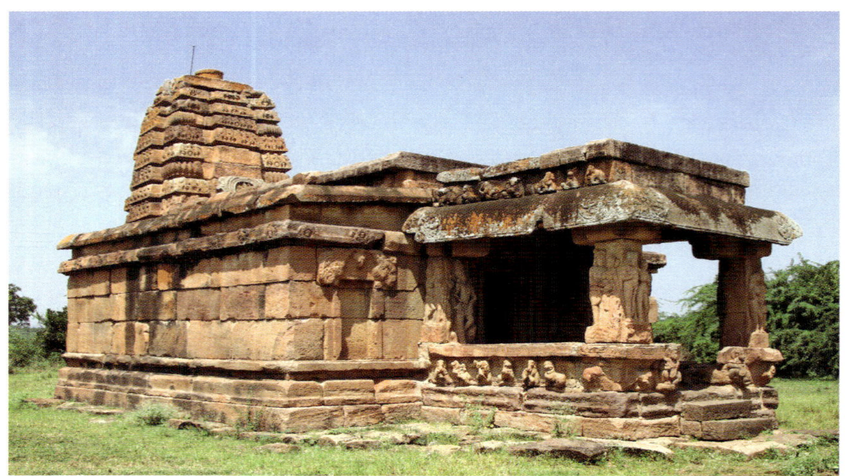

Hucchappayyagudi

doorway. The outer sanctuary walls have icons of Narasimha (west), and Shiva dancing in the skin of the elephant demon he has just slain (north). The tower above is of the Nagara type, with clearly delineated *gavakshas*, but now missing its *amalaka* finial. The three splendid ceiling panels that once graced the *mandapa* interior were removed in the 1920s to the museum in Mumbai. (They depict Brahma together with *rishis*; Vishnu asleep on Shesha; and Shiva and Parvati on Nandi.) Miniature icons of Narasimha, Agni and Yama, however, can still be seen on the beams that once supported these panels.

The track continues southwards through the fields until it passes by the **Galaganatha Complex,** overlooking a modern dam across the Malprabha. The principal temple, after which the group takes its name, however, is an unadorned Early Chalukya structure with a stepped pyramidal tower. The *mandapa* interior preserves a ceiling panel of Brahma (damaged); another portraying Vishnu is now placed against the tower. (The third panel, showing Shiva, is now also in Mumbai.) Another temple of interest in this group, assigned to the 9th century, is recognised by its almost complete Dravida styled tower. Its small porch has angled balcony seating adorned with auspicious pot motifs. Diminutive carvings on the sanctuary walls portray Durga and Harihara. Typically Rashtrakuta in style are the *makaras* with long foliated tails carved onto the central pairs of wall pilasters. Assigned to the Late Chalukya period is a free-standing portal with finely worked columns and a lintel embellished with looped garlands.

The last monuments to be described in this tour of Aihole are those of the **Ramalingeshvara Complex,** facing west towards the Tungabhadra, more than 1 kilometre south of the town. That these enjoy an active religious life is indicated by the modern wooden chariot with stone wheels parked next to the portal that serves as the entrance to the complex. The portal has sculptures of dancing Shiva and two lions on top of the lintel. The main temple of the complex comprises three shrines, two with pyramidal towers topped by *kuta*-roofs, opening off a common *mandapa*. An arched gate of later construction gives access to a path that leads down to the river.

From the Ramalingeshvara it is possible to return by car to the main road that runs south of Aihole.

SIDDANAKOLLA

The route to Guddur, 2 kilometres south of Aihole, leads by way of a side road to Siddanakolla, a sacred spot picturesquely situated at the top of a wooded ravine on the edge of the Malprabha valley. The first building to be seen here is a modern rest-house, with a festival chariot parked in front. Steps from here descend to a rocky ledge with a waterfall. Partly hidden in the trees is the whitewashed Sangameshvara Temple dating back to Early Chalukya times. The temple is topped by a Nagara-styled tower but preserves little original detail. A shrine tucked into the adjacent cliff accommodates a brightly painted set of the Saptamatrikas. Its doorway is flanked by ram- and goat-headed attendants holding staffs.

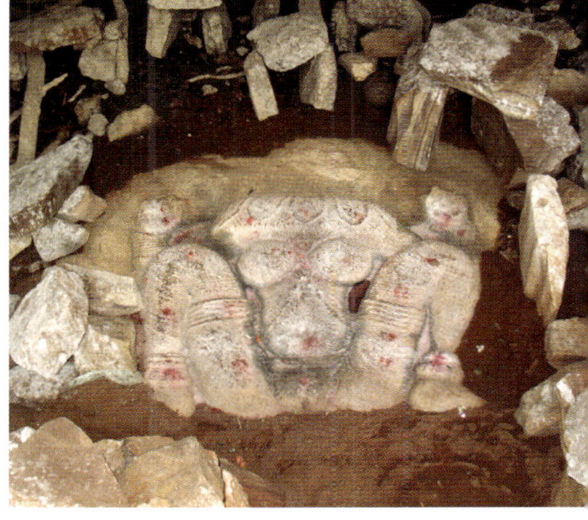

Lajja Gauri, rock carving at Siddanakolla

Beneath a rocky overhang nearby is an image of Lajja Gauri. This is carved onto a boulder, over which water flows during the rainy season; a modern *linga* is placed nearby. The Siddheshvara temple perched on the rocky shelf above is a Late Chalukya structure with a whitewashed upper chamber. Loose sculptures are disposed around the entrance to a lower chamber directly beneath.

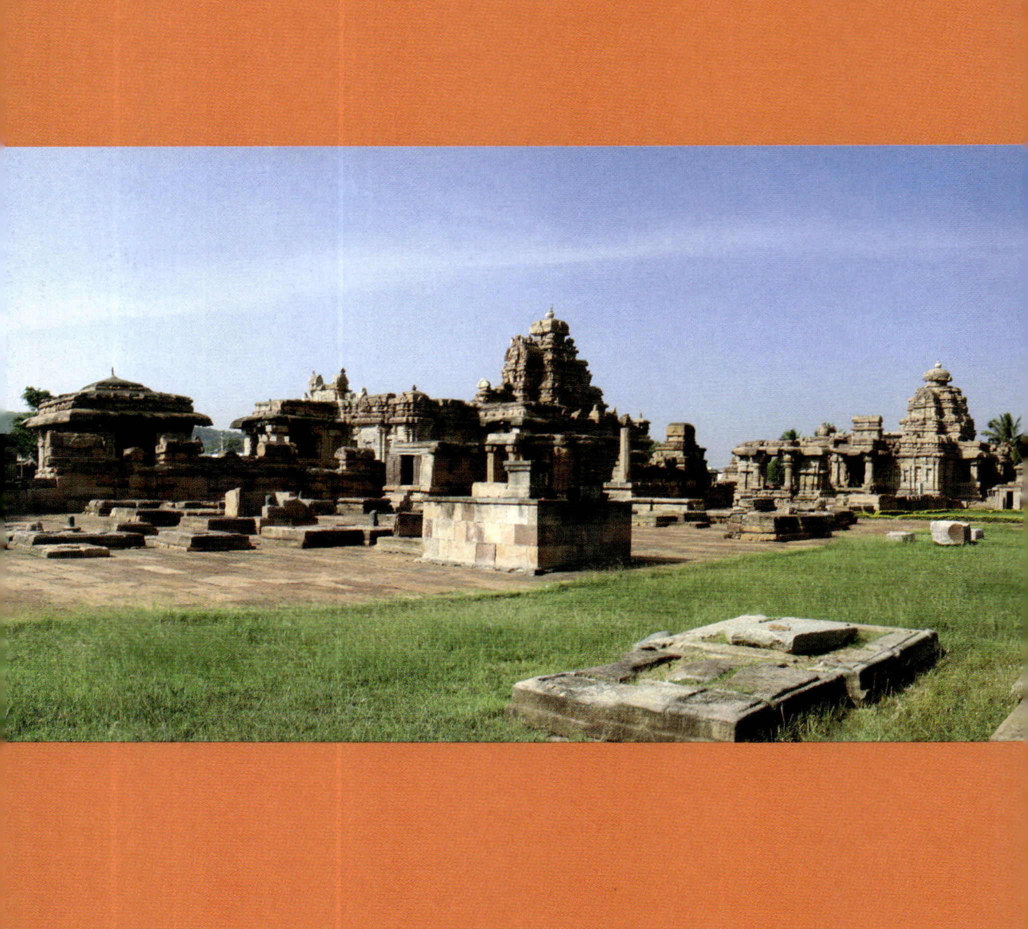

PATTADAKAL

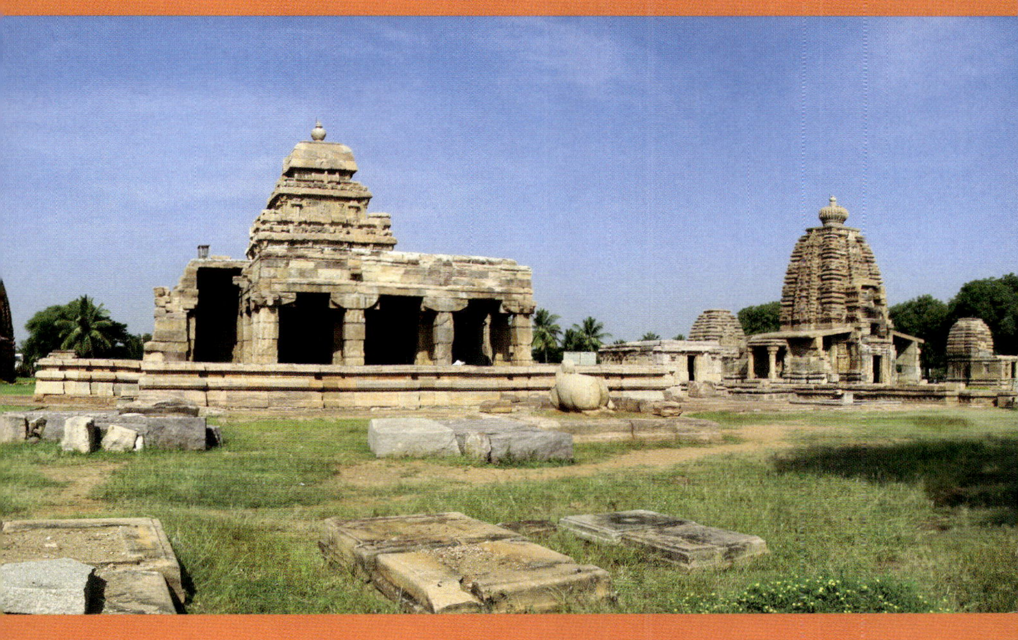

Preceding Pages & Opposite: **Main group of temples**

The temples at Pattadakal on the left bank of the Malprabha, 22 kilometres from Badami, now enjoy international prestige. Not only do these monuments represent the greatest achievement of the Early Chalukya builders and sculptors in the first half of the 8th century, they signal a climactic moment in the overall development of Hindu architecture and art in the Deccan. In their day, the Pattadakal temples must have represented the grandest, most stylistically evolved illustrations of the Dravida style in all of Southern India. As for the sculpted panels and decorative designs on the walls, columns and ceilings, these far exceed in number and variety those on any earlier temples.

The inscription on a column set up in the middle of the site by Kirttivarman II, the last of the Early Chalukya rulers, indicates that the three largest temples at Pattadakal were conceived as commemorative monuments, suggesting that the site may have served as a coronation place for the Early Chalukyas. This would explain why Pattadakal was virtually abandoned after the downfall of the dynasty, even though there was some attempt to rehabilitate the temples there during the 9th-10th centuries.

The tour of Pattadakal described here begins with the main group (ticket required). This complex has now been cleared of the village houses that once encroached onto the temples, with the monuments standing in the middle of landscaped lawns. The group is dominated by three major temples, the Sangameshvara, Virupaksha and Mallikarjuna; however, regular worship is conducted only in the Virupaksha. These three edifices are built in the Dravida manner, in striking contrast to the Nagara styled Kadasiddheshvara, Jambulinga, Galaganatha and Kashivishvanatha temples with which they are juxtaposed. A path beside the river leads to the Papanatha, of interest for its hybrid idiom combining Dravida and Nagara features. It is worth noting that the names by which the temples are known today are not original.

Before reaching Pattadakal, when travelling from Badami, visitors may wish to stop along the road to inspect a number of other features, including a dolmen dating back to prehistoric times, and a Jain temple of the Rashtrakuta period. On the flank of nearby Bachinagudda, the hill that rises to the west of Pattadakal, is another Rashtrakuta shrine. For those with more time and greater interest a visit is recommended to the rocky overhang of Hulligemmanakolla at the edge of the Malprabha valley. A small temple of recent date stands beside the road at Mangalagudda, a short distance beyond Pattadakal.

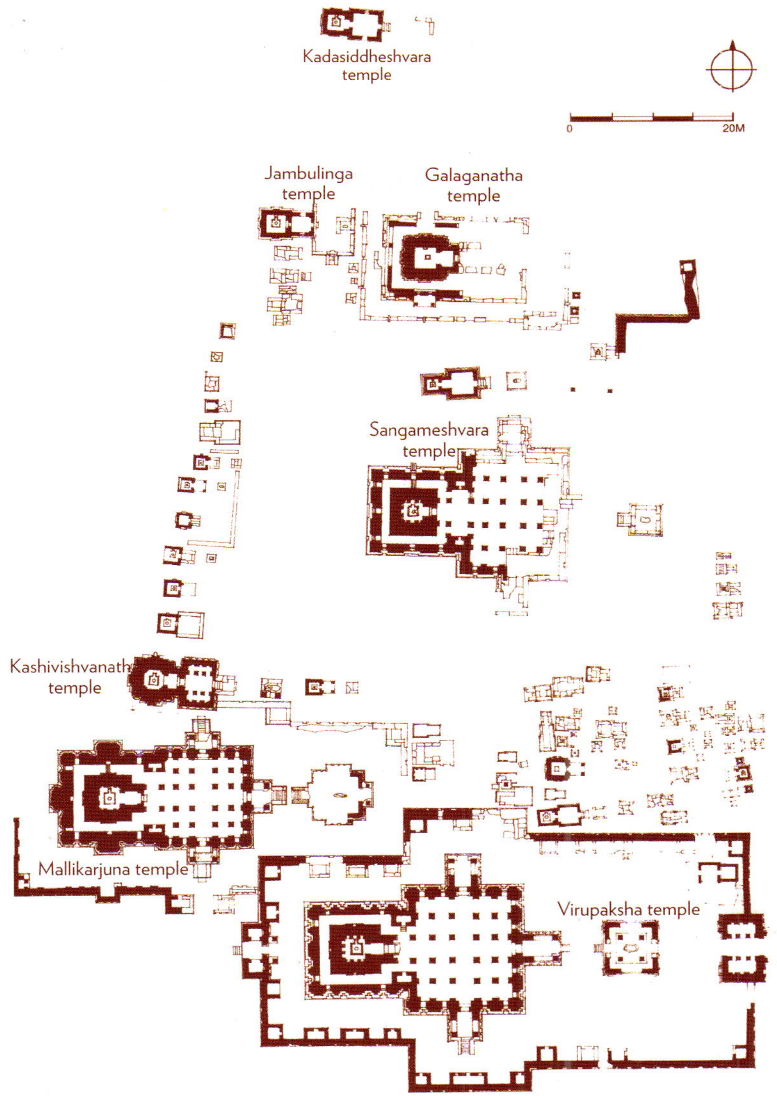
Kadasiddheshvara temple
0
20M
Jambulinga temple
Galaganatha temple
Sangameshvara temple
Kashivishvanath temple
Mallikarjuna temple
Virupaksha temple

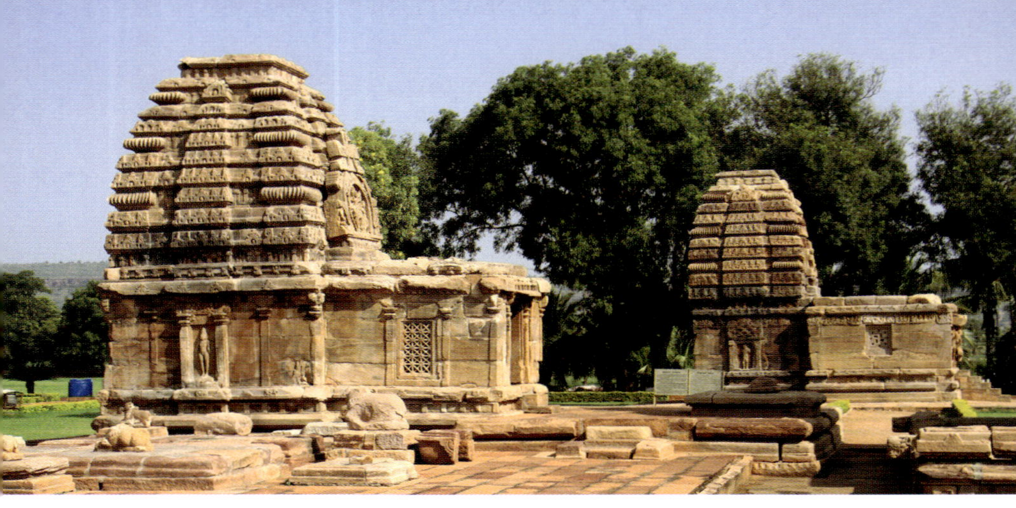

Kadasiddheshvara and Jambulinga temples

MAIN GROUP OF TEMPLES

Eight temples consecrated to Shiva, all facing east towards the river, constitute the main group at Pattadakal. Surrounded by numerous minor shrines, of which only the plinths survive, these monuments are not coordinated in any obvious way, except for the Virupaksha and Mallikarjuna temples, which occupy interlocking walled compounds. The temples are described in a north-to-south sequence, beginning with those nearest to the entrance gate (ticket required).

The **Kadasiddheshvara Temple** is assigned to the first decades of the 8th century. Its small sanctuary is approached through a vestibule lit by side windows with swastika motifs (one window is a replacement). The doorway on the east is flanked by guardian figures, now damaged. Pilastered projections on the sanctuary walls accommodate icons of Lakulisha, recognised by his locks of hair (south), Harihara (west, defaced), and Ardhanarishvara leaning on Nandi (north). Each of these is headed by a pediment composed of interlocking *gavaksha* motifs. The walls are terminated by a frieze of looped garlands containing dwarfs and flying figures. A standard Nagara type tower rises above, devoid of its *amalaka* finial, but with a frontal arched projection containing an icon of dancing Shiva (damaged).

Tower detail of Jambulinga temple

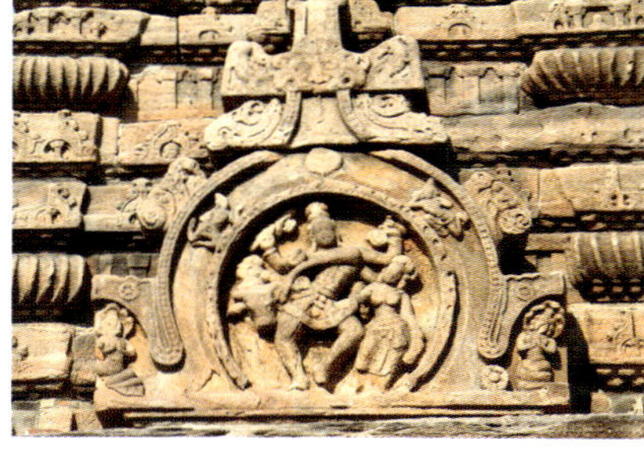

A few metres to the south stands the **Jambulinga Temple**, of similar size, date and style to the Kadasiddheshvara just noticed. Minor differences are seen in the frieze of *ganas* and birds on the basement, and the pilasters that mark the corners of the sanctuary and vestibule walls. Sculptures on the sanctuary represent Lakulisha (south), Surya (west, damaged), and Vishnu (north). These icons are framed by pilasters on which sit *makaras* with foliate tails, ridden by miniature figures. The tower is identical to that of the Kadasiddheshvara, though its profile is slightly more curved and the image of dancing Shiva in the frontal arch better preserved. A raised platform defined by a plinth extending to the east supports a Nandi sculpture. From here an irregular line of minor shrines extends southwards.

The ruined, possibly never finished **Galaganatha Temple** stands to the east of the Jambulinga. A date towards the end of the 7th century seems appropriate, since the Galaganatha is an almost exact copy of the Svarga Brahma temple dated 689 at the Early Chalukya site of Alampur in Andhra Pradesh. Raised on a broad terrace, the Galaganatha consists of a sanctuary and antechamber surrounded on three sides by a passageway with projecting porches on three sides. Only the southern porch survives complete, inside

Galaganatha temple

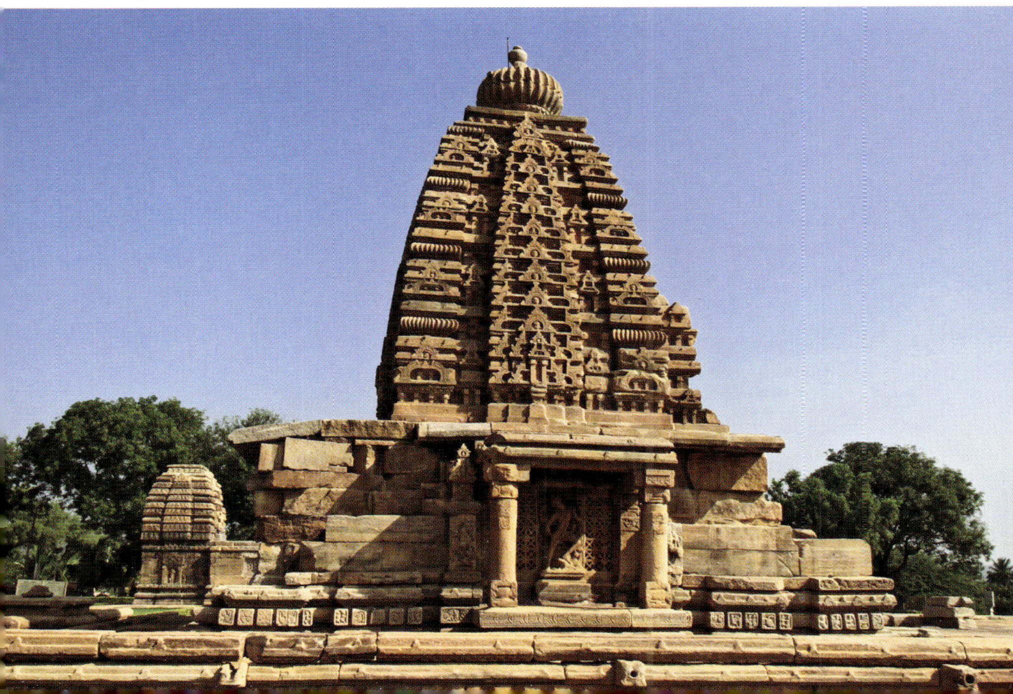

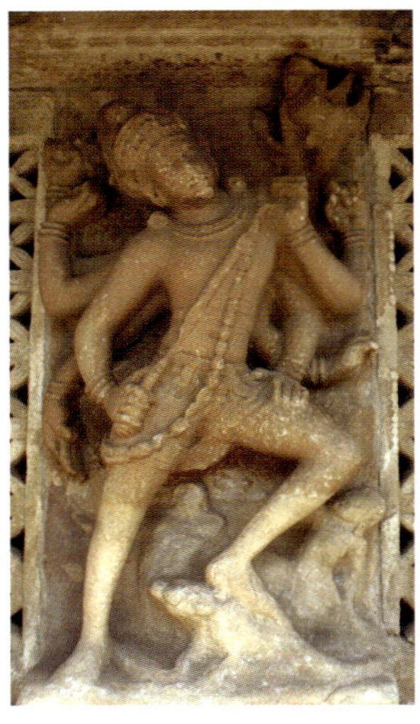

Shiva spearing Andhaka; wall panel from the Galaganatha temple

which is a sculpted slab portraying Shiva wearing a garland of skulls, energetically spearing the demon Andhaka, set between perforated windows. The sanctuary once opened into a *mandapa*, but only the doorway is preserved, with river goddesses beneath at either side. The piers of the vestibule within have palmette and petal-like motifs carved onto the brackets; a black stone *linga* is installed in the sanctuary.

In spite of its incomplete condition, the Galaganatha has a remarkably well preserved tower of the curved Nagara type, with all of its precisely carved details intact. These include outer bands with tiny *amalaka* motifs, as well as central bands with ascending tiers of full *gavaksha* motifs between split-*gavakshas*. The tower is surmounted by an *amalaka* finial rising almost 15 metres above the terrace. Projecting blocks on the east face of the tower indicate a frontal projection, now lost, leaving a gap through which it is possible to glimpse the hollow interior of the superstructure. Significantly, the tower may be considered a stylistic advance on the more rudimentary examples of the Nagara idiom presented by the Kadasiddhesvara and Jambulinga, even though these temples may actually be slightly later in date.

A few metres south of the Galaganatha is the small **Chandrashekhara Temple**, devoid of any tower. This is the only structure within the main group that postdates the Early Chalukya era. A late 9th- or early 10th-century date within the Rashtrakuta era is suggested by the crisp details of its pilastered walls and the total absence of carved ornament, except for pairs of *makaras* sitting on pairs of pilasters in the middle of the sanctuary walls. A small square plinth with a seated Nandi is seen to the east.

The next monument to be described is the **Sangameshvara Temple**, a few metres south of the Chandrashekhara. The pillar inscription of Kirttivarman II, already referred to, records that the Sangameshvara was erected by Vijayaditya, and dedicated to Shiva under the name Vijayeshvara. Though the building was left unfinished at the death of its royal patron in 734, there was an attempt to complete it in Rashtrakuta times; an inscribed slab set up within its *mandapa* indicates that the monument also received attention during the Late Chalukya era. In spite of its incomplete condition the temple is noteworthy for its imposing proportions and clarity of design, giving expression to the monumental Dravida style developed by Early Chalukya architects in the first third of the 8th century.

The Sangameshvara has a *linga* sanctuary entered from the east, surrounded on three sides by a broad passageway lit by three windows on each face A vestibule in front of the sanctuary has a pair of minor shrines, now empty, possibly intended for Durga and Ganesha. The vestibule opens into a spacious *mandapa* with 16 columns, additions of the Rashtrakuta era. The *mandapa* was intended to be entered through porches on three sides but only the basements of those on the north and south were completed.

The outer walls of the sanctuary and tower above are fully preserved. Raised on a moulded basement with a frieze of elephant, *yali* and *makara* torsos, the walls are divided into four projections, those in the middle

Sangameshwara temple, with the inscribed pillar in the foreground

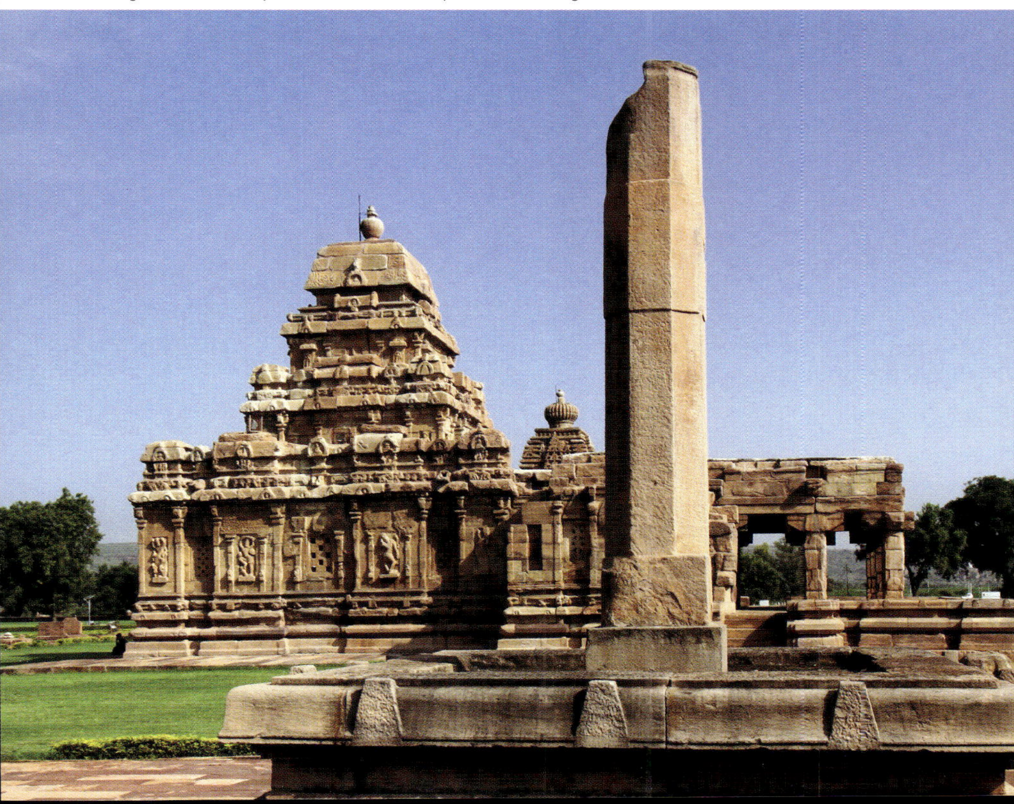

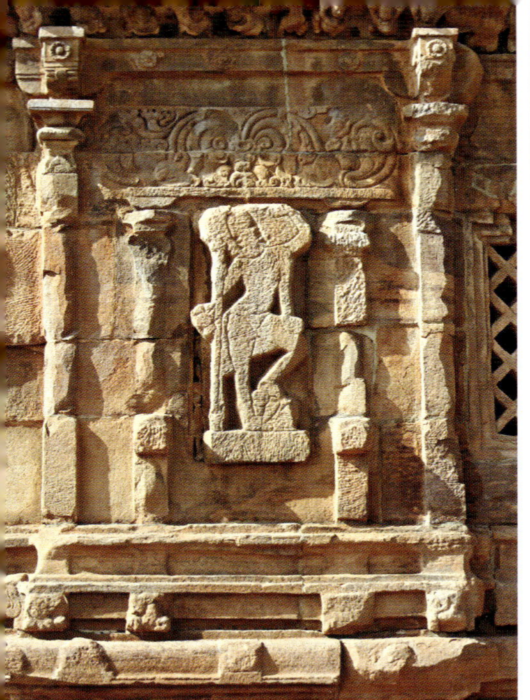

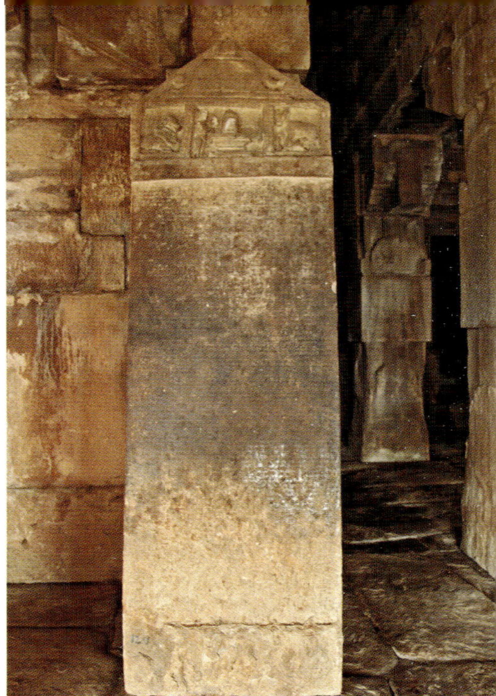

Left: Incomplete panel on the Sangameshvara temple; *Right:* Inscribed slab inside the temple

being somewhat broader, defined by shallow pilasters. The projections are marked by figural panels, some blocked out, others only partly carved. They depict, on the south, Shiva spearing Andhaka, dancing Shiva with a twisted body, and Shiva with hands upraised; on the west, Lakulisha holding the club, Ardhanarishvara, and Shiva with Bhringi (particularly well finished); and on the north, Vishnu, and Varaha. Perforated windows with bold geometric designs are set in the intervening recesses. The walls are overhung by a curved *kapota* eave supporting a parapet with clearly defined *shalas* over the two central projections, and *kutas* over the corner projections. The two diminishing storeys of the tower exhibit increasingly simplified pilastered walls with sculpture panels (difficult to make out), each topped by a *kapota* and parapet; there is no frontal projection. The tower is crowned by a large *kuta*-roof with incised foliation at the corners, carried on a frieze of geese. The capping, pot-like finial is positioned almost 16 metres above the ground.

The sanctuary doorway within the Sangameshvara temple is flanked by unfinished, damaged four-armed guardians leaning on clubs; the doorway itself, however, seems to be an addition of the Rashtrakuta era. So, too, the *mandapa* columns, with three-quarter circles incised onto their shafts, and the angled plain brackets. The roof slabs are horizontal and set at the same level throughout. An inscribed slab set up within the *mandapa* records a gift to the god Vijayeshvara in 1164 by Devaladevi, wife of Nirmadi Tala, one of the Late Chalukya rulers. A few metres to the east of the temple is a small plinth on which is placed a naturalistically carved, but headless Nandi.

From the Sangameshvara it is but a few paces to the Virupaksha temple, the largest and most elaborate monument at Pattadakal. On the way visitors will notice the broken octagonal shaft of the **Inscribed Pillar** with Kirttivarman's edict. This gives the information already noticed about the Sangameshvara; it also explains that the temples now known as Virupaksha and Mallikarjuna were commissioned by two sister queens of Vikramaditya II to commemorate their husband's successful raids on the Pallava capital at Kanchipuram. Though no date is specified, these military campaigns were completed in about 745, after which these projects are likely to have been undertaken.

Known originally as the Lokeshvara, after its sponsor, the queen Lokamahadevi, the **Virupaksha Temple** marks a significant advance on the earlier Sangameshvara in terms of building design, scale and constructional technique, as well as range and quality of sculptural imagery. At the time it must have been recognised as an outstanding achievement since the architect mentioned in an inscription on the east porch of the gateway to the complex is accorded the title of Tribhuvanacharya, Master of the Three Worlds. Many of the artists involved also have their names engraved beneath the carved panels that they worked on.

The Virupaksha temple forms the centrepiece of a grandly-scaled, formally panned complex, incorporating an entrance gateway, Nandi pavilion, porch, *mandapa*, and *linga* sanctuary preceded by an antechamber, all aligned on an east-west axis. The temple stands in a paved compound bounded by walls, laid out as a rectangle with projections on the north and south echoing those of the *mandapa*, with a gap on the north side through which visitors now enter. Minor shrines are built up to the inner face of the compound walls. The temple itself is entered from the east through a porch with high balcony seating; additional porches are provided on the north and south, but are not normally used today. The porches give access to a spacious *mandapa* with 18 columns. Two rows of five columns define the central east-west aisle that leads to the sanctuary doorway, flanked by minor shrines set into the side walls. The sanctuary is surrounded by a passageway lit by pairs of windows with diverse and beautiful designs on each of three sides.

Main shrine of the Virupaksha temple, Pattadakal

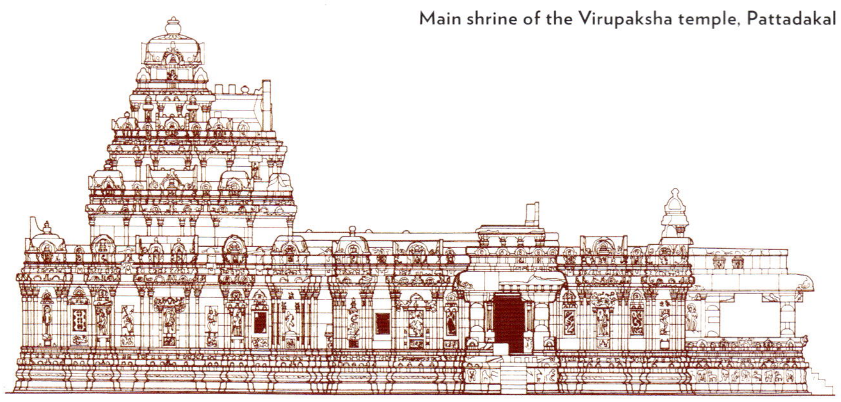

Balcony seating in the three porches of the Virupaksha temple is raised on a high basement, the lower part enlivened with elephant torsos and lions. The porch columns have fluted brackets and outstretched *yalis* that carry deeply-curved eaves, with the undersides treated as timber-like ribs. Enlarged *shalas* rise upon the roofs at the rear of each porch. The *mandapa* walls, as well as the walls encasing the passageway around the sanctuary, are divided into projections framed by single or double pairs of pilasters, with intervening recesses. These projections and recesses are echoed in the basement, which employs a prominent part-octagonal moulding decorated with a continuous creeper motif, above which is a frieze of lion and *makara* torsos. The walls are sheltered by a curved *kapota* eave carrying a parapet, with *kutas* over the corner projections, and *shalas* over the central projections, both with *kudus* filled with model temple towers; larger *kudus* are positioned in between. Sculptures adorn the wall projections, those in the

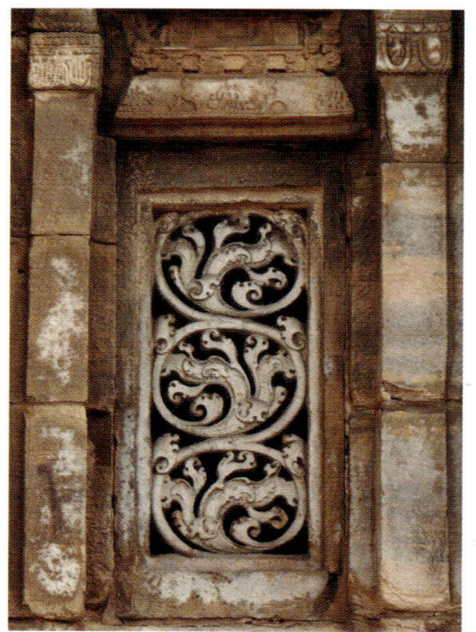

Perforated stone window on the Virupaksha temple

central projections on four sides of the building being framed by secondary pairs of pilasters carrying ornamental compositions. The recesses are marked by perforated windows with a range of designs, surmounted by *kudu* pediments. The tower that rises over the sanctuary is an imposing pyramidal composition consisting of three diminishing storeys. The lower two storeys repeat at a diminishing scale and in simplified form the pilastered projections, eave and parapet elements of the walls beneath. These two storeys are extended eastwards where they are carried on the walls of the antechamber beneath. The third story, with only *kutas* in the parapet, is topped by a squat *kuta*-roof with decorated *kudus* on each face. The crowning pot-finial, which rises more than 17.5 metres above the pavement, is the highest point attained by any Early Chalukya temple tower. The frontal face of the tower is marked by a large, horseshoe-shaped arch filled with a model temple facade, rather than the more usual dancing Shiva icon.

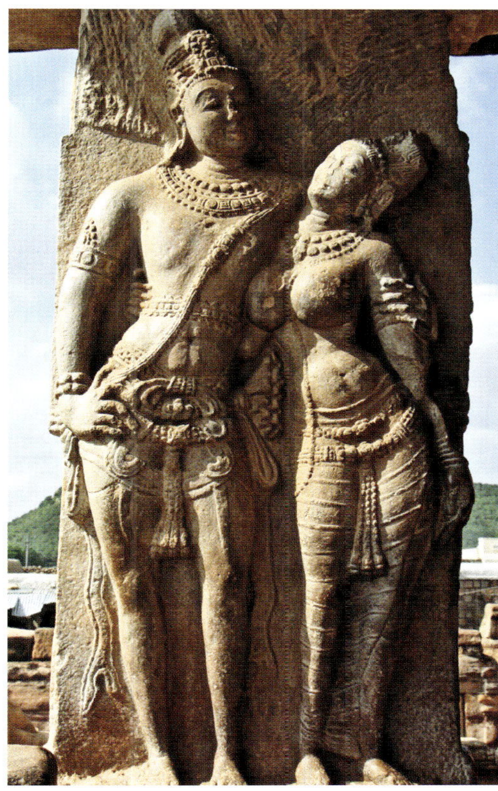

Courtly couple on a column in the east porch of the Virupaksha temple

The walls and porch columns of the Virupaksha Temple Exterior are vehicles for diverse sculptural compositions, by far the most numerous to be found on any Early Chalukya monument. The description of the carvings begins at the east porch. Its outer columns are graced with courtly couples, with the females wearing long patterned cloths, their hair arranged into ornate buns. The inscriptions here are by Lokamahadevi; one mentions a grant to the musicians of the temple. On the *mandapa* walls either side of the porch are two matching compositions. To the right, six-armed

Vishnu appears as Trivikrama, his leg kicked straight up, the foot acrobatically touching his outstretched hand. *Makaras* with riders and gorgeous foliated tails are carved in shallow relief above. The windows at either side employ designs based on fanciful foliage and entwined knots. To the left of the porch, Shiva emerges from a *linga* fringed with flames. The god is flanked by diminutive boar and goose, representing Vishnu and Brahma. Peacocks with extravagant foliate tails are seen above, together with Lakshmi and elephants flanked by flying figures. The windows here have swathes of foliage and swastikas set between lotuses. The side walls of the east porch have carvings of Ardhanarishvara and a dwarf (north), and a couple beneath a tree (south).

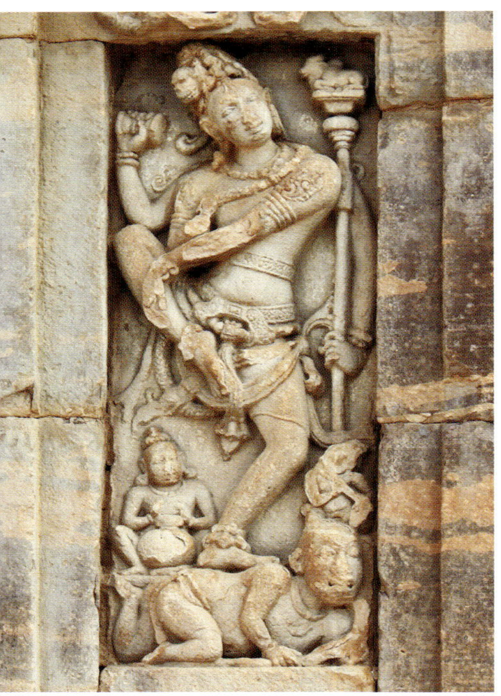

Dancing Shiva; wall panel on the Virupaksha temple

The next panel to be seen when proceeding in a clockwise direction around the *mandapa* of the Virupaksha temple is that at the south corner of the east wall. This shows eight-armed Shiva standing on a dwarf, in the company of a grotesque attendant with a face on his stomach. The panels on the south *mandapa* wall begin with dancing Shiva holding drum and staff, his right leg raised high. The flowing drapery and the arm flung across the body convey the vigorous motion of the steps, paralleled in the flying figures above. Then comes Shiva with Parvati in affectionate embrace, the god's hand placed gently on the right shoulder of the goddess; Lakshmi and elephants in foliation are seen above. Flowing foliate designs are seen in the windows on either side. Next comes the south porch. Panels on its side walls portray Shiva and Parvati on Kailasa (east), and Narasimha disembowelling his victim (west). The porch columns present vigorous compositions. That on the right shows a fight between two (unidentified) men with interlocked legs. That on the left portrays multi-headed Ravana with 20 arms shaking rocky Kailasa.

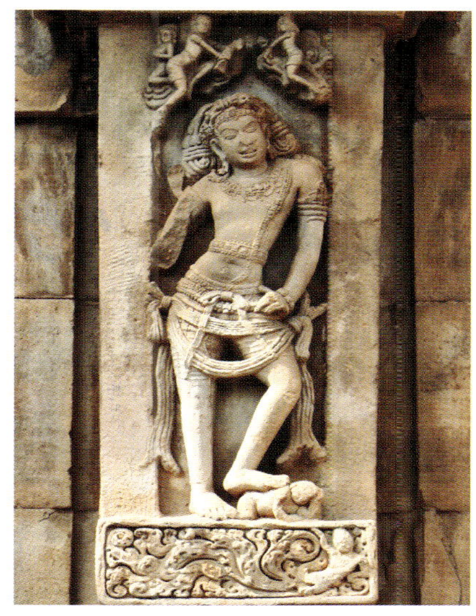

Bhairava with matted hair; wall panel on the Virupaksha temple

The panels that extend up to and around the south-west corner of the *mandapa* depict episodes of the *Ramayana*, arranged in anti-clockwise sequence. They show Vali and Sugriva (monkey heads lost) engaged in violent combat. Then comes Ravana holding up a shield, his head tilted dramatically backwards, being attacked from behind by Jatayu with angrily fanned wings. A diminutive horse-drawn aerial chariot above shows Sita being abducted by Ravana. The *Ramayana* sequence concludes on the west face of the *mandapa* wall with the episode of the golden deer; above, Lakshmana rejects the advances of Ravana's sister, the ogress Shurpanakha.

The panels on the passageway walls around three sides of the *linga* sanctuary of the Virupaksha temple are mostly devoted to Shiva: thus, Bhikshatana, and Bhairava with matted hair (south); the god spearing Andhaka, and Lakulisha with curling tresses (west); and Bhairava and Harihara (north). This sequence is interrupted in the middle of the north side with a formally posed, eight-armed icon of Vishnu holding a full range of weapons. That this may be a replacement icon is suggested by the figures of Shiva and Parvati between exquisitely modelled *makaras* with cascading tails above, and a panel of Durga slaying Mahisha below. A modest image of Varaha occupies the adjacent niche, followed by two further icons of Shiva, one with matted hair, wearing head- and chest-bands in the manner of an ascetic.

Panels on the north *mandapa* wall begin with an icon of Shiva holding a drum and a staff with a fluttering banner, leaning comfortably against Nandi (west corner). This is followed by a superbly modelled Harihara, with trident and conch, with a disc seemingly floated above. Then comes a somewhat masculine Ardhanarishvara, next to a window with quartet of cut-out petals. The side walls of the north porch are carved with Ravana beneath a scene of *linga* worship (west), and Shiva with sages (east). The columns of the north porch are embellished with representation of Vishnu with a *rishi* (right), and the same god descending on Garuda to vigorously rescue the elephant Gajendra, which is shown trapped in a lotus pond (left). Panels on the remaining

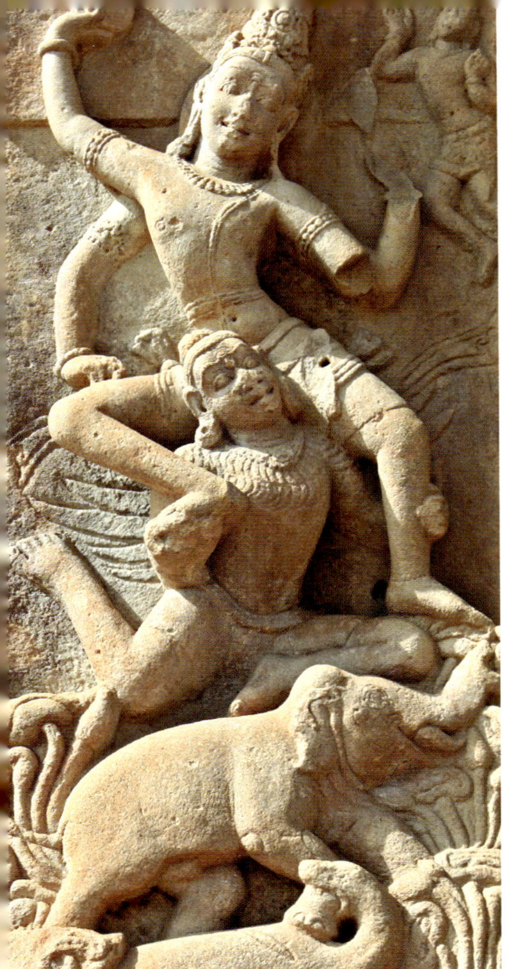

Vishnu on Garuda; column in the north porch of the Virupaksha temple

projections of the north *mandapa* wall begin with Shiva holding an ornate trident, dancing on a prostrate dwarf. Windows at either side employ swathes of foliation and foliated peacocks. The series concludes with Shiva and Parvati, the god leaning on Nandi, and, at the extreme northern end of the east *mandapa* wall, Vishnu with devotee.

The porch interiors of the Virupaksha temple are also richly supplied with sculptures. This is immediately apparent from the east porch, the ceiling of which portrays Surya riding in the chariot through the clouds, the horses being directed by Aruna, with archers aiming their bows outwards to either side. The engaged columns at the rear have guardian figures dressed in flowing drapery, leaning on fluted clubs. An inscription on the left-hand column gives the name of the architect who has already mentioned. Wall extensions here are treated as shallow niches housing pot-bellied *nidhis* holding conch and lotus. The doorway in between is framed by fluted pilasters supporting an eave, and topped by a parapet in shallow relief crowded with celestials. Doorways within the north and south porches are of similar design,

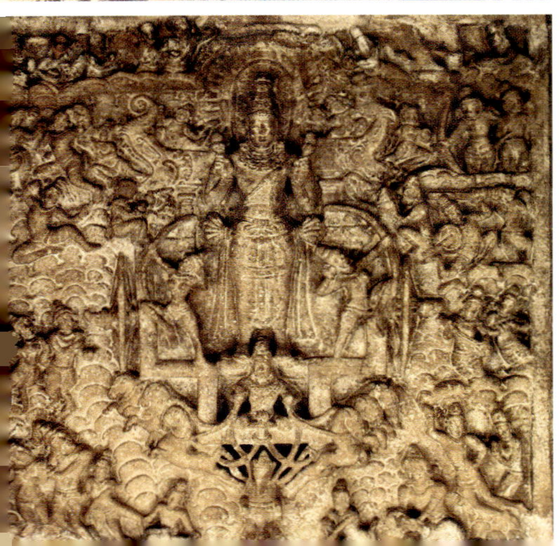

Surya riding in the chariot; ceiling panel in the east porch of the Virupaksha temple

being flanked by almost three-dimensional guardian figures, several with angry expressions, furled brows and roaring mouths. Ceiling panels here portray Brahma on a lotus (south porch), and Shiva in the company of *rishis* and female attendants (north porch).

Further sculptural imagery is to be seen on the *mandapa* columns of the **Virupaksha Temple Interior**. Cubical blocks topped with semicircles, linked by bands to bottom circles, are filled with reliefs illustrating a rich assortment of divinities, legendary stories (not all identifiable), accessory figures and decorative designs. Settings vary from palace interiors to forest hermitages in rocky landscapes with lotus ponds and wild animals and birds. Narratives employ successive episodes separated into bands and compartments, or assembled in continuous friezes. This imagery also includes courtly couples wearing elaborate costumes in affectionate embraces, *ganas* dancing in garlands, animals fighting, and a seemingly inexhaustible range of fantasy vegetal motifs incorporating human, animal and bird themes.

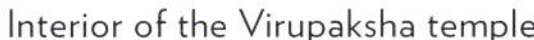

Interior of the Virupaksha temple

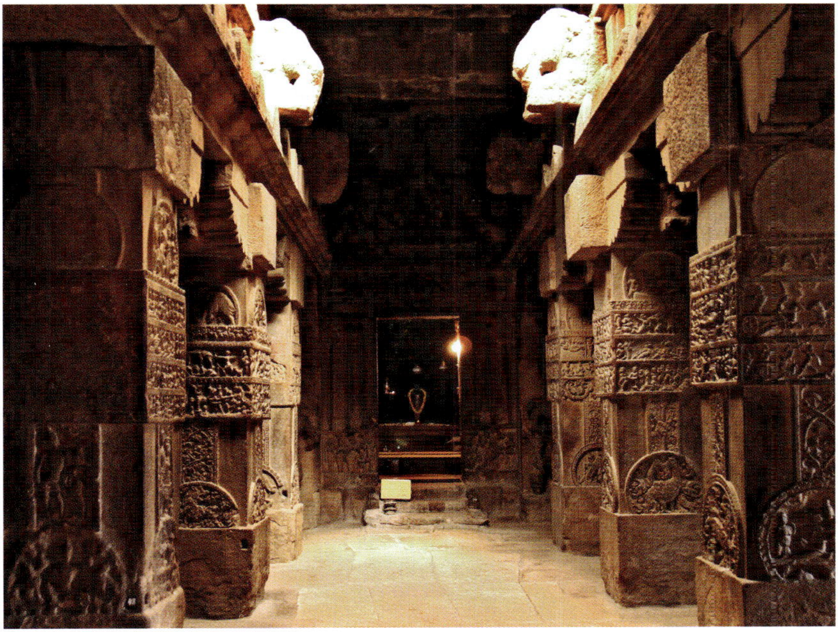

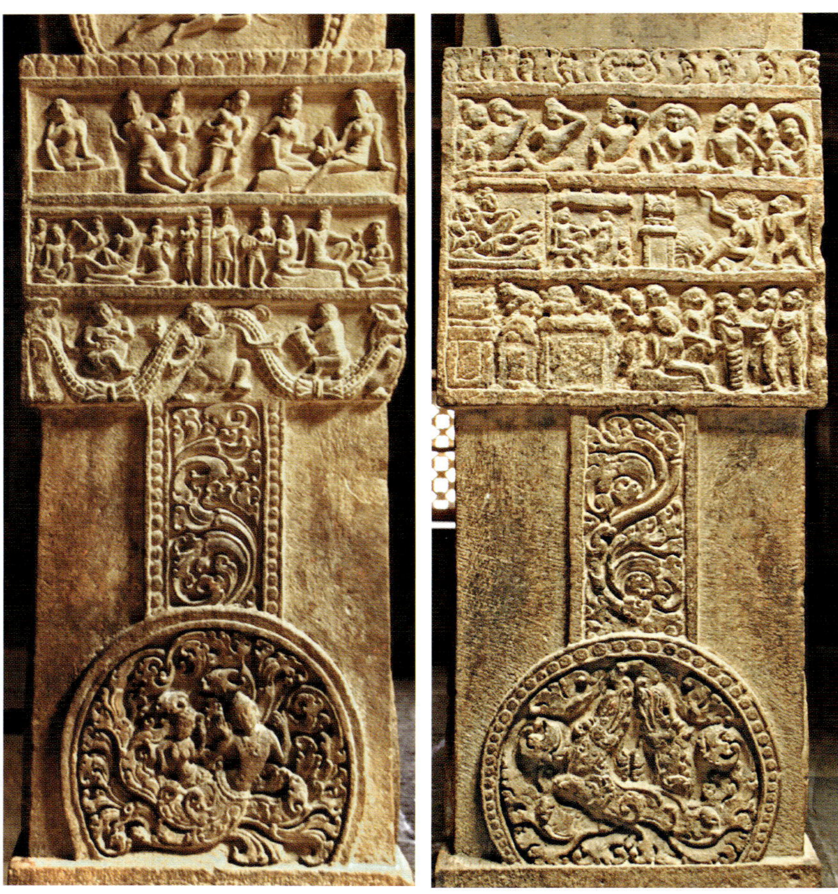

Columns with legendary scenes and foliate decoration in the Virupaksha temple

The selection of narrative reliefs described here begins with those on the columns flanking the central east-west aisle of the *mandapa*. (The columns are numbered in rows, beginning at the east entrance to the *mandapa*, and then from south to north; that is, from left to right when facing towards the *linga* sanctuary.) *Ramayana* scenes in four bands cover the north face of the second column in the third row. In the first (top) band, Lakshmana cuts off the nose of Shurpanakha, who then holds up her hands in horror; in the second band, Shurpanakha complains to Ravana, and then joins the demons to battle with Rama and Lakshmana. The story of the golden deer is reserved for the third band, the animal being depicted three times. In the fourth (bottom) band, Ravana appears as an ascetic before Sita, and then abducts her in his aerial chariot before being attacked by Jatayu; Rama then meets the dying bird.

Comparable *Mahabharata* scenes cover the south face of the opposite column (third column in the third row). A council of war takes place in the first (top) band, with Bhishma, the great Pandava warrior, shown dying on a bed of arrows in the broader second band. In the third (bottom) band Bhima and and Duryodhana fight with clubs. Scenes representing further stages in the war between the Pandavas and Kauravas cover the other three faces of the same column. The climactic confrontation between Arjuna and Karna, the protagonists riding in war-chariots, is reserved for the east face.

The Kirtarjuniya episode from the *Mahabharata* occupies the upper band on four faces of the second column in the next (fourth) row. The story begins on the east face with Shiva as a hunter and Arjuna shooting arrows at the same boar. This leads to the fight between Shiva and Arjuna; Arjuna overpowering Shiva; and then Shiva presenting Arjuna with the magic axe, all shown on the north face. The story then jumps to the south face where Arjuna leaves the forest in a chariot, and is then entertained by celestial females. Finally, on the west face, Arjuna shows Shiva's weapon to Duryodhana and his brothers.

Ramayana scenes are resumed on the third column in the fourth row, on the other side of the central aisle of the *mandapa*. On the south face, Hanuman battles with two ogresses, one of which he has already slain (middle band), and then sits up high on his coiled tail before Ravana (bottom band). This sequence properly begins on the west face with Jatayu narrating Sita's abduction (unfinished). It continues onto the north face where Rama and Lakshmana meet with Sugriva (top band), and then with the monkeys, after which Hanuman leaps across the monster-infested ocean (middle band) to find Sita in Ravana's garden (bottom band). The fight between Sugriva and Vali takes place on the east face (top band), with Shurpanakha drowning in the ocean (middle band).

The celebrated legend of the churning of the cosmic ocean appears on the second column in the fifth row (north face). Gods and demons are shown tugging the serpentine body of Shesha, which is wrapped around the pole-like shaft of Mount Mandara. The scene is repeated in an abbreviated form in the circle above. Here, Garuda pulls at Shesha's serpentine body while the gods look on.

Further narratives are discovered on the columns in the outer aisles of the *mandapa*. Scenes from the childhood of Krishna are seen on three faces of the first column in the first row: the youthful god overthrowing the demon who had trapped the two brothers (east face); subduing Kaliya, and holding up Mount Govardhana (south face); and killing the crow demon, sucking at the breast of Putana, pulling the mortar tied to two trees in which the brothers were trapped, and confronting the horse demon (all on the west face).

The story of the descent of the Ganga is illustrated on the first column in the second row, where there are scenes on three faces showing ascetics in forest settings. The south face depicts the river flowing past Bhagiratha onto Shiva's outstretched lock of hair. Shiva's rescue of Markandeya is found on the first column in the third row (east face).

Among the other topics portrayed on the *mandapa* columns are the marriage of Shiva and Parvati, and an elephant fight (second column in the first row, north face); an energetically striding elephant with rider pursuing a horse (third column in the first row, east face, top block); Shiva dancing in the company of Parvati and drummer (second column in the second row, east face, top circle); elephant and boar ingeniously combined, and three entwined dancers (second column in the fourth row, circles); and an elephant savagely goring a human victim (third column in the fifth row, circles).

Only two raised ceiling slabs with carvings are preserved over the central aisle of the *mandapa* of the Virupaksha temple: they portray a *nagaraja* bearing garlands surrounded by its coiled serpentine body; and Lakshmi between elephants. Sloping slabs roof the outer aisles in two tiers. Visitors should ensure that they do not miss the icon installed in the minor shrine to the right (north) of the sanctuary doorway (torch required), which may be regarded as

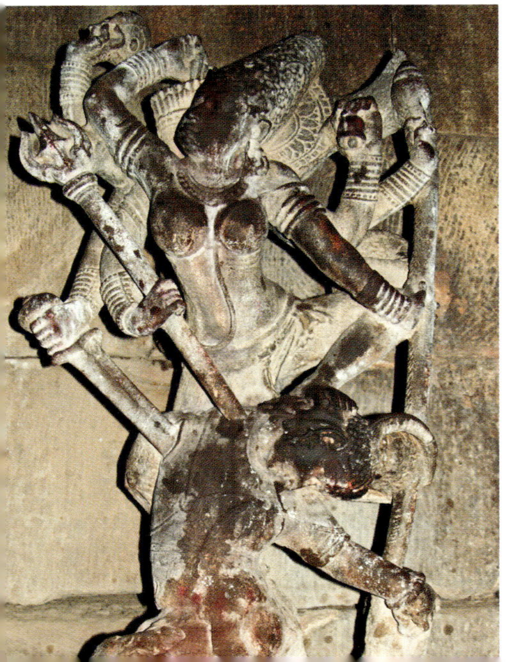

Durga spearing Mahisha; sculpture in minor shrine in the Virupaksha temple

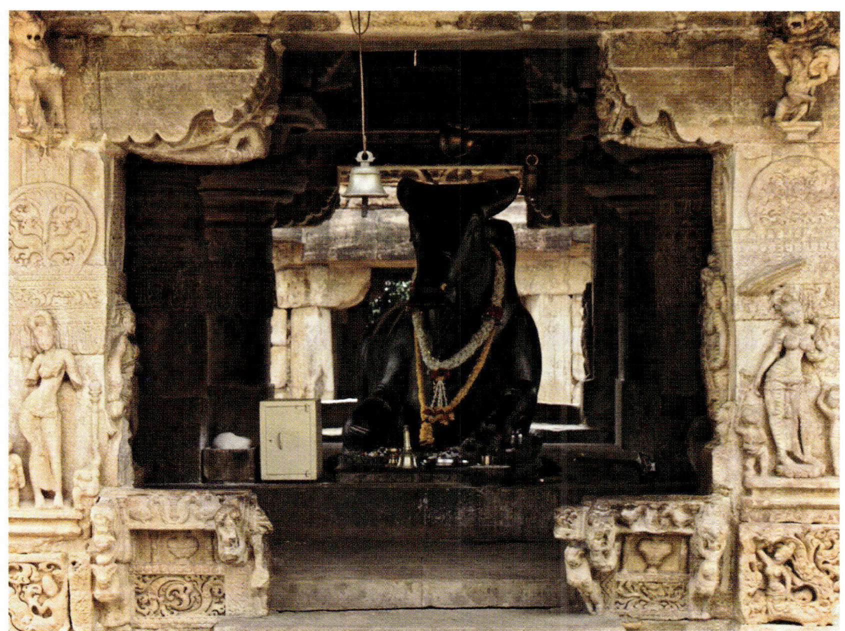

Nandi pavilion of the Virupaksha temple

one of the great masterpieces of Early Chalukya art. This cut-out sculpture depicts eight-armed Durga savagely thrusting her trident and sword into Mahisha, who recoils backwards in shock. Fully modelled guardians, facing away from each other, embellish the engaged columns either side of the sanctuary doorway. The entrance has pilasters carrying *makaras* spewing garlands that meet in a medallion containing Shiva with Parvati and Nandi. Dancing Shiva is carved onto the ceiling of the vestibule that precedes the sanctuary, in which an imposing, polished black stone *linga* now receives worship.

The **Nandi Pavilion** of the Virupaksha complex accommodates a huge sculpted bull, no less than 3 metres long and 1.8 metres high, facing towards the east porch of the temple. Carved out of a single block of black granite, its surface is oiled and somewhat restored. The corner walls of the pavilion, raised on a high basement, have niches with attendant females, some in alluring postures; other maidens as well as amorous couples adorn the columns framing the openings. The foliate panels beneath these figures are especially imaginative. The walls are sheltered by a deeply curved eave with cut-out ribs and rafters on the underside. The Nandi within is seated between four substantial circular columns, the shafts decorated with petals and garlands. Cushion-like capitals and projecting square capitals carry the lotus medallion ceiling above.

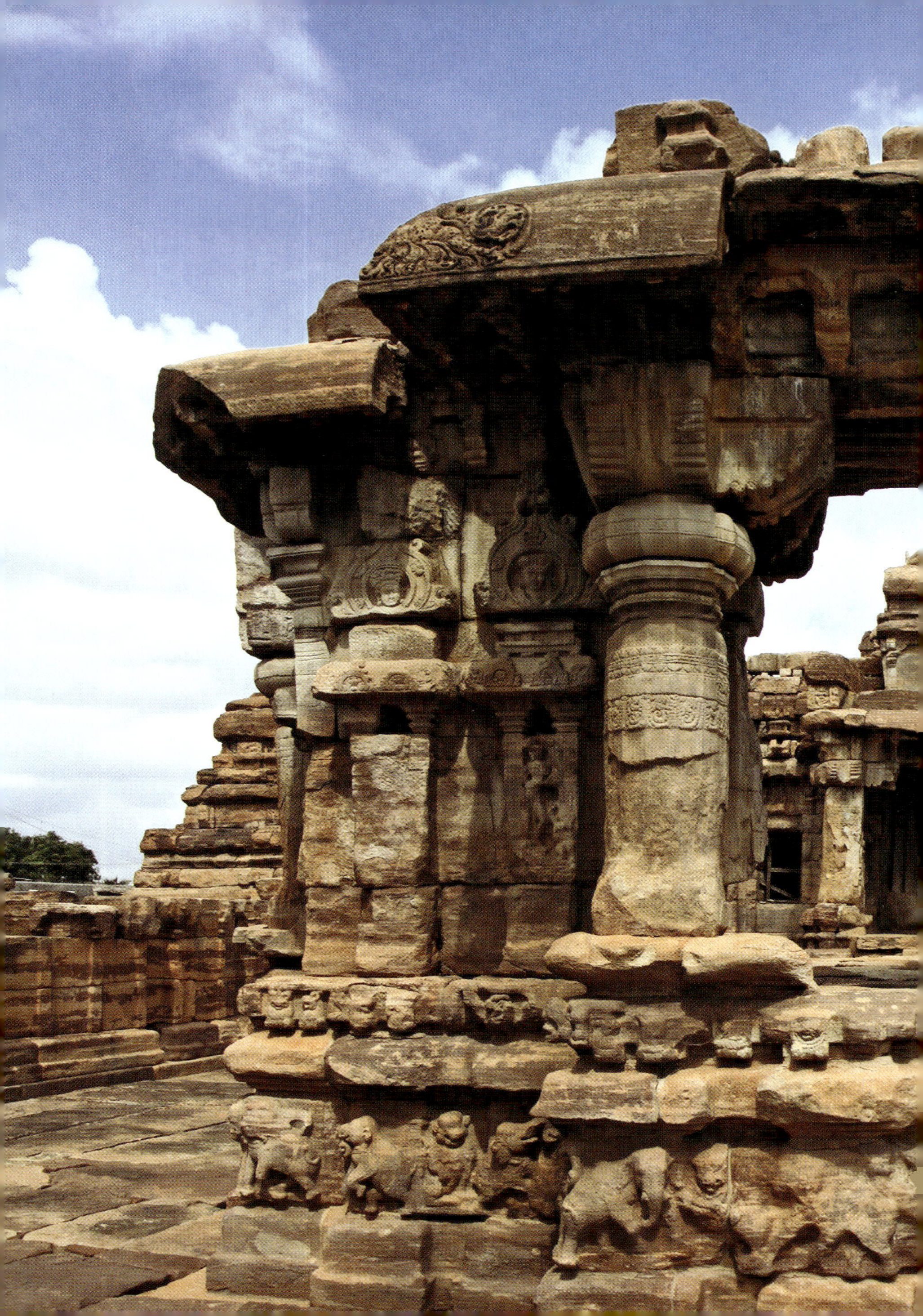

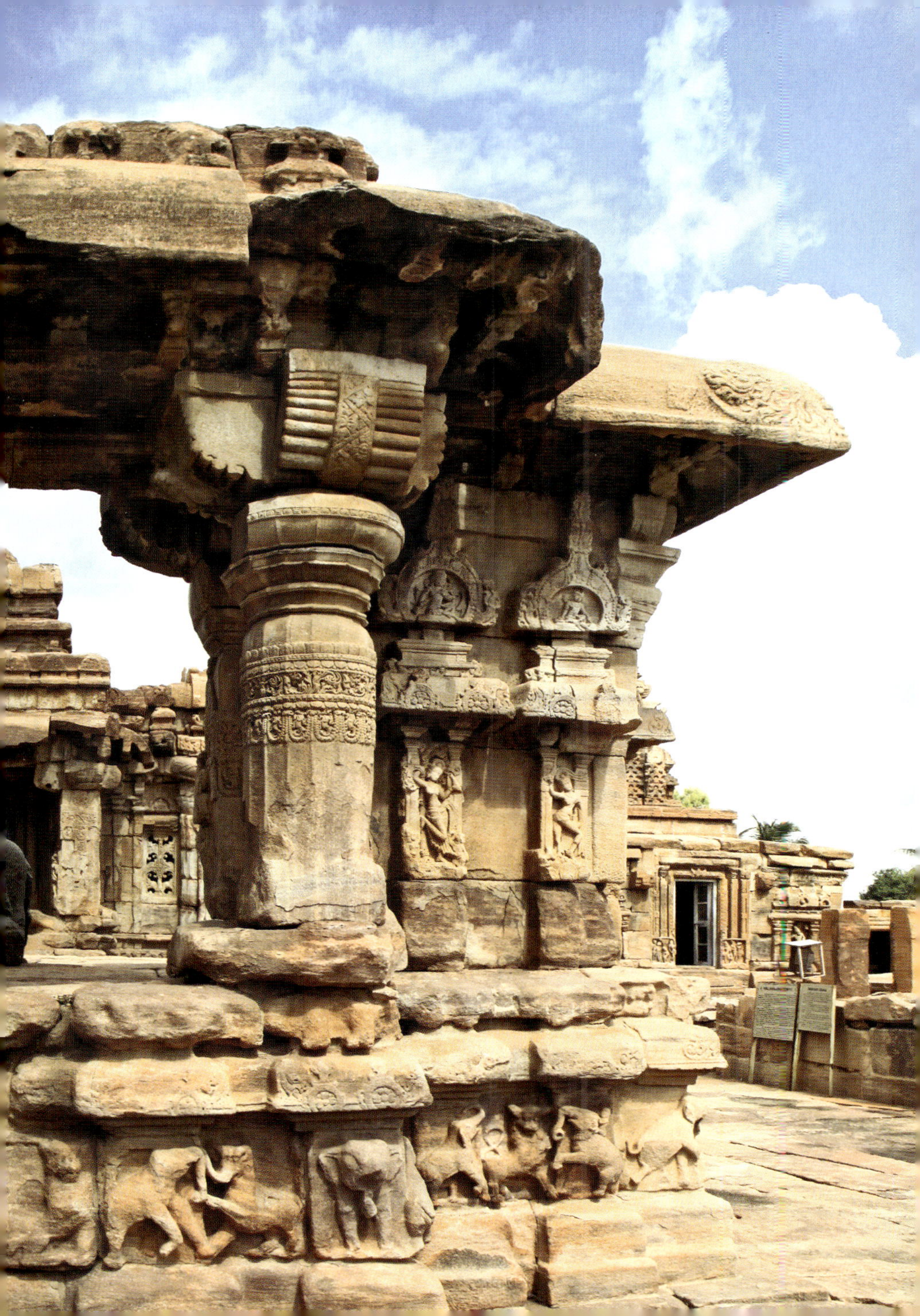

Previous pages: Mallikarjuna temple

Immediately east of the Nandi pavilion is a monumental Gateway, through which the Virupaksha complex is entered from the river bank. The inscription on its outer wall mentioning the temple architect has already been noticed. Visitors to the complex should be encouraged to pass through the gateway and follow the path leading to the Papanatha temple (described below).

Before they leave the main group of temples at Pattadakal visitors should take time to inspect the Mallikarjuna Temple, erected by Trailokamahadevi, the sister of Lokamahadevi, originally named after her as the Trailokeshvara. The historical link between the Mallikarjuna and Virupaksha temples is borne out architecturally, since the two projects were obviously conceived as matching monuments with almost identical layouts, even though the Mallikarjuna is slightly smaller in scale and lower in height. Like the Virupaksha, it too is contained within a walled compound with Nandi pavilion and gateways, though these seem never to have been completed.

The elevation of the Mallikarjuna imitates that of the Virupaksha in all essential respects. Slight differences are seen in the triple sets of pilasters that frame the central wall projections, and the increased articulation of the parapet elements at each level of the tower that results in a greater three-dimensional massing, highlighted by the capping hemispherical roof. Another variation is the frontal arched projection of the tower accommodating a dancing Shiva icon. Unlike the panels on the walls of the Virupaksha, those of the Mallikarjuna are incomplete or badly damaged, and many of the perforated windows are missing. Among the finest icons are Shiva with matted hair, and the same god with Nandi, at the east end of the south *mandapa* wall. A remarkable icon of Bhikshatana, with twisted body, is seen on the south passageway wall. Here, too, is an incomplete, but vigorously posed sculpture of Shiva spreading out the skin of the elephant demon, possibly removed from the Sangameshvara temple. The same may also be true of the icon of eight-armed dancing Shiva in the middle of the west passageway wall. However, the adjacent Ardhanarishvara image with a delicately chiselled face seems to be an original panel. Additional images of Shiva, mostly incomplete, are set into the north wall.

Porch columns on three sides of the Mallikarjuna temple are raised on friezes of spirited lions and elephants. Eight-armed Narasimha grappling with his victim is carved onto one column of the frontal east porch; the column opposite shows maidens with gracefully attenuated bodies, one with a musical instrument. Guardians holding a snake and trident frame the doorway within. An icon of

Column in the Mallikarjuna temple depicting scenes of the churning of the ocean, and Durga battling Mahisha

Vishnu riding on Garuda graces one column of the north porch.

As in the Virupaksha, the Mallikarjuna *mandapa* columns are covered with carvings. Here, too, is found is a broad range of narratives, including the Kiratarjuniya story (first column in the second row from the entrance, west face); and the Krishna legend, the latter showing Krishna stepping on Kaliya in a lotus pond, and holding up Mount Govardhana (second columns in the third and fourth rows, bands and top circles). More unusual are illustrations of stories taken from the *Panchatantra*: a monkey sitting at a desk (fourth column in the second row, west face, top circle); and a monkey with a crocodile, and a mongoose killing a snake that threatens a sleeping child (third column in the fourth row, south face, top circle and band beneath). The curious tale of a pigeon bearing a love note to a queen from an admirer, and then the queen being beaten and killed by her husband, is found on the first column in the fifth row (north face). Two versions of the churning of the ocean story are seen (second column in the fifth row, south face, top circle and band beneath). Here, too, there is a panel imitating a Pallava period composition at Mamallapuram, which depicts Durga riding on the lion advancing towards

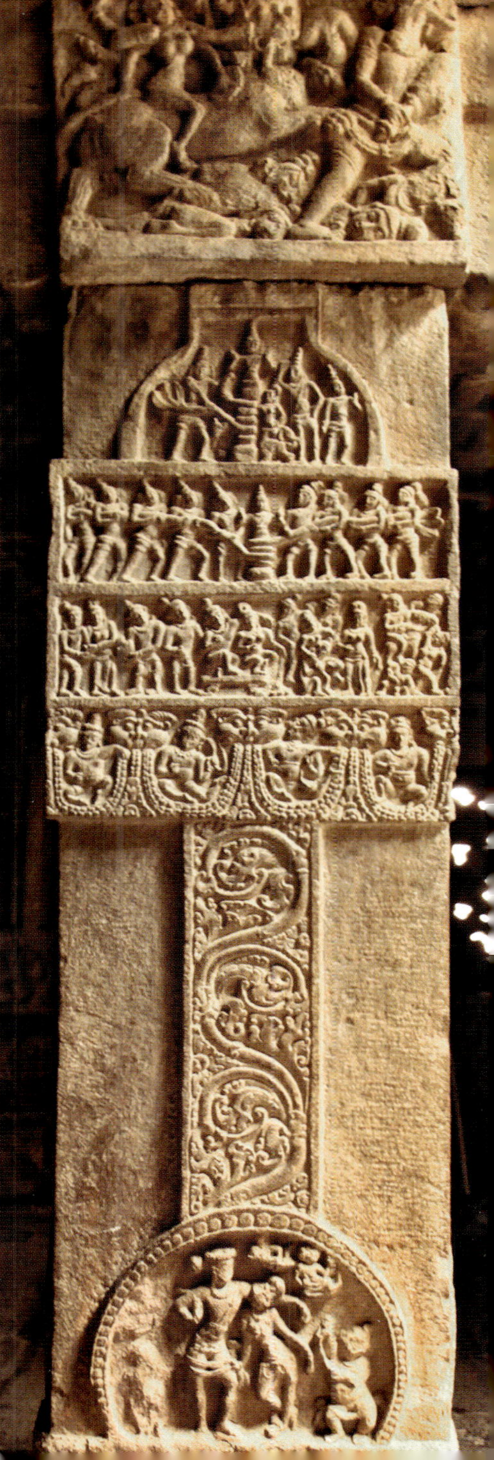

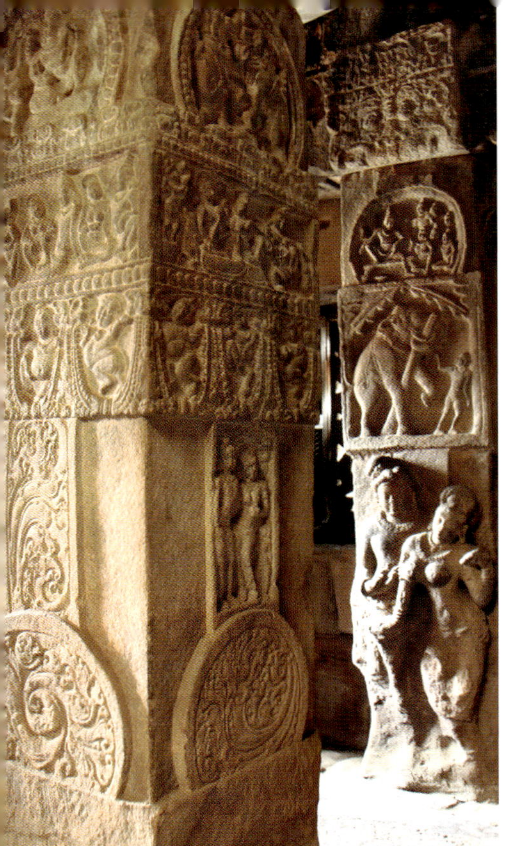

Mandapa columns of the Mallikarjuna temple

the buffalo-headed Mahisha, who recoils backwards (second column in the fifth row, bracket on the south face). Elsewhere, the brackets of the columns lining the central aisle are adorned with flying couples. Three ceiling panels over the central aisle portray eight-armed dancing Shiva accompanied by Parvati and Nandi; *nagaraja* with coiled serpent body; and Lakshmi between elephants within a ring of lotus ornament.

Wall columns of the *mandapa* interior are embellished with refined courtly couples attired in a variety of costumes and headdresses. Some are posed in affectionate embraces, such as the male who delicately touches the chin of his companion, on one of the columns beside the north doorway. The columns flanking the doorway to the *linga* sanctuary have fierce guardians with protruding eyes and tusks. The figures are symmetrically posed, one leg bent behind the other. The ceiling panel within the vestibule shows Shiva and Parvati surrounded by celestials.

The dilapidated pavilion in front of the Mallikarjuna temple accommodates two fragmentary, green-stone Nandis.

The Kashivishvanatha Temple, probably dating from the first decades of the 8th century, stands barely 2 metres distant from the north porch of the Mallikarjuna, but at a slightly lower level, thereby suggesting that it may be somewhat earlier. Consisting of a sanctuary and small rectangular *mandapa* only, the Kashivishvanatha is the most advanced example of the Nagara style at Pattadakal. Its outer walls have regularly spaced, shallow niche projections topped by pediments with varied *gavaksha* designs. The niches are mostly devoid of carvings, except for damaged icons of Ardhanarishvara and Lakulisha on the north *mandapa* wall, and the river goddesses flanking the entrance doorway on the east. A complicated mesh pattern derived from interlocking *gavakshas* entirely covers the central facets of the curving, *shikhara*-type tower that rises above; regularly spaced flattish amakala motifs are seen on the outer facets. The *amalaka* finial is not preserved.

Of interest within the Kashivishvanatha temple are the four columns with elegantly fluted shafts, interrupted by sculpted maidens. Cubical blocks are mostly embellished with Shaiva topics. These include the marriage of Shiva and Parvati; Shiva killing various demons; the god appearing out of the *linga*; and the god as a yogi with sages. In contrast, the outer right-hand column has scenes from, the childhood of Krishna, and Vishnu sleeping on Shesha. Vase-and-foliage motifs adorn three of the column capitals. Fluted brackets and *yali* brackets carry the raised ceiling over the middle of the *mandapa*. This is carved with Shiva with Parvati and Nandi surrounded by the Dikpalas. A black stone *linga* is installed within the sanctuary.

Left: Tower of the Kashivishvanatha temple *Right:* Interior columns of the temple

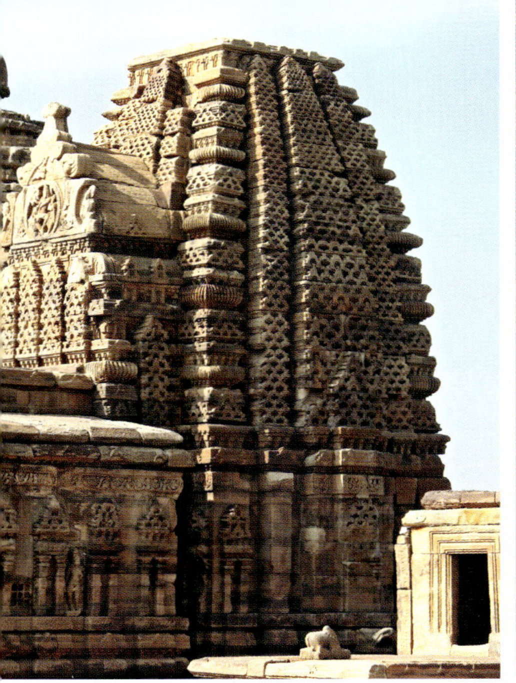

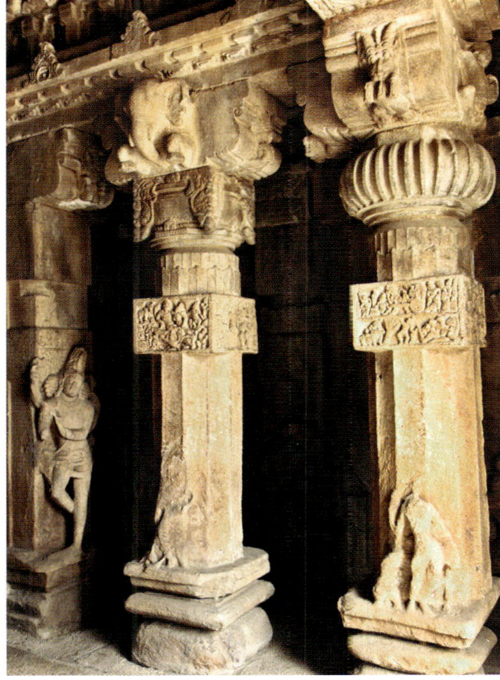

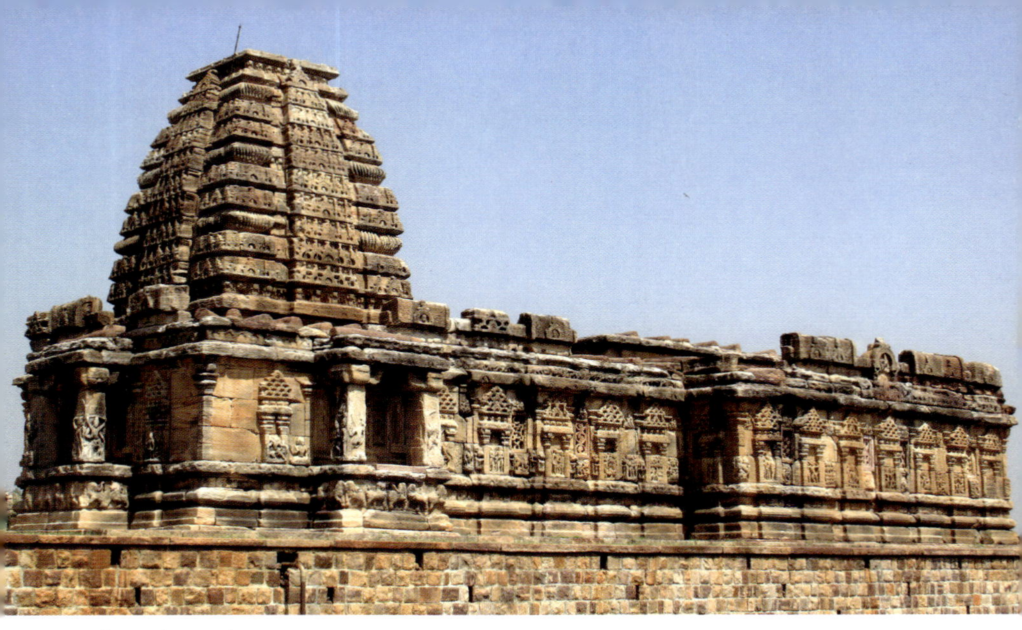

Papanatha temple

ALONG THE RIVER

A few minutes walk from the gateway to the Virupaksha complex brings visitors to the Papanatha Temple. Dating from the very end of the Early Chalukya era, this monument is of particular interest for its mix of Nagara and Dravida features. Another curious feature is the pair of interconnecting *mandapas*, the inner one with four columns, the outer one with 16 columns, entered from the east through a small porch with balcony seating. A narrow passageway with porch projections on three sides surrounds the sanctuary at the western end of the temple. This uncommon scheme is best explained by three successive phases of construction, unified through consistent architectural and sculptural detail.

The outer walls of the Papanatha, much elongated on the north and south, are lined with pilastered niches headed by triangular *gavaksha* pediments. These Nagara features contrast with the *shalas* and *kutas* of the Dravida styled parapet. A simple Nagara styled tower, with a frontal arch projection containing an icon dancing Shiva, rises over the sanctuary. Porches on three sides shelter perforated windows either side of sculpted panels showing Shiva in various aspects, now badly damaged, with images of the Dikpalas carved on the walls at either side. Of particular interest are the narrative panels at the eastern end of the temple illustrating the *Ramayana* and Kiratarjuniya stories, both series proceeding towards the entrance porch. The *Ramayana* series begins in the middle of the south wall of the inner *mandapa*, with Dasharatha meeting

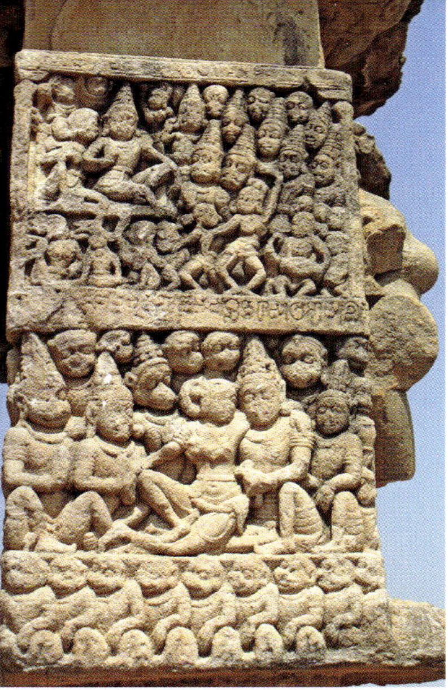

Ramayana scenes on a porch column of the Papanatha temple

a sage, and then conducting a fire sacrifice. The story continues with the education of Rama and Lakshmana; Rama and Lakshmana combatting demons in the forest; the shooting of the golden deer; Ravana appearing before Sita as an ascetic; Sita's abduction; and Jatayu intercepting Ravana. Then come the scenes of Rama and Lakshmana at the monkey court; the combat between Vali and Sugriva; Rama killing Vali; and, at the eastern end of the south wall, monkeys hauling boulders in the act of building the bridge to Lanka. Progressing onto the east *mandapa* wall, the scenes show the battle between Rama and Ravana, the latter riding in his chariot. The narrative concludes with the scene of Rama's coronation on the south column of the entrance porch.

Episodes from the Kiratarjuniya storey are less extensive. They commence towards the eastern end of the north wall of the outer *mandapa* and continue onto the east wall. They begin with Arjuna and Shiva as the hunter aiming bows towards a boar, then fighting over the killed animal; they conclude with the scene of Arjuna's victory on the north column of the entrance porch. Compared with these vividly composed compositions, the damaged carvings of various deities in the other wall niches are of lesser artistic interest, with the exception of the entrance porch which is richly embellished. The porch is raised on a dramatic frieze of fighting elephants and lions, while the outer columns have carvings of full modelled human couples, one showing a horse-headed woman and companion beneath a tree. (The final scenes from the *Ramayana* and the Kiratarjuniya story on these columns have already been noticed.) The doorway within the porch has fluted pilasters carrying *makaras* with foliate tails, with a tiny image of Lakshmi in the central medallion. The ceiling panel above showing dancing Shiva is carried on an ornate entablature and parapet, with fully-bodied elephants and lions angling inwards at the corners.

The first feature to be noticed within the first (outer) *mandapa* of the Papanatha temple is a finely carved Nandi, possibly displayed on an external plinth when the temple was conceived with a single *mandapa* only. Columns lining the central aisle have 16-sided shafts, with attendant maidens. Capitals are of the cushion type, or are cubical with vase-and-foliage motifs.

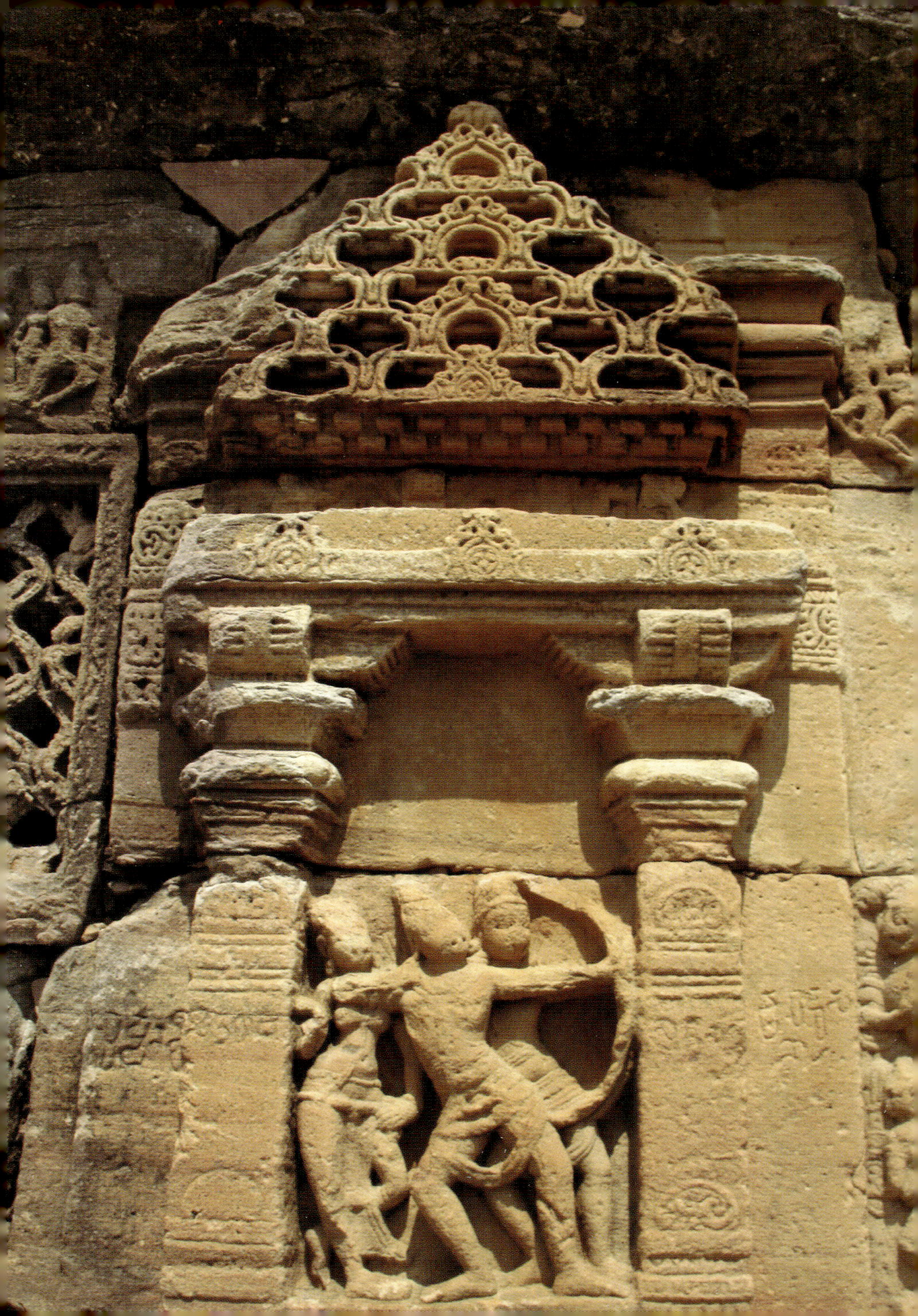

Opposite: *Ramayana* scene on the Papanatha temple

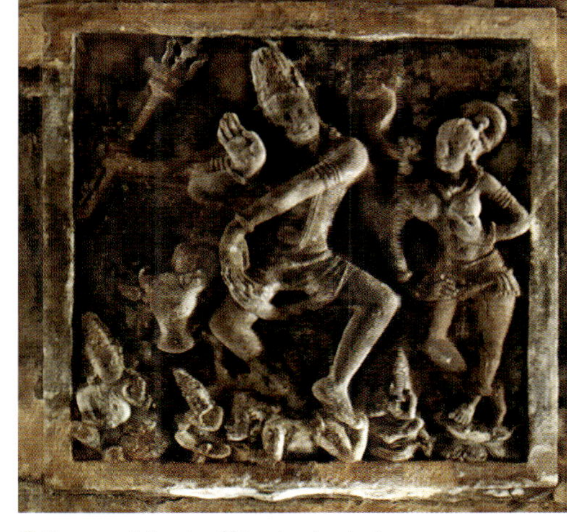

Ceiling panel showing Shiva dancing in the Papanatha temple

Extended fluted brackets and *yalis* carry beams of highly intricate workmanship, with angled *yalis* at the corners, as in the porch. The three central ceiling slabs represent Vishnu on Shesha surrounded by the Dikpalas; *nagaraja* holding a garland; and Lakshmi between elephants surrounded by a ring of flying celestials. Wall columns are vehicles for richly dressed, embracing couples, distinguished by their naturalistic modelling and lyrical poses. Small side niches accommodate icons of Ganesha (south) and Durga (north). Guardians leaning on clubs, in complimentary poses, flank the doorway to the second (inner) *mandapa*. This *mandapa* is of interest for the ceiling panels of dancing Shiva and of *nagaraja*, the finest versions of these themes at Pattadakal. The narrow passageway around the *linga* sanctuary accommodates icons of Shiva (south), Surya (west), and Vishnu (north).

Interior of the Papanatha temple

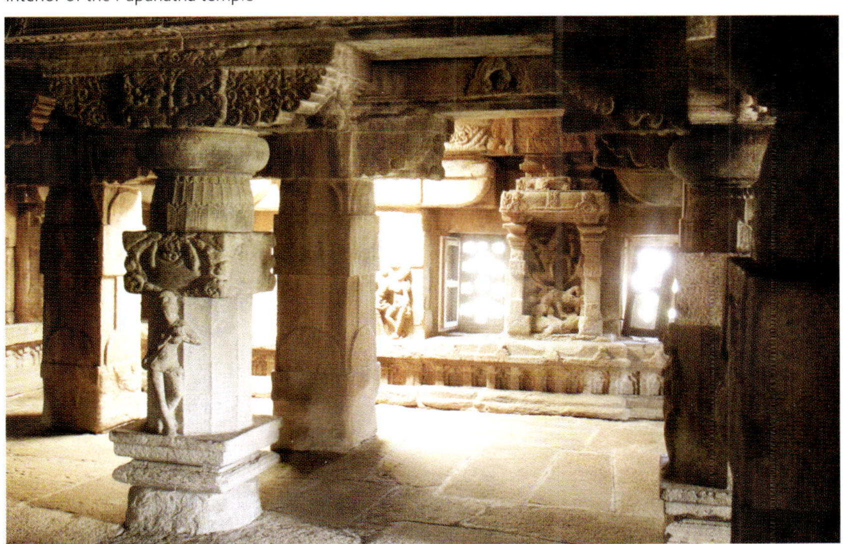

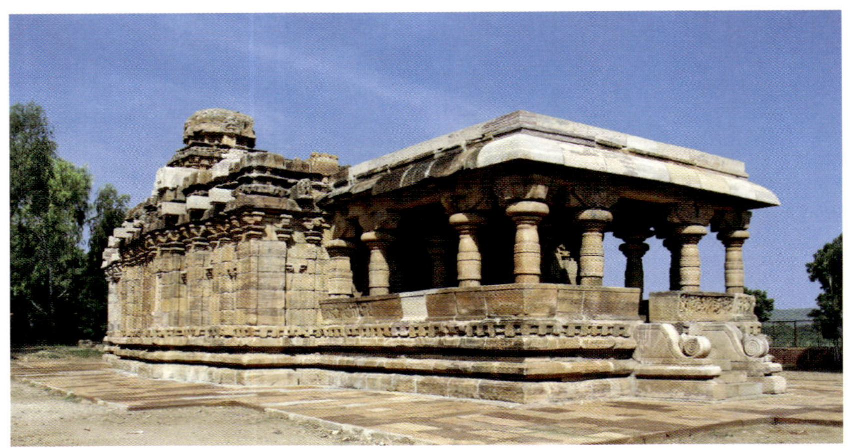

Jain temple near Pattadakal *Opposite:* Sculpted elephant in the temple

AROUND PATTADAKAL

Other monuments and historical sites of interest are located in the vicinity of Pattadakal. The first to be visited is the **Jain Temple**, less than 500 metres from the main group of temples, to the right of the road when returning to Badami. This displays distinctive attributes of the Rashtrakuta style: crisply modelled basement mouldings and pilasters; blocked-out parapet elements on the outer walls and tower; and squatly proportioned columns with massive circular shafts and capitals in the open porch through which the *mandapa* is entered. The remarkable, naturalistic elephant torsos with riders carved onto the walls within the porch recall similar animals on other Rashtrakuta monuments, notably those at Ellora in Maharashtra; so too the *makaras* with exaggerated foliated tails above the sanctuary doorway. As for the Jaina dedication of the temple, this relies on a single Jina figure carved onto the *kapota* eave (north side), and a total absence of panels portraying Hindu divinities. The tower, containing an upper chamber, is crowned with somewhat compressed *kuta* roof. The walls containing the narrow passageway around the sanctuary, once entirely missing, have now been altogether rebuilt.

Dolmen beside the road leading to Pattadakal

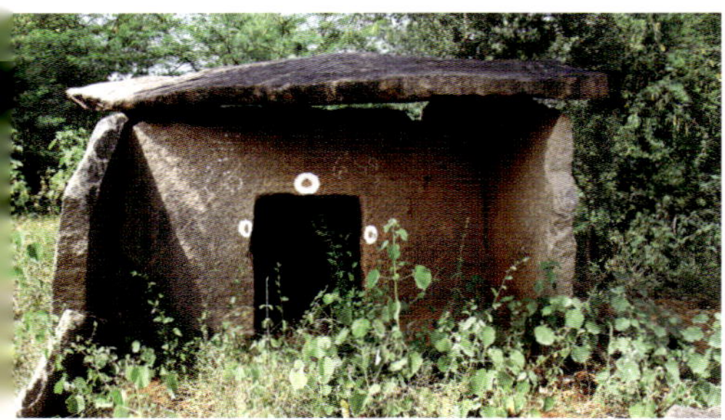

Continuing along the road in the direction of Badami for another 1 kilometre visitors will come across

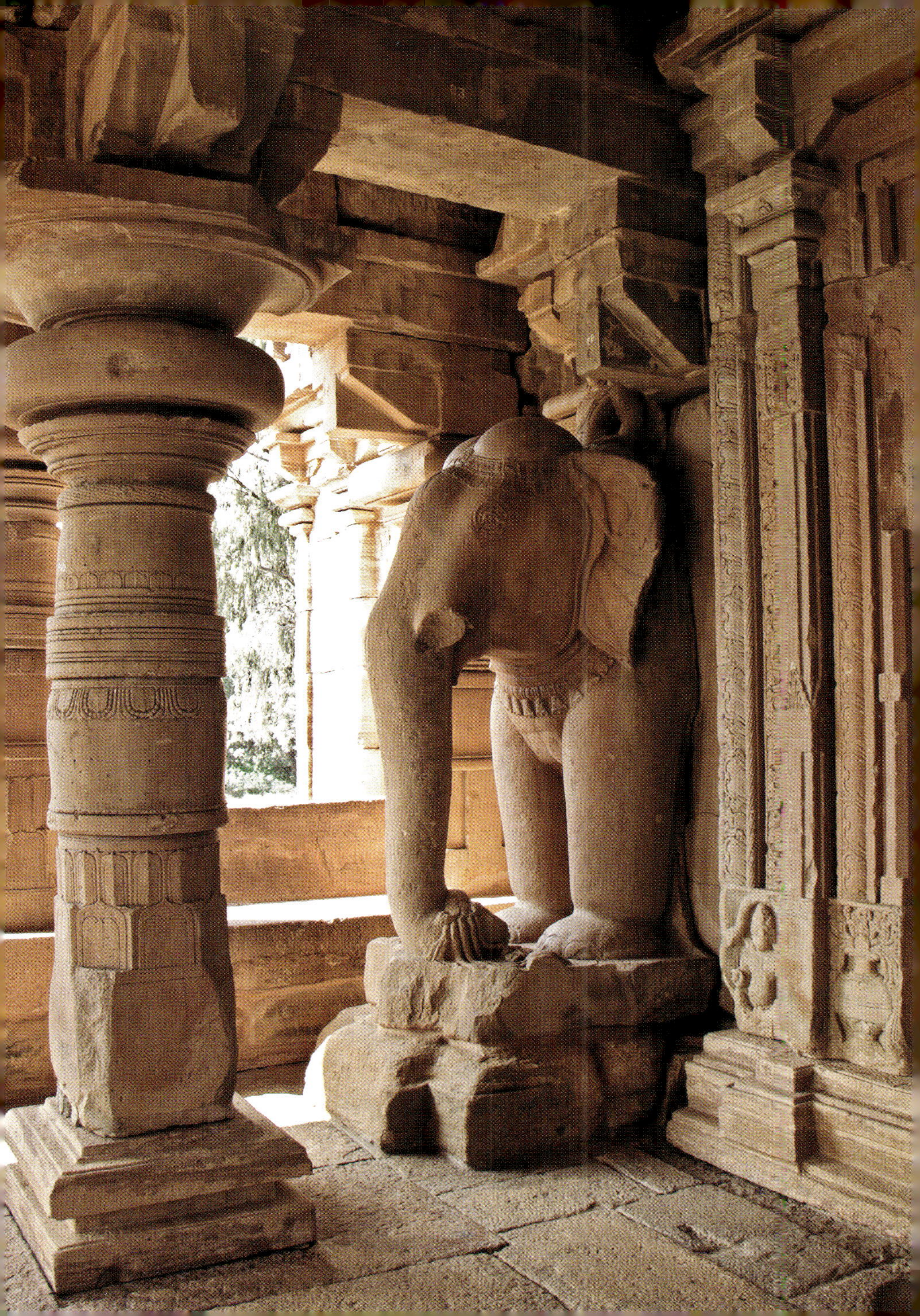

a **Dolmen**, partly hidden by bushes. This is the most accessible and best preserved vestige of the Megalithic period in the Malprabha valley, dating back to the 1st millennium BCE, if not earlier. The dolmen consists of an approximately 2-metre square chamber with a doorway opening on the front (east). It is assembled out of four massive sandstone slabs, laid vertically, topped by a huge, irregularly shaped capping slab. A few years ago, archaeologists uncovered traces of brick structures about 300 metres away from the dolmen, which they assigned to the 3rd-4th centuries CE. (These remains have been filled in and are no longer visible.) The hill that rises steeply nearby is known as **Bachinagudda**. On its northern flank, reached by a rough path, stands a small cubical *linga* shrine without tower, dating from the late 8th century. Its walls are articulated by sharply modelled pilasters in the typical Rashtrakuta manner. Carvings of Narasimha and Brahma set into the central niches on the west and north sides appear to have been taken from one of the Pattadakal temples.

A further site to be visited in the area is **Huligemmanakolla**. This is a 2-kilometre diversion from the village of Bhadranayakana Jalihal on the Badami road, 7 kilometres west of Pattadakal. The site consists of a partly constructed

Rock carvings at Huligemmanakolla

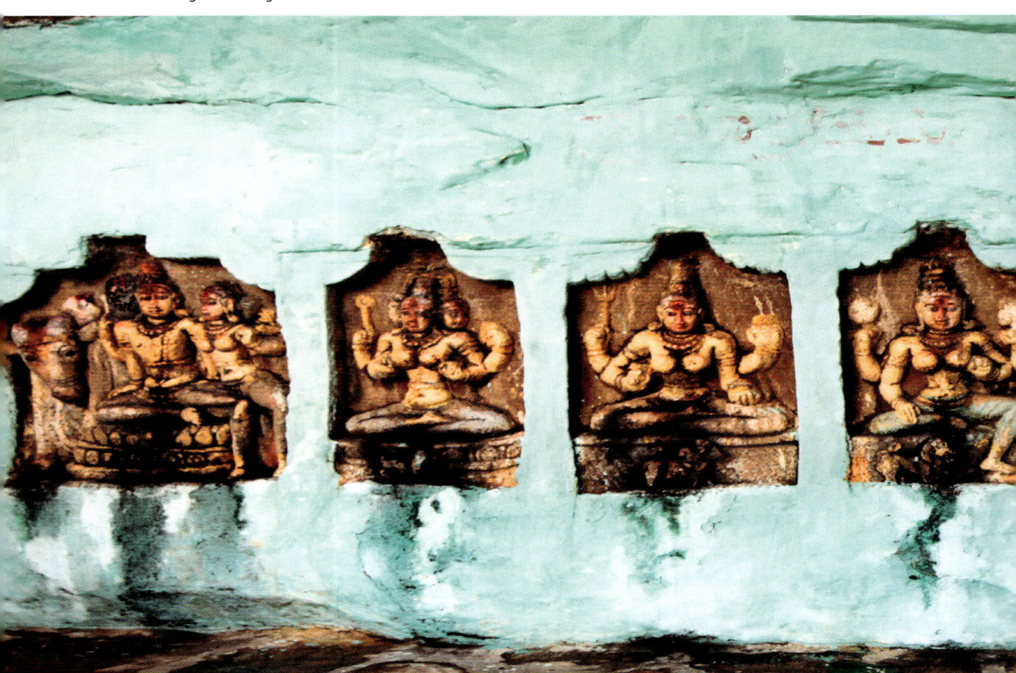

terrace set beneath a dramatic natural overhang with a refreshing waterfall. Here are seen a modern shrine for the goddess who gives her name to the site, as well as rock-cut images, including two of Lajja Gauri. Eleven tiny *linga* sanctuaries from the Early Chalukya period, some with low pyramidal towers, are concealed in the forest beneath. One example, without tower, has an inscription stating that it served as the 'funerary-casket-bearing shrine' of Vikramaditya II. From this record it seems that Huligemmanakolla may have functioned as a royal memorial site.

The last feature to be described here is the Mangalamma Temple at Mangalagudda, a small hamlet 3 kilometres from Pattadakal, beside the road to Aihole. This goddess shrine is of local importance for its festival with animal sacrifices held every three years. No earlier than the 18th or 19th century, the temple is recognised by its Maratha styled octagonal tower crowned with a diminutive bulbous dome. The tower has five diminishing tiers of brightly painted niches filled with Devi figures, especially Durga. Standing freely in front of the temple is a lamp-tower with two storeys of arched openings. This is topped by battlements with corner finials.

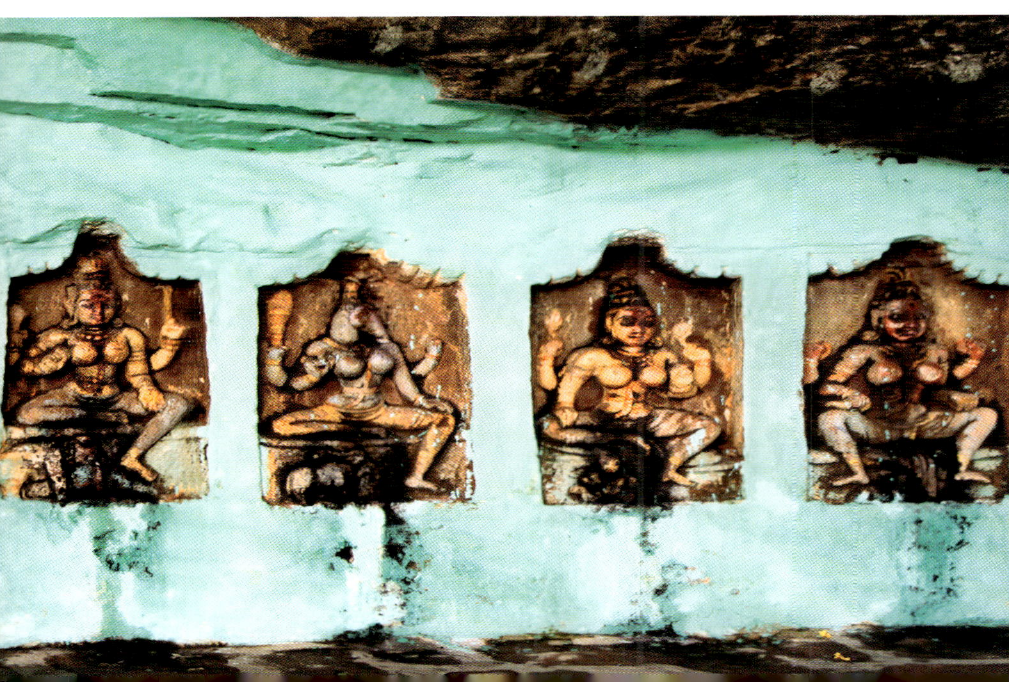

LIST OF EARLY CHALUKYA RULERS

Pulakeshin I	544-567	**Vikramaditya I**	655-681
Kirttivarman I	567-598	**Vinayaditya**	681-696
Mangalesha	598-610	**Vijayaditya**	696-734
Pulakeshin II	610-642	**Vikramaditya II**	734-745
(Pallava interregnum)	642-655	**Kirttivarman II**	745-757

GLOSSARY *Restricted to Indian names and terms*

abhaya-mudra, gesture of protection
Adil Shahis, 16th-17th century line of *sultans* based at Bijapur
Adinatha, the first Tirthankara
amalaka, circular ribbed finial in Nagara styled temples
Ambika, goddess associated with Adinatha
Andhaka, demon speared by Shiva
Ardhanarishvara, Shiva and Devi joined
Arjuna, hero of the Mahabharata; fights Shiva in the Kiratarjuniya story
Aruna, charioteer of Surya
Bahubali, Jain saint, son of Adinatha, the first Tirthankara
Banakshankari, name of Devi
Bhagiratha, ascetic who compelled the Ganga to descend to earth
Bhairava, demonic form of Shiva
Bhikshatana, Shiva as a wandering ascetic
Bhima, mighty Pandava hero in the Mahabharata
Bhishma, great warrior in the Mahabharata
Bhringi, skeletal sage who attends on Shiva
Bhudevi, earth goddess rescued by Varaha
Bhutanatha, name of Shiva
Brahma, four-headed creator god
Brahmi, one of the Matrikas
bund, dam wall
chaitya, Buddhist shrine
Chandrashekhara, name of Shiva
chauri, fly-whisk
dargah, Muslim shrine
Dasharatha, father of Rama in the Ramayana
Dattatreya, triple-headed form of Vishnu combined with Shiva and Brahma
Devi, great goddess
Dikpalas, regents of the eight directions of space
dipa-stambha, lamp-column
Dravida, temple style of Southern India
durga, fort
Durga, name of the goddess who slays the buffalo demon Mahisha
Duryodhana, mighty Kaurava hero in the Mahabharata
Early Chalukyas, line of kings ruling from Vatapi (Badami) in the 6th–8th centuries
Gajalakshmi, Lakshmi flanked by elephants
Galaganatha, name of Shiva
ganas, dwarfish imps in Shiva's retinue
Ganesha, elephant-headed god, considered the son of Parvati
Ganga, the river goddess Ganges
Garuda, eagle mount of Vishnu
Gauri, name of Devi
gavaksha, horseshoe-shaped false arch in Nagara temples
gudda, hill
gudi, temple
Hanuman, monkey hero in the Ramayana
Harihara, Shiva and Vishnu joined
Indra, god of the heavens; one of the Dikpalas
jali, perforated stone screen or window
Jambulinga, name of Shiva
Jatayu, vulture who intercepted Ravana when he abducted Sita
Jina, Jain saint
Kala, destructive form of Shiva
Kailasa, mountain home of Shiva
Kali, destructive form of Devi
Kaliya, serpent demon subdued by Krishna
kapota, curved eave above a wall
Karttikeya, warrior god, son of Shiva
Kashivishvanatha, name of Shiva
Kiratarjuniya, Arjuna fighting Shiva disguised as a *kirata*, or hunter

kolla, tank or pond
Krishna, popular god in Hinduism
Kubera, god of the underworld; one of the Dikpalas
kudu, horseshoe-shaped false window in Dravida temples
Kumbhakarna, giant demon in the service of Ravana
kuta, square-to-domed roof
Kalachuris, 5th–6th century line of rulers in peninsular India
Lajja Gauri, squatting lotus-headed goddess
Lakulisha, form of Shiva holding the club
Lakshmana, brother of Rama in the *Ramayana*
Lakshmi, goddess of wealth; consort of Vishnu
Late Chalukyas, line of kings ruling from Kalyana in the 11th–12th centuries
linga, Shiva in the form of a phallic emblem
Mahabharata, epic story of the battle between the Kauravas and the Pandavas
Mahakuteshvara, name of Shiva worshipped at Mahakuta
Mahisha, buffalo demon slain by Durga
makara, aquatic monster with crocodile-like jaws and fanciful tail
Mallikarjuna, name of Shiva
mandapa, columned hall of a temple
Mangalamma, name of Devi
Marathas, warrior rulers from Maharashtra in the 17th–18th centuries
Markandeya, youthful devotee of Shiva
Matrikas, set of mother goddesses
naga, cobra
nagakal, snake-stone
nagaraja, cobra king
Nagara, temple style of Northern India
Nandi, bull mount of Shiva
Narasimha, man-lion incarnation of Vishnu
nidhi, pot-bellied guardian
Padmapani, Buddhist saintly figure holding a lotus flower
Pallavas, rulers of Tamil Nadu based at Kanchipuram in the 6th–9th centuries
Panchatantra, set of popular animal fables
Parshvanatha, second last of the 24 Tirthankaras
Parvati, wife of Shiva
phadi, rock
pipal, fig tree
Ramayana, popular epic recounting the story of Rama
Rashtrakutas, 8th–9th century rulers of Maharashtra
Ravana, multi-headed demon who shakes Kailasa, and who abducts Sita in the *Ramayana*
rishi, ascetic or sage
Sangameshvara, name of Shiva
Saptamatrikas, set of seven mother goddesses
Shaiva, pertaining to the cult of Shiva
shala, barrel-vaulted roof
Shesha, cosmic serpent which shelters Vishnu
shikhara, curved tower in Nagara temples
Shiva, major Hindu cult
Shurpanakha, sister of Ravana in the *Ramayana*
Sugriva, rightful monkey king in the *Ramayana*
Surya, sun god
tirtha, sacred spot with a pond or pool
Tirthankaras, set of 24 Jain saviours
Tripura, triple cities with demon kings killed by Shiva
Trivikrama, incarnation of Vishnu pacing out three cosmic steps
urs, death anniversary celebration of a Muslim saint
Vamana, dwarf incarnation of Vishnu who transforms himself into Trivikrama
Vaikuntha, form of Vishnu
Vaishnava, pertaining to the cult of Vishnu
Vali, wrongful monkey king in the Ramayana
Varaha, boar incarnation of Vishnu
Varahi, one of the Matrikas
Varuna, god of the ocean, one of the Dikpalas
Virabhadra, warrior form of Shiva
Vijayanagara, capital of a dynasty of powerful rulers of southern India in the 14th–16th centuries
Virupaksha, name of Shiva
Vishnu, major Hindu cult
Yamuna, the river goddess Yamuna
yali, leonine monster
Yama, god of death, one of the Dikpalas
Yellamma, name of Devi

FURTHER READING

Bolon, Carol Radcliffe. "The Mahakuta pillar and its temples". *Artibus Asiae*, 41/2-3 (1980), pp 253-68.

----. "Calukyas of Badami: Karnata", in Michael W Meister, MA Dhaky and Krishna Deva, eds., *Encyclopaedia of Indian Temple Architecture North India, Foundations of North Indian Style, c. 250 BC–AD 1100*. New Delhi, American Institute of Indian Studies, 1988, pp 276-311.

----. "Two Chalukya queens and their commemorative temples: Eighth century Pattadakal", in Vidya Dehejia, ed, *Royal Patrons and Great Temple Art*. Bombay: Marg Publications, 1988, pp 61-76.

Dhaky, MA. *Encyclopaedia of Indian Temple Architecture: South India, Upper Dravidadesa, Later Phase, AD 973-1326*. New Delhi, American Institute of Indian Studies, 1996.

Gupte, RS. *The Art and Architecture of Aihole*. Bombay: Taraporevala & Sons, 1967.

Hardy, Adam. *Indian Temple Architecture, Form and Transformation: The Karnata Dravida Tradition, 7th to 13th Centuries*. New Delhi: Indira Gandhi National Centre for the Arts, 1995.

Lippe, Aschwin, "Some sculptural motifs on Early Calukya temples", *Artibus Asiae*, 29/1 (1967), pp 5-24.

----. "Early Chalukya icons", Artibus Asiae, 34/4 (1972), pp 273-330.

Meister, Michael W and **MA Dhaky**, eds, *Encyclopaedia of Indian Temple Architecture: South India, Upper Dravidadesa, Early Phase, AD 550-1075*. New Delhi: American Institute of Indian Studies, 1986.

Michell, George. *An Architectural Description and Analysis of the Early Western Chalukyan Temples*. London: Art and Archaeology Research Papers, 1975.

----. "Temples of Early Chalukyas", *in In Praise of Aihole, Badami, Mahakuta, Pattadakal*. Bombay: Marg Publications, 1979, pp 55-130.

----. *Monumental Legacy, Pattadakal*. New Delhi: Oxford University Press, 2002.

Nagaraja Rao, MS. *Kiratarjuniyam in Indian Art, With Special Reference to Karnataka*. Delhi: Agam Kala Prakashan, 1979.

Nagaraja Rao, MS and **KV Ramesh**, "A royal memorial to Chalukya Vikramaditya II", in MS Nagaraja Rao, ed, Madhu: *Recent Researches in Indian Archaeology and Art History*, Shri MN Deshpande Festschrift. Delhi: Agam Kala Prakashan, 1981, pp 175-9.

Nilakanta Sastri, KA. "Part IV. The Chalukyas of Badami", in Gulam Yazdani, ed, *The Early History of the Deccan*. Oxford: Oxford University Press, 1960, pp 201-46.

Padigar, Srinivas, "The Durga Temple, Aihole: an aditya temple", *Archaeological Studies*, II (1977), pp 59-64.

Rajasekhara, S. *Early Chalukya Art at Aihole*. New Delhi: Vikas, 1985.

Rambach, Pierre and **Vitold de Golish**. *The Golden Age of Indian Art, Vth-XIIIth Century*. London: Thames and Hudson, 1955.

Ramesh, KV. *Chalukyas of Vatapi*. New Delhi Agam Prakashan, 1984.

Rao, SR. "A note on the chronology of Early Chalukyan temples", *Lalit Kala*, 15 (1972), pp 9-18.

Ray, Himanshu Prabha. "Creating religious identity: Archaeology of early temples in the Malprabha valley," in Himanshu Prabha Ray, ed, *Archaeology and Text: The Temples in South Asia*. New Delhi: Oxford University Press, 2010, pp 15-37.

Settar, S. "A Buddhist vihara at Aihole", *East and West*, 19 (1969), pp. 126-38.

Soundara Rarajan, KV. *Early Temple Architecture in Karnataka and its Ramifications*. Dharwar: Kannada Research Institute, Karnatak University, 1969.

----. *Cave Temples of the Deccan*. New Delhi: Archaeological Survey of India, 1981.

Sivaramamurti, C. "Western Chalukya paintings at Badami", *Lalit Kala*, 5 (1959), pp. 49-53.

Srinivasan, KR. *Temples of South India*. New Delhi: National Book Trust, 1971.

Sundara, A. *World Heritage Series: Pattadakal*. New Delhi: Archaeological Survey of India, 2008.

Tarr/Tartakov, Gary Michael, "Chronology and development of the Chalukya cave temples", Ars Orientalis, 8 (1970), pp. 155-84.

----. *The Durga Temple at Aihole: a Historiographical Study*. Delhi: Oxford University Press, 1997.

Wechsler, Helen, J. "Royal legitimation: Ramayana reliefs on the Papanatha temple at Pattadakal", in Vidya Dehejia, ed, *The Legend of Rama: Artistic Visions*. Bombay: Marg Publications, 1994, pp 27-42.

ADVICE TO TRAVELLERS

The nearest airport to Badami is at Hubli (115 kilometres distant), with daily connections to and from Bangalore and Mumbai. Direct train links with Badami station are now also available from Bangalore and Mumbai; the station at Gadag, on the Goa-Hospet-Hyderabad line, is only 80 kilometres away. Otherwise, Badami may easily be reached by road from Hubli, or from Belgaum or Hospet (both about 140 kilometres distant). Transport in and around Badami is available in the form of local taxis, public buses and auto rickshaws; sadly, pony-drawn tongas have now almost totally disappeared.

Lack of accommodation at Aihole and Pattadakal means that Badami remains the only options for visitors to be based when visiting the region. To date the best hotels are Badami Court (tel: 08357 220230; email: rafiqmht@dataone.in) and the newly opened Heritage Resort with stylish cottages (tel: 08357 220250; email: info@theheritage.co.in), as well as the older, but renovated Mayura Chalukya (tel: 08357 220046; email: adami@karnatakaholidays.net), all situated slightly out of town. Less comfortable are the Mookambika Deluxe and Rajsangam International across from the bus stand.

The Badami Court and Mayura Chalukya each has a restaurant, but visitors should have no problem finding simple places to eat elsewhere in Badami. Tea, cold drinkss and snacks are available at Aihole and Pattadakal, but barely anything else.

January is the season of the fair at Banashankari, the largest in this part of Karnataka. Otherwise, shopping in Badami is mostly restricted to local stores in the market. Ancient Arts at Badami Court offers a fine selection of silver jewellery and handicrafts.

ACKNOWLEDGEMENTS

In his visit to the Badami region to gather material for the volume the author was greatly assisted by the owner, managers and staff of Badami Court Hotel, whom he thanks for their great kindness and support. Without the expert guidance of Chandru Katageri it would have been impossible to reach many of the lesser known sites in the area. The author benefited greatly from Chandru's profound familiarity with Badami's history and art traditions. He must also acknowledge the information generously supplied by Dr Sheelakant Pattar, a local scholar and friend dating back to the author's student days in Badami. In his exploration of the many wonderful sites in the region the author was accompanied by John M Fritz, colleague, collaborator and life companion.

The maps and town plans were specially prepared for this volume by Graham Reed. The architectural drawings come from the author's dissertation, *An Architectural Description and Analysis of the Early Western Chalukya Temples*. The photographs are all by Surendra Kumar, except for those supplied by John M Fritz (pp. 18 top, 30, 35, 48 right, 55 left, 65, 72 right, 73 left, 73 right, 74 left, 74 right, 99 top, 105, 112, 131, 132 and 134), and Clare Kirkman (pp. 41, 56 right, and 86). Reproductions of the carved panels on pp. 6, 7 and 41 are reproduced with kind permission of the Chhatrapati Shivaji Maharaj Vastu Sangrahalaya, Mumbai.

INDEX *Numbers in bold refer to pages with illustrations*